FAST TRACK ENGLISH

The Business World

Robert Parr

Die Fernsehsendungen zu FAST TRACK ENGLISH, The Business World produzierten die Pilgrim Productions 2000 (Canterbury, England) im Auftrag des Westdeutschen Rundfunks (Redaktion: Peter Teckentrup) für das Telekolleg.
Drehbücher: Gillian Jones: Language Consultant. Rüdiger Deutsch, Keith Jones; Kamera: Georg Pellet; Regie: Brain Earley, David Pick

6. Auflage 2017

Bild- und Textnachweis:
Fotos: Videoprints aus den Fehnsehsendungen
Materialien: Barclays Bank PLC (S. 24, 39); British Tourist Authorize (S. 7); *The Daily Telegraph* (S. 109); *Deutscher Hotelführer* (S. 104); *Fresh* (January 1996); Reed Business Publishing (S. 191); *Ideal Home* (June 1993); IPC Magazines (S. 92); The Prince's Youth Business Trust (S. 58); *Private Eye* (S. 142); *Punch* (S 226); R. Twinings and Company Ltd. (S. 175);
Zeichnungen: Claudia Hofmann, München (S. 49f, 148, 174, 180), Daniel Schwarz, Köln (S. 137)
Umschlaggestaltung: Franziska Schob-Bergmeir, München
Gesamtherstellung: Kessler Druck + Medien GmbH, Bobingen
ISBN 978-3-941282-50-6

Vorwort

FAST TRACK ENGLISH, The Business World bietet Ihnen die Möglichkeit, Ihre Englischkenntnisse in den Bereichen Wirtschaft und Handel auszubauen und zu festigen. Parallel zu den gleichnamigen Fernsehsendungen besteht jede der 13 Lektionen dieses Begleitbuchs aus fünf Abschnitten:

- Die **Module A und B** geben Statements und Dialoge aus den Fernsehsendungen im Wortlaut wieder. Ausgewählte Wörter und Wendungen werden gesondert aufgelistet und übersetzt. In diesen *Wordlists* fehlen bewusst wichtige Ausdrücke - diejenigen, die der sich anschließende Teil *Working with the text* behandelt. Der Übungsblock *Exercises* geht über den jeweiligen Text hinaus und bietet - zusammen mit *Focus on*, das wichtige sprachliche Strukturen aufgreift - zusätzliches Übungsmaterial. Das Hauptaugenmerk richtet sich auch in diesem Abschnitt auf die Wortschatzarbeit.

  Lernende, die sich intensiver mit der englischen Grammatik auseinandersetzen möchten, seien auf die vorausgehenden Bände der Reihe FAST TRACK ENGLISH verwiesen: PART ONE (Lektion 1-13), PART TWO (Lektion 14-26).

- **Modul C** versteht sich vorrangig als Hörverständnisübung. Es empfiehlt sich daher, diesen Teil der Fernsehsendungen mehrmals anzuschauen, bevor Sie sich mit den Übungen beschäftigen.

- In **Modul D** begegnet uns 'Troubleshooter', der Mann, der sich unermüdlich um die Sorgen und Probleme von Geschäftsleuten kümmert. Lassen Sie sich von seinem Humor, Charme und Engagement inspirieren!

- **Modul E** rundet mit Originaldokumenten, Bildern und anderen optischen Elementen die Lektionen ab.

Im Anhang finden Sie die *Tapescripts* zu den Modulen C, sämtliche Lösungen zu den Übungen sowie ein alphabetisches Register aller Wörter aus den *Wordlists*.

Robert Parr

Contents

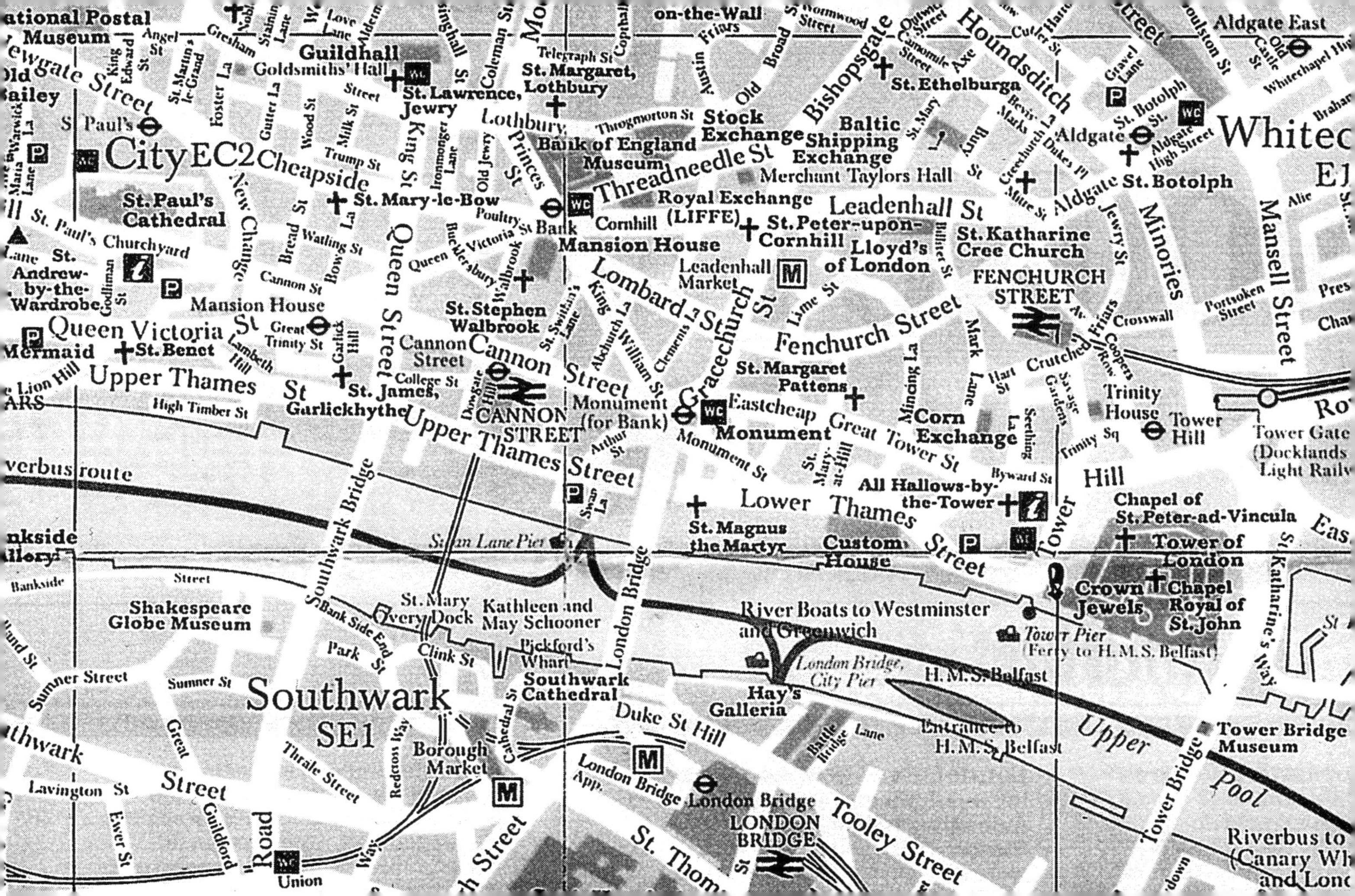
City EC2
St. Paul's Cathedral
St. Paul's Churchyard
Newgate Street
Old Bailey
National Postal Museum
King Edward St
St. Martin's le-Grand
Foster La
Gutter La
Wood St
Milk St
Goldsmiths' Hall
Guildhall
St. Lawrence, Jewry
King St
Ironmonger Lane
Old Jewry
Coleman St
St. Margaret, Lothbury
Lothbury
Telegraph St
Copthall
on-the-Wall
Austin Friars
Old Broad St
Bishopsgate
St. Ethelburga
Houndsditch
Aldgate East
Whitechapel High
St. Botolph
Aldgate
Aldgate High Street
Whitec
Cheapside
New Change
St. Mary-le-Bow
Bread St
Watling St
Bow La
Trump St
Queen Street
Queen Victoria St
Bucklersbury
Poultry
Walbrook
Princes St
Bank
Mansion House
Cornhill
Threadneedle St
Bank of England Museum
Throgmorton St
Stock Exchange
Baltic Exchange
Shipping Exchange
Merchant Taylors Hall
Royal Exchange (LIFFE)
St. Peter-upon-Cornhill
Leadenhall St
Lloyd's of London
St. Katharine Cree Church
Creechurch La
Bevis Marks
Duke's Pl
Mitre St
Minories
Mansell Street
Jewry St
St. Andrew-by-the-Wardrobe
Godliman St
Cannon St
Great Trinity St
Garlick Hill
Queen Victoria St
Mermaid
St. Benet
Lambeth Hill
Upper Thames St
High Timber St
St. James, Garlickhythe
College St
Cannon Street
Dowgate Hill
CANNON STREET
St. Stephen Walbrook
St. Swithin's Lane
King William St
Abchurch La
Clements La
Lombard St
Gracechurch St
Leadenhall Market
Lime St
Fenchurch Street
FENCHURCH STREET
Crutched Friars
Coopers Row
Crosswall
Portsoken Street
Monument (for Bank)
Monument
Eastcheap
St. Margaret Pattens
Great Tower St
Mincing La
Mark Lane
Hart St
Seething La
Savage Gardens
Trinity House
Trinity Sq
Tower Hill
Tower Gate (Docklands Light Railway)
Corn Exchange
Monument St
St. Mary-at-Hill
Byward St
All Hallows-by-the-Tower
Arthur St
Swan La
Lower Thames Street
St. Magnus the Martyr
Custom House
Swan Lane Pier
Upper Thames Street
Riverbus route
Bankside Gallery
Bankside
Shakespeare Globe Museum
Southwark Bridge
Bank Side End
Park St
St. Mary Overy Dock
Kathleen and May Schooner
Clink St
Pickford's Wharf
Southwark Cathedral
London Bridge
River Boats to Westminster and Greenwich
London Bridge City Pier
Hay's Galleria
Tower Pier (Ferry to H.M.S. Belfast)
H.M.S. Belfast
Entrance to H.M.S. Belfast
Crown Jewels
Chapel of St. Peter-ad-Vincula
Tower of London
Chapel Royal of St. John
St. Katharine's Way
Upper Pool
Tower Bridge
Tower Bridge Museum
Riverbus to (Canary Wharf and London
Southwark SE1
Sumner Street
Sumner St
Great Guildford Street
Southwark Street
Lavington St
Ewer St
Union Street
Redcross Way
Thrale Street
Borough Market
Cathedral St
Duke St Hill
London Bridge App.
London Bridge
LONDON BRIDGE
Battle Bridge Lane
Tooley Street
St. Thomas St

‘It is too late to agree with me:
I’ve changed my mind.’

Mahbub ul Haq, 1934-1998

RETAIL AND WHOLESALE 1

1A

Buying and selling

What do these three people do?

David Novell: "I'm the Managing Director of this garden centre. The name of the garden centre is Polhill Garden Centre. We sell *lawnmowers*, we sell plants, garden furniture, in fact everything you need for the garden. There are a number of different departments. There's a Plant Department, a Pet Department and a department that sells all kinds of fish and aquariums. We are a retail business. That means we sell to the general public. We employ about a hundred and thirty staff. Some of them are part-time and some of them full-time."

Brian Archibald: "I'm responsible for buying for the Pet Department and Garden *Sundries*. In our Pet Department we actually sell animals and all products associated with them. Garden Sundries, that means all the products for gardening like compost, pots, seeds and *fertilizers*. The Garden Centre buys plants from local *growers*. We also buy plants from abroad. I purchase a lot of my products from wholesalers. Many of the wholesalers that I use are local but sometimes I purchase from wholesalers that are abroad, in other words, I import. The sort of items that we import are bamboo *canes* from China and many garden tools from Germany."

Colin Cross: "I'm the Manager of this *distribution depot*. I'm a wholesaler. That means that I buy large quantities of products from manufacturers and supply those to garden centres and small retailers in smaller quantities across the *Home Counties*. One of our largest customers is Polhill Garden Centre. We have developed a system with them whereby we are linked by modem through their computer to ours. That enables us to receive an order from them at the end of trading on Sunday so that we can start picking it first thing Monday, and we deliver those products, at the very latest, Monday afternoon after receipt of the order on a Sunday evening."

retail and wholesale	Einzel- und Großhandel	cane	Rohr
lawnmower	Rasenmäher	distribution	Verteilung, Vertrieb
sundries *pl*	Verschiedenes	depot	(Lager)haus
fertilizer	Dünger	Home Counties	*an London grenzende Grafschaften*
grower	Züchter(in)		

■ Working with the text

*I. Are these sentences true or false according to the text? Tick the appropriate box in the grid (*Gitter*).*

	true	false
1. David Novell and Brian Archibald both work at the Polhill Garden Centre.		
2. The Polhill Garden Centre is a retail business.		
3. Brian Archibald is David Novell's boss.		
4. Colin Cross knows Brian Archibald.		
5. Colin Cross does business with retailers and manufacturers.		

II. Complete these sentences. Use two words from the text in each sentence.

1. A retail business sells products to the … … .
2. A wholesale business sells products to … … .
3. A manufacturer sells … … of products to wholesale businesses.

III. Nouns in the text. Which are they? (The first letter is given.)

1. a large part of a company d…
2. all the people who work in a company s…
3. a person who buys something from a shop c…

4. a piece of paper which asks for products to be delivered o...
5. a person or company that makes a product m...

IV. Verbs in the text. Which are they? (The last letter is given.)

1. to offer work to somebody ...y
2. another word for 'buy' ...e
3. to bring in products from another country ...t
4. to deliver products to a person or company ...y
5. to make possible ...e

V. Complete these sentences. Use words from exercises III and IV in their correct form.

1. David Novell ... about 130 people at the Polhill Garden Centre.
2. Some of the ... are full-time, some are part-time.
3. Brian Archibald, the Centre's Buyer, ... products from wholesalers in Britain.
4. He also ... from countries such as Germany and China.
5. Colin Cross is a wholesaler. One of his ... is Brian Archibald.
6. Colin Cross often receives ... by computer.
7. This enables him to ... retailers within 24 hours.

VI. What's the German?

1. managing director (line 2)
2. the general public (line 7)

3. garden tools (line 16)
4. end of trading (line 22)
5. receipt of the order (line 24)

VII. Say these words from the text out loud.

1. staff
2. tool
3. depot
4. modem
5. receipt

VIII. What about you?

1. Do you think having a garden centre is a good business in Britain? Give a reason for your opinion.
2. If you had the choice between doing David Novell, Brian Archibald or Colin Cross's job, which one would you choose? Can you say why?

■ Exercises

Focus on → talking about jobs

Deutsche Berufsbezeichnungen oder Bildungsabschlüsse lassen sich manchmal schwer ins Englische übersetzen bzw. haben keine englischen Entsprechungen. Spricht man über den Beruf, empfiehlt es sich daher, das Aufgabengebiet zu beschreiben bzw. den Arbeitgeber zu nennen.

I'm responsible for buying for the Pet Department.
I work at the Polhill Garden Centre.

I. Say it in English. Start with: 'I work in ...' Use one short sentence only! Don't translate word for word!

1. Ich bin Betriebswirtin und arbeite in der Personalabteilung eines großen Elektrokonzerns in München.
2. Ich bin Anästhesist in einer Kinderklinik in Braunschweig.
3. Ich habe Feinwerktechnik studiert und bin in der Abteilung Forschung und Entwicklung bei einer großen Autofirma in der Nähe von Stuttgart angestellt.
4. Ich bin Sozialversicherungsfachangestellte und arbeite bei einer Betriebskrankenkasse in Berlin. Ich bin verantwortlich für den Bereich Beitragszahlung.

II. Read these job ads. Imagine that three people are working in these jobs and describing their work to English-speaking friends. What might they say? Write two sentences for each job. Don't translate word for word!

1. Zum nächstmöglichen Zeitpunkt suchen wir

eine/n Fachverkäufer/in

mit Eigeninitiative und Engagement, vorzugsweise aus der Juwelierbranche, für unser Geschäft in Hamburg. Wir erwarten mehrjährige Verkaufspraxis und Erfahrung mit anspruchsvollen Kunden.

2. In unserer Niederlassung in Frankfurt suchen wir Ihre qualifizierte Unterstützung als

Sekretär(in).

Sie bearbeiten unsere Korrespondenz und sind für die Erstellung von Statistiken und Berichten genauso verantwortlich wie für die Terminkoordination.

3. *Für die Verkaufsgebiete in Ostdeutschland suchen wir*

Vertriebsingenieure für elektronische Meßsysteme.

Ihre Aufgabe: technische und kaufmännische Kundenberatung und Organisation von Informationsseminaren.

Focus on ➔ compound nouns

Zusammengesetzte Substantive bestehen meist aus zwei Substantiven. Sie bilden gemeinsam einen Begriff, z.B. *garden centre*. Das erste Substantiv beschreibt das zweite. Zusammengesetzte Substantive werden entweder zusammengeschrieben (z.B. *lawnmower*) oder getrennt geschrieben (z.B. *retail business*) - oder, aber viel seltener, mit Bindestrich versehen.

III. What's the difference between ...

1. a 'horse race' and a 'race horse'?
2. 'milk chocolate' and 'chocolate milk'?

IV. Which compound noun is being described? Check the spelling in a dictionary.

1. a clock that wakes you up in the morning
2. people who have poor eyesight wear them (they are not glasses!)
3. you can pay for things with it, it is sometimes called 'plastic money'
4. a simple hotel where young people can stay
5. a person who looks after small children when their parents are away
6. a room where you wash, bath or have a shower

Focus on → defining relative clauses

Relativsätze, die für das Verständnis des ganzen Satzes notwendig sind, werden ohne Kommas geschrieben. Als Objekt des Relativsatzes kann das Relativpronomen entfallen.

There's a department ***that sells all kinds of fish and aquariums****.*
Many of the wholesalers ***(that) I use*** *are local.*

V. *Which of these sentences contain defining relative clauses? Which contain non-defining relative clauses and need commas?*

1. The people we met on our holiday were all really nice.
2. We sometimes work with people who can't even operate a computer.
3. Have you seen the new car they've bought?
4. The garden centre we went to doesn't close until 9pm.
5. Mr Schneider who originally came from Germany has worked here for twenty years.
6. The people who come here want to enjoy themselves.

def	non-def

VI. *Is there an object relative pronoun in the sentence? If so, rewrite the sentence without it.*

1. Is that the woman who you work with?
2. The goldfish which we bought died after three days.
3. The man who came to the door yesterday wanted to sell us insurance.
4. Is there anybody who doesn't like going on holiday?
5. The flowers which are in this part of the garden never get the sun.
6. The accident which we saw yesterday was shown on TV.

VII. *Word families. Complete the grid.*

	verb	noun
1.	receive	...
2.	order	...
3.	produce	...
4.	deliver	...
5.	employ	...
6.	purchase	...
7.	develop	...
8.	use	...

VIII. Complete this paragraph. Use six of the eight words in the box. ●●

chance • company • conference • customer • department • public • staff • travel

"I work for SIP, a medium-sized computer … . I work in the personnel … . I'm responsible for recruiting new … . I like my job because it gives me a … to meet people. The other thing I like about my job is that I … quite a lot. Next week, for example, I'm going to a training … in Berlin."

IX. What do you do?

Now you write a short paragraph in English about your job. Say where you work and what you are responsible for. Finish by saying why you like - or do not like - your job. (If you have not got a job at the moment, write about a job you would like to have!)

1B

Day-to-day business ●●

At the garden centre

▸ Clare Stevens has bought a plant from a garden centre and now she does not want it. What happens when she goes back to the shop?

▸ Can I help you?

▸ Yes, I hope so. I bought this here yesterday and it's just not what my husband wanted. Can I change it or could you give me a refund?

▸ Have you got your receipt?

▸ Yes, I have.

▸ Would you like a refund or would you like to exchange it for something else?

▸ I think I'd like to exchange it for something else.

▸ If you'd like to leave that here and go and choose something.

▸ OK, thank you.

At the post office

Clare needs a new car licence so she goes to a post office. Has she got the right documents with her?

- I hope I filled this in correctly.
- Let's have a look.
- And I hope I have everything I need.
- I'm sure you have. May I have your *registration document*, please?
- Here you are.
- Thank you. And your certificate of insurance?
- This one?
- That's the one, thank you. That's fine. And your *MOT* certificate?
- This one?
- Thank you. Are you paying for a year or six months?
- A year, please.
- That's going to cost you £145, please.
- Thank you.

At the bank

Next Clare goes to the bank. What does she do there?

- Can you check my *current account* for me, please?
- Yes, of course. May I have your card, please?
  (She gives Clare a *print out.*) There we are.
- Thanks. I'd like to transfer some money from my *deposit account* to my current account.

- How much would you like to transfer?
- £500, please.
- If you could just check this and sign it for me, please. That will *go through* for you today.
- Thank you.

day-to-day	Alltags-, täglich	current account	Girokonto
registration document	Kraftfahrzeugbrief	print out	Auszug, -druck
MOT (*abbr for* Ministry of Transport)	*TÜV*	deposit account	Sparkonto
		go through	(*Betrag*) eingehen

■ Working with the text

I. Which ending (a-c) completes the statement best? Tick it.

1. At the garden centre Clare hopes to …
   a) change some money.
   b) exchange one product for another product.
   c) find another husband.
2. At the post office Clare would like to …
   a) buy a new car.
   b) get insurance for her car.
   c) renew her car licence.
3. At the bank Clare wants to …
   a) buy some Austrian money.
   b) transfer money from one account to another account.
   c) pick up a new credit card.

II. Which word in the text is being described?

1. the money that you get back (after you have returned something you have bought)
2. a small piece of paper which shows that you have received a product

III. Complete the definition by adding one word.

1. A … account is a bank account for everyday expenses.
2. A … account is a bank account for savings.

IV. Further questions. Answer them using your own words as far as possible.

1. Why does the woman at the garden centre want to know if Clare has got a receipt for her plant?
2. What three pieces of paper does the woman at the post office want to see before she can give Clare a new car licence?
3. What does Clare do before she transfers money from her deposit account to her current account?

V. And what about you?

1. Do you think people in Germany often go back to shops to exchange goods or get a refund? Say why or why not.
2. Do post offices in Germany offer the services that British post offices do?

■ Exercises

Focus on ➔ polite questions

Um Fragen höflich zu stellen, verwendet man meist die modalen Hilfsverben 'can', 'could', 'may' oder 'would' (+ 'like to') in Verbindung mit dem Infinitiv.

Could *you give me a refund, please?*
Would *you* ***like to*** *exchange it for something else?*

I. Join a sentence on the left to a sentence on the right to form mini-dialogues.

1. Can I help you?
2. Can you check my current account, please?
3. Please choose something else.
4. I hope I've got all the forms.

a. Yes, certainly.
b. Oh, thank you.
c. I'm sure you have.
d. Yes, please.

II. You make some requests. Use polite forms with 'may' or 'could'.
Use the information below - and your own ideas.

1. You want to open the window (because the room is hot).
2. You want to interrupt somebody (who is talking).
3. You want to borrow somebody's pen (to write down a phone number).
4. You want to disturb somebody (who is working).

III. You have a guest. Make polite offers with 'would like'. Use the information below and some of your own ideas to build an eight-line dialogue. Begin like this: 'Hello! Please come in. Let me take your coat ...'

1. Your guest has arrived. Perhaps it's time to offer her/him a drink.
2. You know your guest drinks white wine. Perhaps she/he will have a glass now.
3. You have some new New Zealand wine. Maybe your guest will try some.
4. Ask your guest to come into the kitchen and look at the bottle.

IV. What's the difference in meaning between these questions?

1. Do you like tea?
2. Would you like tea?

V. Ask questions with 'What ...?' to get the missing information.

1. I like gardening but I don't like
2. I wouldn't like a new bicycle but I would like
3. I would like to work in a foreign country but I wouldn't like to
4. I don't like going on holiday but I like

VI. Rewrite the conversation. Use short forms of the auxiliaries (eg 'is', 'shall', 'would' etc) wherever possible.

- Is John arriving in the evening or in the afternoon?
- I think he is coming at half past five.
- Shall I book a table for us?
- Yes, that is a good idea.
- What time would be best?
- We could eat at eight, I suppose.
- OK. I will ring the restaurant now.

VII. Because primary auxiliaries ('be', 'do', 'have') don't carry any meaning, they often disappear in informal speech. Which auxiliaries are missing in these questions?

1. ... you going into town this morning?
2. ... they ready to leave?
3. ... you want to know what happened?
4. ... we been here before?

VIII. Using 'please' and 'thanks'. Put each word into the dialogue three times.

- Hello.
- Good morning.
- Could I have ten first-class stamps, ...?
- Ten?
- Yes, ...
- Anything else?
- No, ...
- That's £2.80, ...
- ... . And twenty pence change.
- ... .

1C

David Novell - managing the family business

I. As you listen to David Novell talking about the Polhill Garden Centre, read and answer this question.

Which one of the following things does David Novell <u>not</u> talk about? Mark it.

a) how his business began
b) the Garden Centre's customers
c) his favourite flowers
d) the Centre's departments and products
e) the administrative work at the Centre
f) the staff

II. Listen again. Which is the correct answer? Tick it.

1. David Novell formed his company in the …
   a) 1970s. b) 1980s. c) 1990s.
2. Every week about …
   a) 2,000 customers go to the Polhill Garden Centre.
   b) 20,000 customers go to the Polhill Garden Centre.
   c) 200,000 customers go to the Polhill Garden Centre.
3. One of the most popular departments at the Centre is …
   a) the Pet Department. b) Garden Sundries. c) the restaurant.
4. The number one product at the Centre are …
   a) plants. b) aquarium fish. c) cups of coffee.

III. What do the underlined words in sentences 1-4 refer to? Choose an answer (a-d).

1. They love pottering around places like this …	a. the butcher
2. It acts as a customer draw to our Centre …	b. the office staff
3. He is a good attraction for the Centre …	c. the customers
4. They're also responsible for ordering the products …	d. the restaurant

IV. Word family. Read the definitions and complete the sentences below using one of the words in its correct form.

- To *produce* /prəˈdjuːs/ something is to make something in large quantities.
- A *product* /ˈprɒdʌkt/ is something which is produced and sold. (countable)
- *Produce* /ˈprɒdjuːs/ is something which comes from a farm. (uncountable)

1. The company I work for sells a range of beauty … .
2. Where does the butter come from? - On the packet it says: '... of France'.
3. Outside the farm shop there's a sign that says: 'Fresh ... daily'.
4. Last year Germany ... more cars than ever before.

1D

Troubleshooter starts up in business

Troubleshooter is sure that he will soon be making a living out of troubleshooting - solving other people's business problems. He's almost ready to begin. All he needs is the signmaker to finish putting a sign on the side of his van. Suddenly the phone rings. Troubleshooter's first customers are on the line.

A young couple would like to go into business. They want to open their own garden shop. However, before the bank will lend them any money, it wants to see their *business plan*. Troubleshooter cycles out to talk to the young man and woman. As they know very little about profit and loss forecasts, *overheads*, fixed costs and things like that, they want Troubleshooter to help them.

Troubleshooter goes back to his office and starts work. Soon he's able to *present* the couple *with* a business plan. The couple, however, are not prepared to give Troubleshooter his money yet. They want to wait until they have shown the plan to their bank.

In the meantime Troubleshooter goes to the signmaker to pick up his van. Clearly the signmaker has been in business longer than Troubleshooter has because he asks for his money immediately. "Payment on completion of work," he says. Troubleshooter writes out a cheque and hands it over to the signmaker. He thinks the £280 have been well invested. "It pays to advertise," he says.

troubleshooter	Krisenmanager(in)	overheads	allgemeine Kosten
business plan	Geschäftsplan	present with	präsentieren, überreichen

I. Answer the questions.

1. Why does Troubleshooter visit the young couple?
2. How can we see that Troubleshooter is not a very experienced businessman?
3. What is Troubleshooter's financial situation like at the moment?

II. Which is the correct answer? Mark it.

1. 'Overheads' (line 8) are …
   a) lights.
   b) regular costs (for rent, light, heat etc) when you run a business.
   c) a small management team.
2. The expression 'Payment on completion of work' (line 16) means …
   a) after the work is finished you must pay.
   b) after you pay the work is finished.
   c) you must not pay if the work is completed too slowly.
3. The expression 'It pays to advertise' (line 18) means …
   a) you must pay if you want to advertise.
   b) advertisements are too expensive.
   c) it's good for business if you advertise.

III. Match the underlined idiomatic expressions with their explanations.

1. Politicians pay lip-service to environmental issues.
2. You pay through the nose for food in this part of London.
3. We paid an arm and a leg for our summer holiday last year.

a. to pay a lot of money
b. to pay too much money
c. to say that you support something (but not to support it in practice)

1E

Have you got what it takes?

Assess whether or not you have what it takes to set up and run a business.

1. I often feel I'm the victim of outside forces I cannot control.

   Yes ☐ No ☐

2. I often work later than planned.

   Yes ☐ No ☐

3. Some days seem to go by without me having achieved a thing.

   Yes ☐ No ☐

4. Given a bad situation, I'll always try to get something out of it.

   Yes ☐ No ☐

5. I think a well ordered pattern of life with regular hours suits me best.

   Yes ☐ No ☐

6. I'm much happier not having to rely on other people.

   Yes ☐ No ☐

7. I'm prepared to take risks only when I've carefully thought through all the consequences.

   Yes ☐ No ☐

8. There's no point starting something unless you're going to see it through.

   Yes ☐ No ☐

9. People often tell me how good I am at seeing things from their point of view.

   Yes ☐ No ☐

10. I tend not to be too ambitious to avoid being disappointed.

    Yes ☐ No ☐

11. It's very important to me that people recognise my success.

    Yes ☐ No ☐

12. When I find myself talking to a telephone answer machine, I usually hang up.

    Yes ☐ No ☐

13. I've never been one to follow the crowd.

    Yes ☐ No ☐

14. All that matters is how much I earn regardless of how hard I work to get it.

    Yes ☐ No ☐

How to score

For questions 2, 4, 7, 8, 9, 11 and 13, score 2 points for every YES response and zero points for every NO. For questions 1, 3, 5, 6, 10, 12 and 14, score 2 points for every NO response and zero points for every YES. The maximum score is 28 points. The higher your score, the better equipped you are likely to be for your future business venture.

A VARIETY OF FIRMS 2

2A

Four types of business

What do these four people do? What sort of company do they work for?

Tony Shaw is the proprietor of Red Signs and Stripes. He is a *sole trader* who works on his own, organizing and running his own business. "I was made redundant so I decided to set up my own company as a sole trader. I mean it's quite complicated starting your own business. I really didn't want the *hassle*. Being a sole trader, on the financial side I take all the responsibility. The Hopewell Business Centre can help with advice, financial advice, legal advice, any worries of that sort. Each company is responsible for security, each of us responsible for making sure that the unit is clean and tidy."

David Huggins is one of the partners at Winch & Winch, a firm of *solicitors* which gives advice to companies at the Hopewell Business Centre. "Winch & Winch is a *partnership*. I'm one of the partners and there are four partners all together. In the case of a legal practice, we are not permitted to work together in any other way.

We're not allowed to become limited *liability* companies. The advantages of a partnership, of course, are that you share a common view and you have colleagues on whom you can rely and with whom you can share your business problems. The disadvantage is that you are not able to limit your personal liability, that if in fact you get into trouble then you are liable to the full extent of your *personal assets*. You cannot protect yourself behind limited liability."

Putting the finishing touches to a fountain

Ian Kirkpatrick is the Managing Director of another company at the Hopewell Business Centre. "The Fountain Workshop is a limited liability company. A limited liability company generally has a *board of directors*. For our company we have two directors. The advantage to those directors is that your liability is limited, as the name suggests, and each director has legal obligations towards the company. Every limited company needs to display a certificate of *incorporation* upon its *premises*. Every company which has a *turnover* of greater than £350,000 has to *file accounts* at *Companies House*."

Nicola Foulston is the *Chief Executive* of Brands Hatch, a famous racing circuit. "Brands Hatch Leisure PLC is the largest organizer and promoter of motor sport events across Europe. PLC stands for 'public limited company' and means that a company is listed on the *stock exchange* within the UK. The *shares* are *quoted* on the London Stock Exchange. The advantages of being a PLC are that you are able to raise money more easily and more efficiently than as a private company. Brands Hatch Leisure PLC turned over £14.2 million in 1996 and made an operating profit out of that of £3 million."

sole trader	Einzelunternehmer(in)	turnover	Umsatz
hassle	Ärger	file accounts	(Geschäfts)bücher einreichen
solicitor	Rechtsanwalt, -anwältin		
partnership	Personengesellschaft	Companies House	*Handelsregister in GB*
liability	Haftung	chief executive	Geschäftsführer(in)
personal assets *pl*	persönlicher Besitz	stock exchange	Börse
board of directors	Vorstand	share	Aktie
incorporation	Gründung	quote	(*Aktien*) notieren
premises *pl*	Firmengelände		

■ Working with the text

I. Which part of the (brackets) is correct according to the text? Read out the correct sentence in full.

1. Tony Shaw (has got/has not got) his own business.
2. David Huggins has got a business with (three/four) other people.
3. Ian Kirkpatrick runs a business. He is (also/not) the owner of the business.
4. Nicola Foulston (works/doesn't work) at the London Stock Exchange.

II. Complete these sentences. Use a word from the text.

1. Tony Shaw is a s… trader. That means he owns and runs a business by himself and takes all the r… for it.
2. David Huggins is a s… . He works with three other colleagues. Their small firm is a p… .
3. Ian Kirkpatrick is the d… of a company that specializes in f… .
4. Nicola Foulston works for Brands Hatch Leisure, which is a p… limited company. That means you can buy s… in the company.

III. Which word or phrase from the text is being described?

1. the owner of a business
2. to lose your job
3. everything a person owns and has a value and which can be used to pay debts
4. a business which belongs to a doctor or a lawyer
5. the obligation a person in business has to pay debts
6. the total sales of a company
7. a place where people can buy shares in a company
8. the money which is made by a company

IV. Questions on the text. Answer them.

1. What advantages does Tony Shaw have by being part of the Hopewell Business Centre?
2. What's the main legal difference between the companies Winch & Winch and The Fountain Workshop?
3. When does a limited liability company have to file its accounts?
4. What are the advantages of being a PLC rather than a private company?

V. Further questions. (The answers are not in the text.)

1. Tony Shaw says that he 'didn't want the hassle' (line 5). What does he mean exactly?
2. David Huggins talks about 'getting into trouble' (line 18). What sort of trouble is he referring to?
3. Ian Kirkpatrick speaks about the directors 'having legal obligations towards the company' (line 24). What legal obligations could these be?
4. Nicola Foulston mentions 'raising money more easily and more efficiently' (line 33) as a PLC. Why would a company like Brands Hatch Leisure want to do this?

■ Exercises

Focus on ➔ focusing structures

Eine gebräuchliche Form von Aussagesätzen:

Article	**Noun**	**to be**	**that**	**...**
The	*disadvantage*	*is*	*that*	*you are not able to limit ...*
The	*advantages of a PLC*	*are*	*that*	*you are able to raise ...*

I. Join the two halves of the sentences. (The four sentences make a short story.)

1. The fact is	a. that the bank gave me another loan.
2. The problem was	b. that I went to see my bank manager.
3. The thing is	c. that I started my own business last year.
4. The result was	d. that the business got into financial difficulty.

II. Make one sentence out of two.

1. A sole trader takes all the responsibility for the financial side of the business.
   That's a fact.
2. In a partnership you are not able to limit your personal liability.
   That's a problem.
3. In a limited liability company you are not liable with all your assets.
   That's an advantage.
4. A PLC is affected by the price of its shares. That's the thing.

III. Write a short paragraph in English describing the advantages and disadvantages of different types of transport (bicycle, bus, car). Write 60 to 80 words.

Example: *The main thing about bicycles is that they are cheap.*
The disadvantage is that ...

IV. Complete the table.

	noun	adjective
1.	finance	...
2.	commerce	...
3.	law	...
4.	variety	...
5.	efficiency	...
6.	fame	...

*V. Say these words out loud. Can you stress (*betonen*) them properly?*

1. company
2. business
3. colleagues
4. advantage
5. liability
6. premises
7. turnover
8. executive

Focus on → comparisons

Einsilbige Adjektive werden durch Anhängen von '-er' und '-est' gesteigert. Zwei- und dreisilbige Adjektive steigert man durch 'more' und 'most' (Ausnahme: Adjektive, die auf '-er', '-le', '-y' und '-ow' enden sowie unregelmäßige Formen).

*Every company with a turnover of **greater** than £350,000 has to file accounts.*
*The advantages are that you are able to raise money **more efficiently**.*

VI. Complete these comparisons. Use the correct form of the words in (brackets). Where you see a question mark (?), think of a word yourself.

1. Would you say that it is (good) working for yourself (?) for other people?
2. It's probably (comforting) to work with other people (?) being completely on your own.
3. Do sole traders have (?) many responsibilities (?) members of a partnership?
4. Limited companies whose turnover is (great) (?) £350,000 must register at Companies House.
5. Most people agree that it is (easy) for a PLC (?) for a limited company to raise capital.

VII. Look at this short extract about partnership agreements. Where do the four expressions in the box go?

capital • disagreements • duties • profits and losses

"A partnership agreement covers the relationship between the partners themselves. It can cover such matters as the … of the partnership, that is what one or more partners put into the business. It can cover the … of the partnership, how much they can take out, how much they have to put in and if there's a loss. It can cover their …, such as what hours they should work on the business of their partnership. It can also deal with such matters as … between the partners, by setting out the procedures to deal with that."

2B

Working at Empire Property Services Ltd

One of the companies at the Hopewell Business Centre is Empire Property Services. Here are three conversations which take place at the firm.

Giving instructions for the day's work

▸ Morning Harry. Morning Bert. This is today's job. This is the *paperwork*. It's a painting job. Painting the outside of the house, the windows, the doors. You'll find it all down here.

▸ What's the address?

▸ 23, Ashley Drive. Do you know where that is?

▸ Yes, I know. It's near the old sports ground.

▸ What kind of a place is it?

▸ It's a two-*storey* house, wooden windows. You have to paint the outside of the house, the doors and the windows.

▸ What's the colour scheme then?

▸ It's all written down here. Beige for the walls, light blue for the windows and the doors.

▸ How long will it take us?

▸ We've allowed a week but I'll see you back here tonight and you can tell us how you're getting on. OK?

▸ OK, let's go then!

Harry and Bert go off to work

Asking the boss for a day off work

▸ Have you got a moment, Alan?

▸ Yes, Theresa?

▸ Do you think I could take a day off work at the end of the month?

▸ Which day is it?

▸ Friday week. The 31.

▸ We're rather busy then. Is it something important?

▸ My cousin's getting married and she asked me to be a bridesmaid.

▸ Well, I suppose I'll have to say yes then, won't I?

▸ Thanks very much.

▸ But remember to fill in a holiday form!

Asking an employee to work overtime

- Tara, we're going to be very busy at the end of the month and Theresa wants to take the Friday off. Can you work a couple of hours' overtime?
- Oh dear, um, yes, I suppose so. How late would you want me to work?
- Hopefully only a couple of hours. Until seven o'clock.
- Yes, all right then.
- All right, thanks, because we're going to be very busy at the end of the month.

paperwork	Unterlagen
storey	Stock(werk), Etage

■ Working with the text

I. Complete these sentences using the information in the text.

1. Harry and Bert's job today is to … .
2. It's quite a big job and it should take them … .
3. Theresa wants a day off work because … .
4. Her boss, Alan, agrees but asks her … .
5. Alan would like Tara to … .
6. One reason is because Theresa is not at work on that day.
   The other reason is that … .

II. Answer these questions on the text.

1. What will Harry and Bert find on the piece of paper the supervisor gives them?
2. Why must Theresa fill in a holiday form?
3. When does Tara usually finish work on a Friday?

III. Say these words from the text out loud.

1. colour scheme
2. beige
3. Friday, 31st
4. won't I?
5. employee

IV. Further questions.

1. Alan says: 'Well, I suppose I'll have to say yes' (line 28) when Theresa asks him for a day off work. What does Alan's sentence say about how he really feels?
2. Explain the expression 'Friday week' (line 25).
3. What does a 'bridesmaid' (line 27) do?

V. What do you think?

1. Should employees always be allowed a day off work when somebody in their family gets married?
2. Is it possible for an employee not to do overtime when the boss asks him or her?

■ Exercises

Focus on ➔ asking difficult questions

Eine Bitte oder heikle Frage leitet man mit 'Would you …?' oder 'Could you …?' ein. Sehr höflich sind die Bitten 'Would you mind if …?', 'Do you think I could …?' und 'I was wondering if …?'.

***Would you** mind if I took a day off work?*
***Do you think I could** take a day off work?*
***I was wondering if** I could take a day off work?*

I. Match the two halves of these sentences.

1. Do you think	a. to leave work earlier today?
2. Would it be all right	b. if I could leave work earlier today?
3. Would it be possible for me	c. I could leave work earlier today?
4. I was wondering	d. if I left work earlier today?

II. Look at Alan's question and Tara's answer. Does Tara agree to Alan's request?

Alan: Would you mind if I closed the window?
Tara: No, not at all.

III. Look at the underlined verb in Tara's question. It's a past tense form but is it also past time?

Tara: Would it be all right if I came later tomorrow?
Alan: I suppose so.

*IV. Ask questions using the prompts (*Helfer*) below. Include a structure in the box. (Be careful with sentence 6!)*

Would it be all right if ... • Would you mind if ... • Would it be OK if ...

1. You want to use your boss's phone.
2. You would like to go home at one o'clock on Friday afternoon.
3. You are planning to have two weeks' holiday in January.
4. You are thinking of working at home tomorrow.

5. You are wondering if you could start work later in the morning.
6. You don't like the idea of moving office.

Focus on ➔ verb + object + infinitive

Nebensätze vermeiden hilft die im Deutschen seltenere Satzkonstruktion Verb + Objekt + Infinitiv mit 'to'.

She expects him to call.
Remind me to buy some milk.

V. Now you're the boss! Translate these sentences into good English.

1. Ich möchte, dass Sie heute etwas länger bleiben.
2. Ich will, dass wir an diesem Sonntag arbeiten.
3. Ich möchte, dass du klopfst, bevor du eintrittst.
4. Ich hätte gerne, dass jeder zur Weihnachtsfeier kommt.

VI. Complete the mini-dialogues using the question words from the box and the correct form of the words in (brackets).

How • How far • How long (x2) • How often • What • When • Where • Whose • Why

1. ... (you/come/from)?	From a small town in Saxony-Anhalt.
2. ... (motorbike/this)?	It's my brother's.
3. ... (the journey/take)?	About three hours but we had one stop.
4. ... (this/call/in English)?	It's a hole puncher.
5. ... (it/from/Glasgow to Edinburgh)?	About 50 miles, I think.
6. ... (you/see/each other)?	Usually twice a week.
7. ... (you/work/in this company)?	For about three years now.
8. ... (you/get/here)?	By car.
9. ... (you/smile)?	I'm sorry. I can't tell you.
10. … (your train/arrive)?	Just after 10.30.

VII. Complete Alan Winter's text. Use the correct forms of the words in (brackets). Where there is a question mark (?), think of a word yourself.

"I … (make redundant) from a large multi-national company and I … (begin, operate) from my own house in the back bedroom. I set up a small office there and started working … (?) a sole trader. The business … (grow) to such an extent that after a twelve-month period I … (find) that I had so much … (?) that I couldn't cope with it myself and I needed to look for … (?) to work with me. It was that time that I set up a … (?) with somebody who is now my co-director. The business … (continue, grow) and it … (be) then appropriate to become a limited company. As a limited company we … (carry on, grow) and last year our … (?) exceeded £1 million."

2C

Hugh Pierce - helping young people in business

Hugh gives Ben some advice

I. As you listen to Hugh Pierce talking about the The Prince's Youth Business Trust, read and answer this question.

What is Hugh Pierce's job? Tick the most appropriate answer.

a) He's a teacher.
b) He's a business advisor.
c) He's a photographer.
d) He's a lorry driver.

II. Listen again. Which is the correct answer? Tick it.

1. How long has Hugh Pierce had a career in banking?
   a) Over 15 years.
   b) Over 20 years.
   c) Over 35 years.
2. The Prince's Youth Business Trust supports young people in two ways. These are ...
   a) with a loan and a business advisor.
   b) with a business advisor and lots of publicity.
   c) with a computer and office furniture.

3. Who is Ben?
   a) He's one of Hugh's sons.
   b) He's one of Hugh's clients.
   c) He's one of Hugh's friends.
4. Hugh Pierce mentions one very important aspect of his work with the clients. This is ...
   a) choosing the right name for the business.
   b) finding the right premises.
   c) working out a business plan.

III. Look at these three sentences from the interview. What does the underlined word 'it' refer to? Match it with the answer below (a-c).

1. It frees me up to talk objectively about his business from my perspective.
2. It can sound a theoretical exercise. I can assure you, it's not. It's hard work.
3. When it's up, it's very, very good but don't get over-optimistic.

   a. doing a business plan
   b. the business cycle
   c. not being in the same profession as the client

IV. Say these words out loud. Make sure you stress them properly.

1. average
2. photographer
3. expertise
4. recommendation
5. decision

V. Complete this table.

	noun	**verb**
1.	advisor, advice	...
2.	...	succeed
3.	loan	...
4.	...	support
5.	photographer	...
6.	...	contribute
7.	recommendation	...
8.	decision	...
9.	...	meet
10.	...	prepare

2D

Troubleshooter advises a young photographer

Troubleshooter has got an important appointment this morning. He has been asked to give some advice to an *up-and-coming* portrait photographer.

When he arrives at the photographer's door, Troubleshooter is surprised to find that his services are no longer required. His client is already receiving advice from another organization: the Prince's Trust. Troubleshooter does not give in, however. He walks into the photographer's studio, takes out a piece of paper and pen and begins to ask questions.

The photographer is busy. He is taking photographs of a young model. All he really wants to know is whether he can afford a larger studio. Troubleshooter suggests the photographer cuts out any unnecessary costs: no more chocolate biscuits, no more sugar in his coffee. He should also remember to recycle his *paper clips* and not to take too many photographs. Troubleshooter is proud to *quote* his professor: "Take care of the pennies and the pounds will take care of themselves."

Troubleshooter is interested in the overheads: *rates*, rent, gas and electricity, phone and fax bill. However, to work out whether the photographer can afford a new studio, he needs to borrow a calculator. As the photographer doesn't have one, Troubleshooter takes out an *abacus* from his *briefcase*. He suggests that the young model might help with the calculation.

The young model, however, has had enough of this strange man disturbing the photographic session. She stands up and punches Troubleshooter on the chin. Troubleshooter falls to the ground. The photographer steps forward to take a photograph of him for 'The Daily Splash'. The cover reads: 'Troubleshooter *counted out*!'

up-and-coming	kommend, aufstrebend	abacus	Abakus (*Rechenbrett*)
paper clip	Büroklammer	briefcase	(Akten)tasche, -mappe
quote	zitieren	punch	schlagen
rates *pl*	Kommunalsteuern	count out	(*Sport*) auszählen

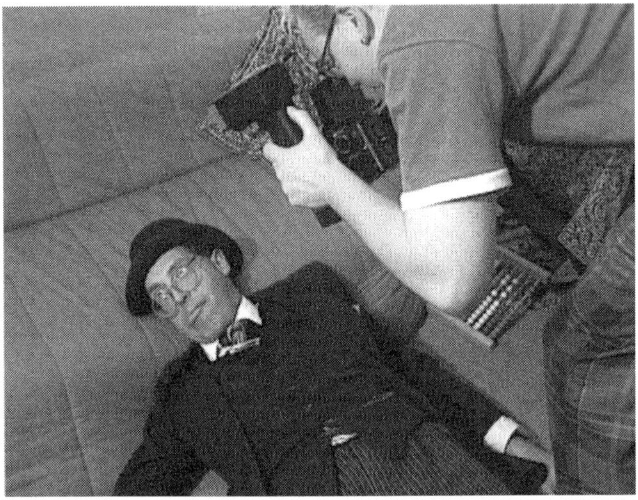

I. Answer the questions.

1. Who does Troubleshooter visit and why?
2. Why does the client give Troubleshooter such a cool reception?
3. What happens to Troubleshooter at the end of his visit?

II. Which is the correct answer? Mark it.

1. What does 'Take care of the pennies and the pounds will take care of themselves' (line 13) mean?
   a) If you go shopping with a lot of pennies you don't have to take many pounds with you.
   b) If you spend a lot of pennies you will not spend many pounds.
   c) If you save money on small items you will automatically save money on large items.
2. What does the phrase 'Troubleshooter counted out!' (lines 22-23) mean?
   a) He can't stand up. b) He has got no money. c) He has received a loan.

III. Choose the correct answer.

1. Which of these people will you probably <u>not</u> have an appointment with?
   a) your boyfriend/girlfriend b) your dentist c) your tax advisor

IV. Explain these idiomatic phrases in English. Use a dictionary if you wish.

1. Cheap houses are two a penny where we come from!
2. I had to explain the joke three times before the penny dropped!
3. Excuse me a second. I'm just going to spend a penny.

2E

A profit and loss forecast

	Month	
	Budget	Actual
Sales (net of VAT) (a)		
Less: Direct Costs		
Cost of Materials		
Wages		
Gross Profit (b)		
Gross Profit Margin ($^b/_a$ x 100%)		
Overheads		
Salaries		
Rent/Rates/Water		
Insurance		
Repairs/Renewals		
Heat/Light/Power		
Postage/Printing/Stationery		
Motor & Travel		
Telephone		
Professional Fees		
Interest Charges		
Bank Charges		
Other		
Total Overheads (c)		
Trading Profit (b)-(c)		
Less Depreciation		
Net Profit Before Tax		
Cumulative Net Profit		

TECHNOLOGY AT WORK 3

3A

How magazines are produced

John Pitt is the *Commercial Director* at Invicta Press, a printing company owned by Headley Brothers. During a tour of the firm, John explains the production process.

"This is the pre-press department. Nigel is using a drum scanner to convert photographic prints or *transparencies* into digital *files* on computer. Here Hugh is working on a page of a customer's magazine. The customer has prepared the page on computer and has transmitted it by modem or ISDN to Headley Brothers. Hugh is now adding a picture to the page. This is the printing department. All the presses at Headley Brothers are manufactured in Germany. This press can produce a complete section, printed in four colours, on both sides of the paper. Once the *ink* is dry the printed work can be sent to the folding machines in the *bindery* department. The sections are *fed into hoppers*, here, and dropped onto a *conveyor belt*. The sections of the magazine are gathered together and glued into the cover. The purpose of the conveyor belt is to allow time for the glue to dry. This is the *dispatch* hall. Here completed magazines are packed individually in *polythene* envelopes with an address label. They are sorted into post codes and placed into mail sacks for the post office. Headley Brothers also sorts mail to meet German post office requirements. Production continues around the clock and frequently at the weekend as well. Our staff operate on a shift system. We have two daytime shifts, a night shift and weekend shifts. Staff are sometimes asked if they will work overtime to make up an extra shift."

Ingrid Eissfeldt has worked at Headley Brothers as a European *Sales Representative* since 1994. She explains the work of the office staff.

"This is not exactly the paperless office, but the secretary-less office. Every member of staff has his or her own PC linked to a printer. We are all responsible for our own letters and paperwork. There are approximately thirty-five PCs in the office. We have customers all over Britain and we have an increasing volume of work in Europe. Anita has a *database* with details of all our customers. Computers are used to produce customers' *invoices*. All our personal computers are linked in a network and there is also a *mainframe* network for handling magazine *subscriptions*. Our customers can communicate with us by e-mail or by fax or they can communicate with us in the traditional way by sending us their material by courier or by mail."

commercial director	*etwa*: Bereichsleiter(in)	dispatch	Versand
transparency	Dia(positiv)	polythene	Polyäthylen, Plastik
file	Datei	sales representative	Vertreter(in)
ink	Druckfarbe, Tinte	database	Datenbank
bindery	Buchbinderei	invoice	(Waren)rechnung, Lieferschein
feed into	zuführen		
hopper	Einfülltrichter	mainframe	Groß-
conveyor belt	Förder-, Fließband	subscription	Abonnement

■ Working with the text

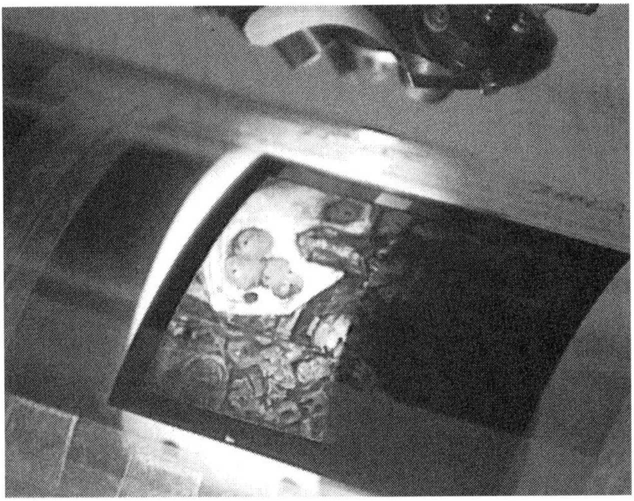

Scanning in a slide

I. Read what John Pitt says about the production process at Invicta Press. Write down the five production stages he talks about. (Part of the exercise has been done for you.)

1.	
↘	
	2. Making up the pages
↙	
3.	
↘	
	4.
↙	
5.	

II. Explain what happens in the bindery department at Invicta.

Example: *The pages are folded and then ...*

III. When does John Pitt use passive forms of the verb when describing the production process? When does he use active forms? Why?

IV. Questions on John Pitt's text. Answer them.

1. What role does modern technology play at Invicta Press?
2. In what sense does Invicta Press help the German economy?
3. How can you see that business is going well at Headley Brothers?

V. Which words from John Pitt's text are being described?

1. letters or parcels sent by post
2. the people who work in a company
3. a period of time worked by a group of workers

VI. Questions on Ingrid Eissfeldt's text. Answer them.

1. Why are there no secretaries in the Headley Brothers' office?
2. What do the office workers use their PCs for?
3. What four ways can customers send their material to Headley Brothers?

VII. Which words from Ingrid Eissfeldt's text are being described?

1. a large amount of information on a computer
2. a list of goods or services and what they cost
3. paying in advance to receive a magazine regularly

VIII. Further questions. (The answers are not in the text.)

1. What's the difference between using a modem or ISDN when transmitting information?
2. What do you think about working shifts (lines 19-21)? Would you do it?

■ Exercises

Focus on → passive forms

Das Passiv ermöglicht es, eine Handlung zu beschreiben, ohne die agierende Person zu nennen.

*The presses **are manufactured** in Germany.*
*The magazines **are sorted** into post codes.*

I. Put the verbs into present passive forms. (There are also some passive forms with modal auxiliaries.)

1. Scanners (use) to convert prints or transparencies into digital files.
2. First, pages (prepare) on computer by the customer.

3. Then they (transmit) by modem or ISDN to Headley Brothers.
4. The paper (can, print) in four colours and on both sides.
5. The printed work (send) to the folding machines in the bindery department.
6. There the sections of the magazine (gather) together and (glue) into the cover.
7. In the dispatch hall the completed magazines (pack), (sort) and (put) into mail sacks.
8. Magazines (produce) around the clock at Headley Brothers.
9. This means that a shift system (have to, use).
10. And sometimes staff (may, ask) to work overtime.

II. Rewrite these sentences using a passive construction of the underlined verb.

1. Somebody told me something very interesting yesterday.
2. Those stupid people in that shop over the road lost our order for forty dictionaries so we had to order them again.
3. The money vanished from his wallet and he never saw it again.
4. A man in his forties carrying a plastic bag and a toy revolver stole $10,000 from a bank in Cleveland, Ohio.
5. Our well-trained staff check all items of clothing before they leave the factory in Lisbon.
6. Tough competition from south-east Asia and high production costs at home have forced the company to reduce the workforce by 20% in the last six months.
7. Someone from our firm will meet you at the airport and drive you to the office.
8. The government cannot renew your work permit if you have been here for more than two years.

III. Read the text about Total Quality Management. Rewrite the passage using passive constructions. Start with: 'Resources ...' (line 4).

Total Quality Management (TQM) means doing a job right the first time. But what does 'doing it right' really mean? It means you mustn't waste resources; no wasted materials, no wasted time and no wasted space. And it means you have to throw out outmoded processes. It's an ongoing process and it has to involve everyone in the company. You have to move responsibility to the point where employees and customers meet. It's the employees - not the management - that have to make the important decisions because they're closest to the customers. And you must give the employees more decision-making powers. The company administration should support them and try to make their life easier. You can only do this through creative teamwork and not in a climate of conflict and tension.

IV. What do these abbreviations stand for?

MJN 400-2 PC98

- Intel 400MHz Pentium® II Processor
- 128Mb SDRAM
- 8.4Gb ultra ATA-33 hard drive
- 8Mb AGP x2 ATI Rage Pro (Expert @ Work) 3D graphics
- DVD-ROM drive with MPEG-2 playback (also functions as fast CD-ROM)
- LS120 120Mb floppy drive (also functions as 1.44Mb drive)

1. RAM
2. CD-ROM
3. ISDN
4. Gb
5. MHz
6. 3D

Focus on → infinitive of purpose

Der Infinitiv mit 'to' wird verwendet, um den Zweck einer Handlung zu beschreiben. Das Gleiche kann mit 'in order to' oder 'so as to' zum Ausdruck gebracht werden. Bei verneinten Sätzen benutzt man 'in order not to' oder 'so as not to'.

*Computers are used **to produce** customers' invoices.*
*Staff are asked if they will work overtime **to make up** an extra shift.*

V. Rewrite the following sentences using a simple infinitive construction.

1. He went outside in order to get some fresh air.
2. We drove along the country roads so as to avoid the traffic.
3. They got up early in order to get to the airport on time.
4. She emigrated to Florida so as to get away from the cold weather.

VI. Make one sentence out of two by using a negative infinitive construction.

1. I'm leaving now. I don't want to be late.
2. They're bringing us the parcel personally. They dislike paying the delivery charges.
3. She is living alone. She's had enough of depending on her parents.
4. We'll be quiet. What would happen if the baby woke up?

VII. Complete the sentences using the correct words from the box. ●●

personnel • personal • people

1. Which of you doesn't have a ... computer at home?
2. The person who interviews you for a job is often the ... manager.

wallet • suitcase • briefcase

3. A ... is something men have to keep money and important documents in. It's small and flat and it fits into a pocket easily.
4. A ... is something you keep books, papers and files in. It is usually made of leather and has a handle on the top so you can carry it easily.

employer • employee • employment

5. An ... is a person or organization which has people working for them.
6. An ... gets money for working for a company, organization or other people.

notebook • diary • calendar

7. A ... is a book where you write down your appointments.
8. You usually put a ... on the wall so you can see what day and date of the month it is.

economic • economics • economical

9. Small cars are usually very ... because they don't consume a lot of petrol.
10. Has the country's ... situation improved in the last year?

3B

Improving the office

▸ Adrian and ▸ Susanna Garrard have a theatre company called The Naked Pony. They run the company from home. They want to improve their office with some new furniture and new office equipment, including a new PC. First Adrian rings a local shop to find out what they stock. Later he and Susanna go to the shop. First the ▸ shop assistant leads them into the furniture department.

▸ If you'd like to come this way there's plenty to choose from. We've got desks, chairs, *filing cabinets*, cupboards, *bookcases*.

▸ Office furniture is the first requirement.

▸ This one has four drawers and space for *hanging files*.

▸ This one's quite good, don't you think? There's room for everything.

▸ It's too big, isn't it? We don't need one as big as that, do we? How about that smaller one?

▸ That would be fine. Now how about a desk? This would fit, wouldn't it?

▸ This one has a drawer which can be used as a filing cabinet.

▸ It's got this drawer for all your *bits and pieces*, paper clips, *drawing pins*, *hole punch*, *stapler*.

- Great!
- And there's room for *stationery* here, *headed notepaper*, envelopes, *compliment slips*, very neat. How about a *swivel chair* as well?

Next, Adrian and Susanna look at computers.

- Perhaps you'd like to come and look at the computers next. I'll show you what the software can do. If you'd like to take a seat. Perhaps you'd like to remind me what you'd like to do with your computer.
- Well, basically there are two main purposes, office work and publicity. For the office work we want a simple *word-processing* facility, for writing letters, *memos* and so on. And we also want a *spreadsheet* facility for *keeping* our accounts.
- That's no problem, this spreadsheet package can actually *monitor* your accounts and *cash flow* forecasts.

- And then there's the question of publicity. As a theatre company, whenever we put on a new production we have to produce posters and programmes.
- We've tried several printers but whichever way we do it it's always expensive.
- And so we want to do it ourselves.
- Again, no problems. With this machine you can also use this software package, you've got a selection of *clipart pictures* and you can import them. And if you want to create your own design you can use the *paint feature* which is part of the same package. And then you can print it out.

filing cabinet	Aktenschrank, -regal
bookcase	Bücherregal, -schrank
hanging file	Hängeregister
bits and pieces	Krimskrams
drawing pin	Reißzwecke
hole punch	Locher
stapler	Hefter, Tacker
stationery	Büromaterial
headed notepaper	Briefpapier mit Briefkopf
compliment slip	Empfehlungskärtchen
swivel chair	Drehstuhl, -sessel
word processing	Textverarbeitung
memo	Notiz, Mitteilung
spreadsheet	Tabellenkalkulation(spro-gramm)
keep	*hier*: führen
monitor	überwachen, kontrollieren
cash flow	Cashflow (*Überschuss nach Abzug aller Kosten*)
clipart picture	Clipart (*Computerbildchen*)
paint feature	Maloption

■ Working with the text

I. Answer the questions.

1. What two things do Adrian and Susanna want to buy?
2. Is the shop assistant helpful? Say why or why not.

II. Explain the underlined phrases from the text in your own words as far as possible.

1. 'Office furniture is the first requirement.' (line 8)
2. 'Very neat.' (line 19)
3. 'This spreadsheet package can monitor your accounts.' (line 28)
4. 'We've tried several printers.' (line 32)

III. Read through the first half of the text again and label the pieces of furniture.

1.

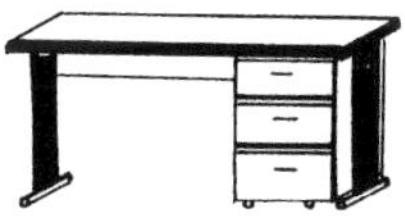

2.

3.

4.

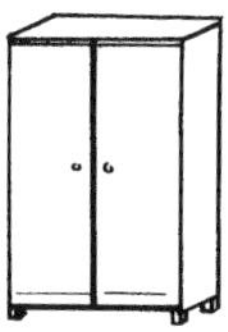

5.

IV. Which bits and pieces can you identify? (They are all in the text - except one!)

1. 

2. 

3. 

4. 

5. 

V. Look at this stationery. What can you see exactly?

1. 

2. 

3. 

VI. Match the two halves of the sentences.

1. If you want to write letters	a. you need a spreadsheet package.
2. If you want to keep accounts	b. you need a word-processing program.
3. If you want to produce posters	c. you need a scanner.
4. If you don't want to type in text	d. you need clipart and paint features.

■ Exercises

Focus on ➔ polite questions

Bitten kann man mit 'If you'd like …' einleiten. Noch höflicher ist 'perhaps'.

If you'd like *to come this way.*
Perhaps *you'd like to look at the computers.*

I. Use 'would like' instead of 'could' to make these sentences sound polite.

1. Could you follow me?
2. Could you wait here for a second?
3. Could you fill in this form?

4. Could you show me what you've brought with you today.
5. Could you come with me?

II. Rewrite this dialogue using more polite structures. The expressions in the box might help you.

• Do you think I could ...?	• Would you like ...?
• Could I ...?	• I'd like to ...

Visitor:	Where's Donald Ryan?
Receptionist:	What's your name?
Visitor:	Jeremy Rushton.
Receptionist:	Sit down and wait.
Visitor:	OK.
Receptionist:	Cup of coffee?
Visitor:	No. I want tea.
Receptionist:	Here.

Focus on ➔ the prop word 'one'

Die Stützwörter 'one' und 'ones' stehen für das entsprechende Substantiv.

*This **one**'s quite good, don't you think? There's room for everything.*
*It's too big, isn't it? We don't need **one** as big as that, do we? How about that smaller **one**?*

III. Replace words with 'one' or 'ones'.

1. I'm going to have a drink. Would you like a drink?
2. I'm going to buy a ticket for the game. Shall I get a ticket for you, too?
3. The postcards from England arrived. The postcards from Ireland didn't.
4. The English apples are more expensive but the French apples are sweeter.
5. This dictionary is not very good. Your dictionary is much better.
6. Are these glasses clean? - No, use the glasses over there.
7. Would you like a chocolate? - Can I have a chocolate with cream in it?
8. Which car is yours? The white car! There are three white cars!
9. My daughter wants a cat. - I wouldn't have a cat in my house!
10. We want to buy her a book when she leaves the firm. - We want to buy her a book, too!

Focus on ➔ question tags

Das Frageanhängsel im Englischen richtet sich nach dem Verb des vorausgehenden Satzes. Auf einen bejahten Satz folgt gewöhnlich ein verneintes Frageanhängsel und umgekehrt.

Bringt das Anhängsel eine echte Frage zum Ausdruck, geht der Sprechende zum Satzende hin mit der Stimme nach oben, sucht er nur Bestätigung, senkt er die Stimme.

IV. Finish the questions. Add the correct tag.

1. You work for a furniture company, .?.
2. You don't work full-time, .?.
3. You have to start at nine o'clock, .?.
4. You've got a nice boss, .?.
5. You haven't worked for her before, .?.
6. The work doesn't pay well, .?.
7. I suppose it's tiring standing on your feet all day, .?.
8. And not all your customers are friendly, .?.

Now read the sentences out in two different ways. Once with rising intonation (↗). And a second time with falling intonation (↘).

Focus on ➔ uncountable nouns

Es gibt Substantive im Englischen, die nur in der Mehrzahl vorkommen (z.B. *trousers*). Das zugehörige Verb steht deshalb in der Mehrzahl.

Einige Substantive im Englischen sind, im Gegensatz zum Deutschen, nicht zählbar (z.B. *information*). Diese Substantive haben keine Mehrzahlform. Es gibt außerdem eine Reihe von Substantiven mit Pluralendung, die als Einheit aufgefasst werden (z.B. *the United States*). Das Verb steht auch bei diesen Substantiven in der Einzahl.

V. Choose the correct word in (brackets) to form complete sentences.

1. The jacket looks fine but the trousers (are/is) too short.
2. Staff (are/is) not expected to wear ties to work.
3. There (are/is) some important news for you.
4. (Have/Has) the new office furniture been ordered yet?
5. Where (are/is) the scissors that (were/was) on my desk a minute ago?
6. (Are/Is) the US hosting the next Winter Olympic Games?

7. The goods you ordered last week (have/has) been delivered.
8. (Don't/Doesn't) the British police carry weapons when (they are/it is) on duty?

VI. Make sentences. Choose the correct form in (brackets).

1. Would you like (some/a) chewing gum?
2. We had (a/some) difficult homework yesterday, didn't we?
3. Your furniture (is/are) very modern! Did you buy (them/it) recently?
4. My luggage (aren't/isn't) here so I suppose (they haven't/it hasn't) come off the plane yet.

VII. Say it in English.

1. Die Informationen über Headley Brothers, die wir erhielten, waren sehr interessant.
2. Vielen Dank für die Ratschläge, die Sie uns gegeben haben.
3. Sie hat seit Weihnachten im Englischen große Fortschritte gemacht.
4. Möchtest du noch einen Toast oder ein Stück Kuchen?

VIII. Complete the sentences by using 'are', 'do', 'does', 'has' or 'have'.

1. … the Netherlands in the European Union?
2. Where … the United Nations Security Council meet?
3. Here … the evening news from the BBC.
4. … all the data been collected?

IX. Give the German equivalent.

1. The data is on the hard disk.
2. The United States is one of the richest countries in the world.
3. No news is good news.
4. Is the media only interested in scandals and disasters?

3C

Ted Roffey - adapting to technological change

I. As you listen to Ted Roffey talking about changes at his place of work, read and answer this question.

What does Ted Roffey think about the changes that have taken place at Headley Brothers over the last forty years?

a) He's unhappy with them.
b) He's pleased about them.
c) He's not interested in them.
d) He's excited about them.

II. Listen again. Which is the correct answer? Tick it.

1. How old was Ted when he started working at Headley Brothers?
   a) He was 15. b) He was 16. c) He was 18.
2. When Ted first started working it was important to be good at English. Why?
   a) Because all the manuals for the machines were in English.
   b) Because the warning signs were in complicated English.
   c) Because pages were made up by hand - not by computer.

3. What happened to the Headley Brothers workforce when new technology came in?
   a) Nobody lost their job.
   b) The older employees had to retire early.
   c) Most people had to share jobs.
4. How does Ted compare his work today with his work forty years ago?
   a) His work today is more frustrating.
   b) His work today is more rewarding.
   c) His work today is more boring.

III. Replace the underlined words with another verb in its correct form from the box below.

to be introduced • to become available • to enter • to discuss • to remove

1. An apprenticeship came up in the composing department.
2. When I came into the trade it was important that you were good at English.
3. Nobody was ever made redundant when new technology came in.

IV. Say these words out loud.

1. apprentice
2. apprenticeship
3. redundancy
4. technology

V. Complete this grid.

	adjective	noun
1.	efficient	...
2.	...	tradition
3.	dangerous	...
4.	...	environment
5.	important	...
6.	redundant	...

3D

Troubleshooter updates his office

Troubleshooter has just finished typing a bill for another satisfied customer. As his typewriter is a bit old, he decides that the time has come to take it to a museum and buy a computer.

He goes to PC World and looks at the latest, state-of-the-art office equipment. The assistant shows him a notebook computer and a mini-fax machine. Troubleshooter wonders if he can do without a printer. "I was rather hoping for a paperless office," he says. The assistant reassures him. "Even the best establishments need hard copy these days, sir." Troubleshooter fills three *trolleys* with computer equipment. "I'm going to be the UK's business success story!" he says excitedly.

At the *till* Troubleshooter remembers that he can set off office equipment against tax. "I will be requiring a *VAT* receipt for my accounts," he says. The bill comes to a massive £36,343.20. However, the assistant is prepared to throw in a free *extension* lead. Troubleshooter is slightly confused. What would he be wanting with an extension lead? The assistant is quick to answer. "To *plug into* the *power*!"

Suddenly Troubleshooter realizes he has got a good excuse to leave the shop without buying anything. "I'm afraid I don't have any electricity in my office," he says.

"I'll have to think about it." He picks up his umbrella and briefcase and says good-bye to the assistant. "Thank you very much for your time and your attention. Good afternoon!"

Troubleshooter hurries back to the museum and picks up his old typewriter. "Just think how much money I've saved today," he remarks.

update	auf den neuesten Stand bringen	VAT	MwSt. (*Mehrwertsteuer*)
trolley	Einkaufswagen	extension lead	Verlängerungskabel
till	Kasse	plug into	anschließen an
		power	Strom

I. Answer the questions.

1. Where does Troubleshooter go and why?
2. What happens at the end of the story?

II. What do these words and expressions mean? Tick one answer.

1. 'State-of-the-art equipment' (line 4) ...
   a) has the most modern designs.
   b) uses the most modern technology.
   c) contains expensive graphics software.
2. 'Hard copy' (line 7) is ...
   a) computer hardware. b) uncomfortable seats. c) printed material.
3. If you 'set off office equipment against tax' (lines 10-11) you want to pay ...
   a) more tax. b) less tax. c) no tax.
4. 'VAT' (line 11) stands for ...
   a) very advanced technology.
   b) value added tax.
   c) violent, aggressive trader.

How much is VAT at the moment in Britain?

III. Give the German translation for the word 'save' in these sentences.

1. He's trying to *save* his marriage.
2. She's *saving up* for a new computer.
3. *Save* some of the chocolate for later!
4. If you order the goods by phone you will *save* yourself a journey.
5. I've *saved* the file on a floppy disk.

3E

Some definitions of success

Name	Stuart Dune
Age	24
Background	Paralysed from the neck down in car accident
Idea	High-performance, lightweight wheelchairs for athletes
The Trust Funding	Test market grant of £250 £1,500 grant £3,000 loan £4,500 loan
Results	Multiple models manufactured in Switzerland
Financial Results	Soon to be a £1 million turnover business

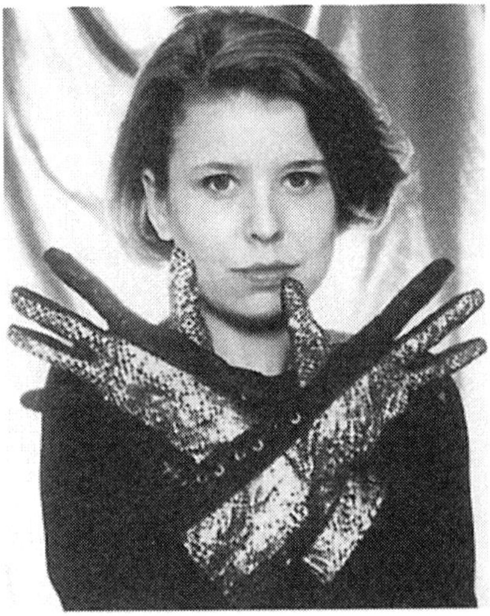

Name	Marie Bernadette Callan
Age	26
Background	Schooled in fashion design. Unemployed for 14 months
Idea	High fashion accessories such as gloves, and hair-bands made from marine leathers
The Trust Funding	£4,000 loan £1,500 grant
Results	Sold in Harrods, US and European department stores.
Financial Results	Expected 1994 turnover, £600,000

BANKING

4

4A

Advising business customers

Claire Wasmuth is a business advisor with Barclay's Bank, one of the United Kingdom's major banks. She's talking to a business customer who has had one of his cheques returned.

- ▸ Good morning, Mr James. How are you today?
- ▸ Hello, Claire, not very happy at the moment.
- ▸ What seems to be the problem?
- ▸ Well, I've received this letter saying that you *bounced* a cheque on one of my clients and it's caused me a bit of *embarrassment*.
- ▸ Oh, right. What seems to have happened is that a *standing order* has gone out of your account the day before this cheque came through. It was for £300. Does that ring a bell with you at all, Mr James?

One of Claire's roles is to help customers who are setting up a new business. "When a customer is setting up a new business or wants to expand their existing business, they might ask the bank to lend them money. When a customer applies for a *loan*, the bank would ask them for lots of information and this would normally come in the form of a business plan. The business plan is then used by the bank to see whether the customer has actually thought through the *proposition* that they're going into. We would then look at the business plan and decide for ourselves whether or not we think the business would be a success. We would also ask the customer to put a *stake* into the business, so in other words, we would ask them to put some of their own money towards it, and this then shows their *commitment* to make it work. Before the bank agrees to lend the money it needs to be sure that the customer is creditworthy. That means will he or she pay back the loan. Sometimes we ask for security with a loan. This might be the person's house, for example. The security is then used as a *safeguard* so that if anything went wrong with the business, the bank would still get its money back."

bounce	(*Scheck*) platzen	proposition	Vorhaben
embarrassment	Verlegenheit	stake	Einsatz, Anteil
standing order	Dauerauftrag	commitment	Engagement
loan	Darlehen	safeguard	Absicherung

■ Working with the text

I. Which is the correct answer to these questions? Mark it.

1. What is Mr James's problem?
   a) He wanted to pay a client by cheque but he had no more cheques in his cheque book.
   b) He wanted to pay a client by cheque but the client does not accept cheques.
   c) He wanted to pay a client by cheque but he had no more money on his account.
2. What does Mr James mean by 'The bank bounced a cheque on my client' (lines 7-8)?
   a) The bank sent another cheque to Mr James's client.
   b) The bank did not transfer Mr James's money to his client's account.
   c) The bank wanted some money from Mr James's client.
3. Why is Mr James embarrassed?
   a) His client might think he has got no money.
   b) His client might think his bank is incompetent.
   c) His client might think he has got no cheques.
4. What is a 'standing order' (line 9)?
   a) A payment from a bank account to another person or organization which is made at a regular time each month.

b) A payment from a bank account to another person or organization which is made by a person standing at the counter.
c) A payment from a bank account to another person or organization which is made automatically by the bank.

5. What does the phrase 'Does that ring a bell with you?' (line 11) mean?
   a) Do you remember?
   b) Do you understand?
   c) Do you feel angry?

II. Answer these questions.

1. Claire says that the bank usually needs three things from a business customer before it can grant a loan. Which three things does she mean?
2. Claire says '... if anything went wrong with the business' (lines 25-26). What does she mean exactly?

III. Explain these expressions from the text using your own words. Give examples if you wish.

1. to think through a proposition	(line 17)
2. to put a stake into a business	(line 20)
3. to be creditworthy	(line 23)

IV. Which does the underlined word refer back to in the text? Choose a word from the box.

the cheque • the standing order • the loan • the customers • the business • security

1. 'It was for £300.'	(line 10)
2. 'They might ask the bank to lend them money.'	(line 14)
3. 'We would ask them to put some of their own money towards it.'	(lines 20-21)
4. 'This might be the person's house, for example.'	(lines 24-25)

■ Exercises

Focus on → multi-word verbs

Bei vielen zusammengesetzten Verben gibt die Grundbedeutung der Einzelwörter keine Auskunft über die Bedeutung des Verbs.

*Claire helps people who are **setting up in** business.*	(gründen)
*We ask them to **put** some money **towards** the business.*	(investieren in)

I. Match the underlined verbs (1-5) with their more formal equivalents (a-e).

1. The government's decision set off protests throughout the country.
2. He set out to walk across the United States.
3. We're setting off early so that we get there before dark.
4. You really ought to set aside some money for when you are older.
5. Banks help people intending to set up a business.

a. keep
b. establish
c. cause
d. start
e. begin a journey

II. Match the underlined verbs (1-5) with their more formal equivalents (f-j).

1. How can they put up with such cheeky children?
2. She's put off her decision until next weekend.
3. Are you going to put in an application for that job?
4. The new government is sure to put up VAT.
5. We had a new boiler put in last month.

f. increase
g. install
h. postpone
i. submit
j. tolerate

III. Rewrite the sentences using the verbs (a-j) from exercises I and II.

1. If we'd set off earlier, we would have arrived on time.
2. Did you know that they're putting up train fares?
3. They've set up a committee to look into inner city violence.
4. It's not easy to put up with that sort of behaviour, is it?
5. They've put off making a statement for 24 hours.

Focus on ➔ 'lend' and 'borrow'

Das Verb 'lend' bedeutet jmdm. etwas geben. Das Verb 'borrow' bedeutet von jmdm. etwas bekommen.

*Did you ask the bank to **lend** you some money?*
*I **borrowed** £10,000 from the bank to expand my business.*

IV. Put in the correct form of 'lend' or 'borrow'.

1. Thanks for the money you … me last week.
2. Would you mind if I … your car for a day?
3. She doesn't like … things from other people.
4. Don't … him any books. You won't get them back!

V. Say these words out loud.

1. cheque
2. proposition
3. commitment
4. safeguard

VI. Now put the words 1-4 in exercise V into the following sentences.

1. We make copies of our files as a … against accidents.
2. Would you like to pay in cash or by …?
3. The company has made a … to pay £5000 to charity.
4. The … is a very attractive one because we don't have to pay interest on the loan.

*VII. Which syllable (*Silbe*) in these compound nouns takes the main stress? Mark it.*

1. a standing order
2. a business plan
3. a current account
4. a cash dispenser

VIII. Complete the sentences below by adding the correct form of 'make' or 'do'.

1. We'd like to ... you an offer.
2. A hurricane is passing over the east coast of the US and tremendous damage has already been ... to people's homes.
3. Can we ... an appointment for some time next week?
4. You're not afraid of ... mistakes, are you?
5. Do you mind ... me a favour?
6. Last week she ... the effort to get to work on time.
7. Do you ... your English homework as soon as you get home or do you leave it until as late as possible?
8. He doesn't like ... decisions unless he really has to.

IX. Brian Capon, the Manager of Press and Information of the British Bankers' Association, talks about the function of banks. Put the six sentences (a-f) into a logical order to form a paragraph. Start with sentence a.

a. "Banks oil the wheels of commerce. They allow it to happen.
b. But banks do a lot more than that nowadays.
c. In fact, they do pretty well everything that affects your normal everyday life."
d. So they allow the manufacturer to make the goods, they allow the retailer to sell them, and they allow the shopper to buy those goods.
e. They now provide mortgages, they provide pensions, they provide health insurance.
f. And they provide a whole range of financial services instead of just the normal banking accounts.

4B

Opening a joint account

A personal banker gives some advice

A couple wants to open a joint account.

- We'd like to open up a joint account.
- I see. Do you have an account with us at the moment?
- I do, but he has his account with another bank.
- So you want to close that account and open a joint account here, is that it?
- Yes, that's right. A current account.
- No problem.
- Do you pay interest on a current account?
- Yes we do, but it's not much.
- Something's better than nothing. Uh, we'd like to pay our monthly bills, gas, electricity ...
- That's no problem. You can pay that by direct debit.
- I think that's about all.
- Hang on a sec ... What about your charges? How much are the bank charges?
- As long as the account *stays in credit* there are no charges, but if you do overdraw then the bank does charge.

- So there's nothing to pay at all unless we go into the red?
- That's right.
- Perhaps we should open a deposit account at the same time?
- That would make sense. You'll get a better rate of interest on your savings.
- OK.
- We can offer you other services: a personal loan for a car, we also do travel insurance for your holidays and we also offer *mortgages* if you wanted to buy a house.
- That's enough for the time being.
- We'll think about it. We've got enough on our plate for the moment.
- Fine. If you'd just like to complete the forms.

joint account	gemeinsames Konto	mortgage	Hypothek
stay in credit	im Kreditrahmen bleiben		

■ Working with the text

I. Which is the best answer to the question? Mark it.

1. Why has the man gone to the bank?
   a) He wants to open a bank account with his wife.
   b) He wants to close his bank account with his wife and open his own bank account.
   c) He wants to close his own bank account and open a bank account with his wife.
2. Why has the woman gone to the bank?
   a) She wants to open a bank account with her husband.
   b) She wants to keep her own bank account and open a second bank account with her husband.
   c) She wants to close her bank account with her husband and open her own bank account.
3. By the end of the conversation how many bank accounts has the couple opened?
   a) One. b) Two. c) Three.
4. Does the couple have to pay for the bank's services?
   a) Yes. b) No. c) It depends.
5. Does a current account offer a better rate of interest than a deposit account?
   a) Yes. b) No. c) It depends.

II. Give the German equivalent for these expressions from the text.

1. interest (line 8)
2. direct debit (line 12)
3. bank charges (line 14)
4. to overdraw the account (line 16)

III. What do these expressions mean? Mark the correct answer.

1. The expression 'I think that's about all' (line 13) means ...
   a) we've got no more time.
   b) we've got no more money.
   c) we've got no more questions.
2. The expression 'to go into the red' (line 17) means ...
   a) to spend more money than is in your account.
   b) to get excited.
   c) to receive an angry letter from your bank manager.
3. The expression 'We've got enough on our plate' (line 26) means ...
   a) we're overweight. b) we're busy. c) we're in debt.

IV. Give an equivalent for the following phrases.

1. 'Hang on a sec ...' (line 14)
2. 'That's enough for the time being.' (line 25)

V. Further questions. Answer them.

1. Explain the difference between a 'direct debit' (4B, line 12) and a 'standing order' (4A, line 9).
2. Do you think the bank advisor does a good job? Say why.
3. Why must the couple fill in some forms? What information will they have to give on the forms?

■ Exercises

Focus on ➔ short answers

Kurzantworten greifen das Hilfsverb aus der Frage wieder auf.

***Have** you got an account with us at the moment?*	***Yes, I have.***
***Do** you pay interest on a current account?*	***Yes, we do.***

I. Complete the short answer. ●●

1. Have you got an account with us? Yes, … .
2. Is it a current account? Yes, … .
3. Would you like to open a deposit account? Yes, … .
4. Do you need a joint account with your husband? No, … .
5. Will you be requiring a credit card? No, … .
6. Are you planning to pay your bills by direct debit? No, … .

Focus on ➔ if-sentences

Es gibt drei Grundtypen von if-Sätzen:

*If you **overdraw** your account, the bank **charges** you.*
*If you **overdrew** your account, the bank **would charge** you.*
*If you **had overdrawn** your account, the bank **would have charged** you.*

II. Complete these mini-dialogues between a customer and a bank clerk by using the correct forms of the words in (brackets). ●●

1. ▸ If we … (open) a deposit account, would we get a better rate of interest?
   ▸ Certainly.
2. ▸ Would you have offered us a mortgage if we … (buy) a house?
   ▸ I suppose so.
3. ▸ … (we, pay) charges if we got into the red?
   ▸ Yes, you probably would.
4. ▸ If we confirm the appointment today, … (you, be able, see) us by the end of the week?
   ▸ I think so.
5. ▸ If I … (be) a regular, would you have given me more favourable conditions?
   ▸ Yes, of course.
6. ▸ Will you ring us back today if you … (not, reach) a decision?
   ▸ Yes, naturally.

Focus on ➔ auxiliaries for emphasis

Die primären Hilfsverben 'be', 'do' und 'have' werden in positiven Aussagesätzen verwendet, um den Kontrast zwischen z.B. etwas Richtigem und Falschem, einer Regel und einer Ausnahme oder etwas Gegenwärtigem und Vergangenem hervorzuheben.

*As long as the account stays in credit there are no charges, but if you **do** overdraw then the bank **does** charge.*

III. Put in the missing word.

1. Why haven't you rung them? - But I ... rung them!
2. He didn't like maths when he was at school but he ... like languages.
3. She doesn't see her parents very much but she ... see her sisters quite a lot.
4. Why weren't you listening when I told you? - But I ... listening!

Focus on ➔ 'unless'

Das Wort 'unless' bedeutet 'if … not' und leitet einen Nebensatz ein.

*There's nothing to pay **unless** you go into the red.*
*There's nothing to pay **if** you do**n't** go into the red.*

IV. Rewrite these sentences using 'unless'.

1. She'll ring you if you don't ring her.
2. He'll take the job if it isn't badly paid.
3. We can go out later if you're not too tired.
4. Come and see us at the weekend if you're not busy.

Focus on ➔ 'will' and 'going to'

Das Modalverb 'will' drückt die Meinung des Sprechenden zum Zeitpunkt des Sprechens aus. Im Deutschen stehen diese meist schnellen Reaktionen in der Gegenwartsform. Die 'going to'-Form wird verwendet, um bereits gefasste Absichten oder in Gang gesetzte Ereignisse auszudrücken.

*We'**ll** think about it.*
*They're **going to** open a joint account.*

V. Complete these mini-dialogues with 'will' or 'going to' and the correct form of the words in (brackets).

1. ‣ Did you buy those stamps for me?
   ‣ Oh no. I completely forgot. I ... (do) it now.
2. ‣ Are you going out?
   ‣ Yes, I ... (buy) something for dinner.
3. ‣ We've decided to paint this room.
   ‣ Really? What colour ... (you, paint) it?
4. ‣ I can't operate this video camera.
   ‣ It's quite easy. I ... (show) you.
5. ‣ Thanks for all your help.
   ‣ You're welcome. I ... (see) you tomorrow.
6. ‣ You look awful.
   ‣ I feel terrible. I think I ... (be sick).

VI. Form opposites using the prefixes in the box.

il- • im- • in- • un-

1. helpful
2. efficient
3. friendly
4. comfortable
5. reliable
6. employed
7. necessary
8. suitable
9. logical
10. possible

It's only a joke!

- Do you know the two nicest words in the English language?
- No? What are they?
- Cheque enclosed!

4C

Pat Daniels - investing in the future

I. As you listen to Pat Daniels, read and answer this question.
What three things does Pat talk about in the interview?

a) How she saved and spent money as a child.
b) How her children took responsibility for their financial affairs.
c) Why her children can't save money.
d) How she invested money later in her life.
e) How she paid for her second wedding.

II. Listen to the interview again. Which is the correct answer? Tick it.

1. When Pat was a child, what did she do with her pocket money?
   a) She spent it all on sweets.
   b) She put it into a savings account.
   c) She gave it back to her parents.
2. When Pat's children were teenagers, how did they receive their pocket money?
   a) Pat gave it to them.
   b) Pat sent it to them.
   c) Pat put it into their bank accounts.
3. When Pat had her first job, what did she do with the money she earned?
   a) She gave it to her husband.
   b) She spent it.
   c) She put it in the bank.
4. How has Pat's attitude towards money changed in recent years?
   a) Now she is not interested in money matters.
   b) Now she likes to plan for the future.
   c) Now she enjoys spending all her money.

III. Complete the sentences.

1. TESSA means 'Tax Exempt Special … …'.
2. PEP stands for 'Personal Equity …'.

IV. What do these expressions mean? Use your own words to explain them.

1. The children did chores.
2. The children had a clothes allowance.
3. Interest is paid net of tax.

V. Do you think it is wise to plan your finances in the way Pat Daniels does? Write a short comment (50 to 60 words) expressing your view.

4D

Troubleshooter's mother intervenes!

Troubleshooter has been strapped for cash for some time so he is delighted that his mother has lent him £500. Now his business is on a firm financial footing.

The phone rings in Troubleshooter's mobile office. It's Sophia of Sophia's Hairdressing Salon. She would like to expand her business and wants to know if Troubleshooter can give her some advice on lending and borrowing money.

At the salon Troubleshooter learns that Sophia would like to add a beauty salon to her hairdressing salon and give training courses. She could pay back a loan in *instalments* over three or four years but she wants to know about interest rates. Troubleshooter is pleased to give Sophia the advice his old professor gave him: "The trouble with banks is that they lend you an umbrella when the sun's shining and they want it back when it rains."

Suddenly Troubleshooter has an idea. He can invest his money in Sophia's expanding business! He tells Sophia that he can offer her a *preferential rate* of interest with no catch, no strings attached, no special conditions and no *small print*. The only thing Troubleshooter wants is to be involved in the day-to-day running of the salon.

Troubleshooter *sets to* work immediately and washes a customer's hair. At that moment Irene, Troubleshooter's mother, comes into the salon. To her horror she discovers that her son has offered to lend Sophia some money. Sophia is worried that Troubleshooter's presence in the salon might drive away the customers. Irene agrees. "If I were you," she continues, "I'd borrow money from a bank!" And with that she *chases* her son out of the salon and down the road.

instalment	Rate	set to	loslegen mit
preferential rate	Vorzugsrate	chase	jagen
the small print	das Kleingedruckte		

I. Answer the questions.

1. How does Troubleshooter want to help Sophia?
2. Who is Irene? What does she think of Troubleshooter's plan?

II. Identify the correct ending to the sentence.

1. If you are 'strapped for cash' (line 1) you …
   a) don't have enough money.
   b) don't carry enough money.
   c) want to become rich.
2. The business is on a 'firm financial footing' (line 2) means …
   a) the business's financial basis is poor.
   b) the business's financial basis is OK.
   c) the business's financial basis is very good.
3. When you pay back a loan 'in instalments' (lines 7-8) you …
   a) pay back the money in one large sum.
   b) pay back the money bit by bit.
   c) pay back the money only if the money is needed.
4. If there's a 'catch' (line 14) there's …
   a) a sudden surprise.
   b) a bad press.
   c) a hidden difficulty.
5. If there are 'strings attached' (line 14) there are …
   a) other people involved.
   b) other banks involved.
   c) special conditions involved.

III. Explain these expressions from the text. Use your own words as far as possible.

1. 'The trouble with banks is that they lend you an umbrella when the sun's shining and they want it back when it rains.' (lines 10-11)
2. a 'preferential rate of interest' (line 13)
3. the 'small print' (line 14)

IV. What is it? Explain or give an example.

1. a cash-and-carry
2. cash box
3. cash desk
4. cash dispenser
5. cash flow

V. Match the idiom (1-3) to the explanation (a-c).

1. We only take hard cash.
2. You have to pay cash down.
3. We send our parcels COD (cash on delivery).

   a. You pay for the goods when you are given the goods.
   b. You can't pay by credit card.
   c. You have to pay immediately.

4E

A letter from a bank

MIDLAND

JH/mrs

Midland Bank plc
Cornmarket High Wycombe
1 Cornmarket
High Wycombe
Buckinghamshire
HP11 2AY

Tel (01494) 656565
Fax (01494) 656599

Mr A W Park &
Mrs S Park
Clovelly
Pretoria Road
High Wycombe
Bucks
HP13 6QW

24-17

12 August

Dear Mr and Mrs Park

Further to my telephone conversation with Mr Park this morning, I am writing to first of all express my sincere personal apologies that your previous requests for monthly statements have not been actioned.

Having reviewed our records today, it is clear that we have not taken the appropriate action to ensure that the right statement diary date has been input to our computer system. We should have taken into account the fact that originally you had a Gold Service account which has, more laterally, been changed to the new Midland Bank Account terms. I have now corrected the error and can confirm statements will be provided as at the end of business on the 3rd of each month and should be with you from our Computer Centre by the 10th of each month. To update you I am enclosing a copy of the more recent statement from 21st July to date.

Please accept my sincere personal apologies once again and whilst I hope that there will not be any further problem please do not hesitate to contact me if the service we provide falls short in any way from the standards which you expect from us.

With kind regards.

Yours sincerely

John Hughes

John Hughes
Branch Manager

Member HSBC Group

Registered in England number 14259
Registered office Poultry London EC2P 2BX

Regulated by the Personal Investment Authority and SFA. Midland only advises on its own life assurance, pensions and unit trusts.

ADVERTISING 5

5A

A variety of media

These three people work for Ogilvy & Mather, an advertising agency located in Canary Wharf, London.

David Muir is a *Business Director*. He talks about *brands*. "You can't really do good advertising unless you understand the nature of the brand. The worst thing you can do is have great advertising for a bad product because people may buy it once but it'll be once only. They'll never ever buy that thing again. The consumer basically at the end of the day is going to be the person who's going to buy that product. Some brands are aimed at the mass market, some other brands are aimed at smaller or *niche* markets. Take a mass-market car like the Ford Fiesta. Now, that is a very high brand awareness. There are a number of products which aren't aimed at the mass market like the Fiesta, and they're aimed at things called the niche market. And I'll give you an example which is Lucozade NRG, which is aimed at a relatively small group, which is sixteen to eighteen years old."

Tim McCabe is responsible for media planning. He explains *targeting*. "Targeting means that, for example, you wouldn't advertise a *nappy* in the financial pages of a broadsheet. It would be far better suited in 'You and Your Baby'. Poster advertising is all around us. We basically target consumers by putting them on the *roadside*. There's obviously key locations so that will have a *bearing* on how much a particular poster will cost. We've currently got between twenty to thirty poster campaigns that are running nationally at the moment, one of them being the advertising for the Ford car. If you're advertising on the television for a *prime time* thirty-second spot, it would cost you on average £100,000 just for one spot. So one network thirty-second television spot on one day would cost the same as five *insertions* for colour pages for the national newspapers which would cost the same as a week advertising on a poster campaign."

Tom Vick is an *Account Director*. He is involved in TV commercials. "The UK advertising industry is very well known for the quality of its commercials, TV commercials or TV ads as we tend to call them. Elements from TV commercials can actually make their way into the language that people talk. The slogan - or the end line as we tend to call it in advertising these days - is important for some brands. Going back into the *mists of time* we have 'Guiness - Pure Genius', very well known, 'Shell - you can be sure of Shell', 'Ford - everything we do is driven by you'. What happens in TV production is that the agency team - myself and the creative people - will meet with a film director. He will talk through a story board of how he or she *envisages* the ad looking eventually. Once the film has been shot, we

then embark upon again a fairly lengthy process of editing. The editing of the film itself is just as crucial as the shooting of the actual commercial so we really need to concentrate on getting our communication as *crisp* and *succinct* as possible."

business director	*etwa*: Bereichsleiter(in)	prime time	Haupteinschaltzeit
brand	Marke	insertion	Anzeige
niche	Nische	account director	*etwa*: Projektleiter(in)
targeting	(*Zielgruppen*) Abzielen, Ansteuern	mists *pl* of time	Dunkel der Vergangenheit
nappy	Windel	envisage	sich vorstellen
roadside	Straßenrand	crisp	frisch, knackig
bearing	Auswirkung	succinct	knapp

■ Working with the text

I. Are these statements true or false according to the text? Mark the correct answer.

1. Brands are products for the mass market.
2. If you target a product, you advertise it on television.
3. Good TV commercials always have a slogan.

	true	false
1.		
2.		
3.		

II. Answer these questions. Use your own words as far as possible.

1. What is a 'niche market' (line 9)?
2. Why is good advertising for a poor product bad for an advertising agency?

3. How much newspaper advertising and poster advertising can you get for a thirty-second spot on prime-time television?
4. Why does the location of posters affect how much a poster campaign will cost?
5. How can you see that slogans are an important part of TV commercials?
6. Producing a good TV commercial means making a good film. But what else must an agency do to make a good TV commercial?

III. Which word is it? Find it in the text. (There are two in each paragraph.)

1. a person who buys or uses goods or services
2. one time
3. a serious newspaper
4. at the moment
5. in the end
6. very important

IV. Say the same thing but change the underlined words. (You may have to change the structure of the whole sentence!)

1. 'You can't do good advertising <u>unless</u> you understand the nature of the brand.' (lines 3-4)
2. 'People may buy the product once but <u>it'll be once only</u>.' (lines 5-6)
3. 'The advertisement would be <u>far better suited</u> in 'You and your Baby'.' (line 16)
4. 'Obviously key locations will <u>have a bearing on</u> how much a particular poster will cost.' (lines 18-19)

5. 'Going back into the mists of time we have 'Guiness - Pure Genius'.' (line 31)
6. 'Once the film has been shot, we then embark upon a fairly lengthy process of editing.' (lines 35-36)

V. Further questions. Answer them.

1. Do you know where Canary Wharf is exactly? (If not, find out!)
2. What is a brand exactly? (Text 5C will help you.)
3. Can you think of other examples of niche markets for teenagers?
4. Can you think of any German slogans which have been used in British advertising?

■ Exercises

Focus on ➔ gerunds after prepositions

Das Gerund ist die einzig mögliche Verbform nach einer Präposition.

*He is interested **in targeting**.*
*We embark upon a lengthy process **of editing**.*

I. Complete these sentences. Add a preposition and form a gerund using the infinitive in (brackets).

1. Have you ever thought ... (live) abroad?
2. They insisted ... (pay) for the tickets.
3. Congratulations ... (land) the job!
4. Are you afraid ... (get) some bad publicity?
5. Let's play cards instead ... (watch) TV.
6. She had no intention ... (hurt) you.
7. You must be proud ... (do) so well.
8. Can you learn a language just ... (listen)?

Focus on ➔ using hyphens

Der Bindestrich wird bei zusammengesetzten Adjektiven verwendet. Enthält das Adjektiv eine Zahl, entfällt das Mehrzahl-s des zweiten Teils des Adjektivs.

*It's a **thirty-second spot**.*
*It was a **five-hour journey**.*

II. Make one sentence out of two.

1. She lives in an enormous flat. (It has got eight rooms.)
2. It was an exhausting flight to Australia. (It lasted 24 hours.)
3. We went on a walk along the Welsh coast. (We walked thirty kilometres.)
4. She gave him an English note. (It had the words 'ten pounds' written on it.)
5. There's a new golf course near our house. (The course has got eighteen holes.)
6. It was a long article. (It was twenty pages.)

Focus on → false friends

‚Falsche Freunde' sind Wörter, die im Deutschen und Englischen ähnlich geschrieben werden, aber unterschiedliche Bedeutungen haben.

Elements from TV commercials can ***actually*** **(tatsächlich)** *make their way into everyday language.*
He will talk through a story board of how he envisages the ad looking ***eventually*** **(schließlich, zum Schluß)**.

III. Complete the table below by putting in the correct equivalents of the German and English words.

	German	←	English	German	→	English
1.	...		chef	Chef		...
2.	...		mustn't	muss nicht		...
3.	...		sensible	sensibel		...
4.	...		meaning	Meinung		...
5.	...		eventually	eventuell		...
6.	...		actual	aktuell		...

IV. Say these words out loud.

1. succinct
2. genius
3. campaign
4. crucial
5. envisage

V. Form common compounds by joining the words on the left (1-12) with those on the right (a-l). Then complete the sentences below (13-17) with five of the compounds.

1. credit — a. vitae
2. crossed — b. conditions
3. data — c. site
4. building — d. cheque
5. curriculum — e. card
6. working — f. processing
7. industrial — g. agency
8. order — h. department
9. forwarding — i. fair
10. raw — j. form
11. accounts — k. materials
12. trade — l. revolution

1.	
2.	
3.	
4.	
5.	
6.	
7.	
8.	
9.	
10.	
11.	
12.	

13. When you apply for a job you send a letter and a ... .
14. A ... ... is a company which transports goods to a customer.
15. If you give somebody a ... ... they have to pay the money into a bank account.
16. The ... ... is the part of a company where a record is kept of all the money which is spent or received.
17. A ... ... is an opportunity for firms and businesses to meet and find out more about each other's products and services.

VI. Read what Tim McCabe says about press advertising.

"The types of press that we advertise in are tabloids and broadsheets. So broadsheets tend to be more on a quality angle and the tabloids tend to be on a mid-market, down-market angle."

Which of these newspapers are broadsheets and which are tabloids? What are some of the differences between these two types of newspapers?

5B

Chairing a meeting

Tom Vick is *chairing* a meeting with Sally, Nicola and David about a poster campaign.

Tom: So, we're here to discuss the developments in the latest Ford poster campaign. Um, Sally, could I ask you to *kick off* by *taking* us *through* the latest research developments?

Sally: Yes, sure. First I'd like to give everyone a copy of the research *debrief*.

Nicola: Thank you.

David: Thank you.

Sally: It shows us that in general the campaign was well received and that it fits in well with the TV campaign.

Nicola: Could I raise a question here?

Tom: Um, I think we'll keep the questions till later actually, Nicola, and, um, let's see what Sally has to say first. So, Sally, if you want to carry on.

Sally: Thanks. I'd also like to draw your attention to page two where we can see the huge increase in Fiesta sales since last year's TV campaign. So, all in all, I think we have a very successful campaign.

Tom: Thanks, Sally. That sounds very encouraging indeed. Now then, Nicola, what did you want to ask?

Nicola: Well, yes, I just wanted to *raise the point* about *branding*. In the last campaign we ran for this client it proved to be a bit of an issue.

Tom: Good point. Does anyone have any thoughts on that?

David: I don't think there's an issue about the branding of Ford company as a whole. I think the bigger issue is about the branding of the product, the branding of Fiesta.

In the next part of the meeting Nicola presents the poster work. Then Tom asks everybody to give their views on the advertising campaign as a whole.

Sally: Well, I'm very enthusiastic on the whole. However, I do have one or two *reservations*, um, mainly in the fact that there's no car in the anti-roll *execution*.

Tom: I'm inclined to agree with you there actually, Sally. Do you think you could sort that out, Nicola?

Nicola: Yes, I could have a look at it.

Tom: Good. Now David. Tell us what you think.

David: Well, *provided* you can deal with the problems I talked about, I think it's fine and I think that Nicola has done a very good job.

Tom: My feeling is that so long as we can deal with one or two small details we should all have a campaign we can be rightly proud of. So if I can just sum up: Nicola, if you could sort out the details about the car on the ad, and David, if you talk to the client about branding or sub-branding, apart from that we're all happy and we can move on to the next stage. OK?

chair	den Vorsitz führen bei	branding	*eine ‚Marke' aus einem Produkt machen*
kick off	beginnen	reservation	Vorbehalt
take through	*hier*: berichten von, vorstellen	execution	Ausführung
debrief	Nachbesprechung	provided	angenommen, gesetzt den Fall
raise the point	auf etw. zu sprechen kommen		

■ Working with the text

I. What are the four main stages of the meeting? (The first one has been done for you.)

1. Sally's debrief

➔ 2.

➔ 3.

➔ 4.

II. Answer these questions. Use your own words as far as possible.

1. What is the group's feeling in general about the poster campaign?
2. Does any member of the group sound unhappy about the outcome of the meeting? If so, why?

III. Which answer is correct? Mark it.

1. A 'debrief' (line 7) is ...
   a) a letter.
   b) a report.
   c) a newspaper article.

2. An 'issue' (line 21) is ...
   a) a problem.
   b) an unpopular idea.
   c) a flop.

3. A 'view' (line 27) is ...
   a) a criticism.
   b) a difficulty.
   c) an opinion.

4. A 'reservation' (line 29) is ...
   a) a piece of land.
   b) a doubt.
   c) a question.

5. The expression 'apart from that' (line 41) means the same as ...
   a) because of that.
   b) except for that.
   c) as well as that.

IV. What does the word 'it' in the following sentences refer back to in the text?

1. 'It shows us that in general the campaign was well received.' (line 10)
2. 'In the last campaign we ran for this client it proved to be a bit of an issue.' (lines 20-21)
3. 'Yes, I could have a look at it.' (line 33)
4. 'Provided you can deal with the problems I talked about, I think it's fine.' (lines 35-36)

V. Use different words for the underlined part of the text.

1. 'Could I ask you to kick off by taking us through the research developments?'
2. 'Could I raise a question here?'
3. 'We can see the huge increase in Fiesta sales.'
4. 'All in all I think we have a very successful campaign.'
5. 'Provided you can deal with the problems I talked about, I think it's fine.'
6. 'We can move on to the next stage.'

VI. Further questions. Write two or three sentences in your answer.

1. To what extent do you think you are influenced by advertising?
2. What is your experience of attending meetings? Are they similar to the meeting in the text above?

■ Exercises

Focus on ➔ writing out sums of money

Das Pfundsymbol £ wie auch das Dollarzeichen $ stehen direkt vor dem Betrag. Bei Pence und Cents schreibt man 'p' und '¢' direkt nach dem Betrag. Für Beträge über 1 Pfund oder Dollar wird ein Punkt verwendet. Für Beträge über 1000 benutzt man ein Komma.

30p	**£20**	£9.99	£2,345
30¢	**$20**	$9.99	$2,345

I. Rewrite these sums of money as numbers.

1. sixty-six cents
2. eight pounds forty-two
3. sixty-three dollars thirty-six
4. one pound eighty-nine
5. a hundred and fifty-one dollars
6. five thousand six hundred and seventy-five pounds

II. Complete these sentences by underlining the correct word or expression in (brackets).

1. A dime is a (10¢/25¢/50¢) coin.
2. The Germans say ‚Schein', the Americans say 'bill' and the British say (pass/note/notice).
3. All US bills are grey on the front and green on the back. That's why the US currency is sometimes referred to as the (greyback/greenfront/greenback).
4. In the year 2002 many European currencies will be replaced by the (US dollar/euro/German mark).

III. Read these prices out loud.

1. £456.00
2. $989.34
3. £65,482
4. $6,125
5. £24,658
6. $679,797

Focus on → describing change

Es gibt eine Reihe von Verben, die Veränderungen beschreiben, z.B. *increase, decrease, fall, rise, raise* usw. Das Verb 'rise' ist intransitiv, d.h., es kommt ohne ein direktes Objekt vor. Das Verb 'raise' dagegen ist transitiv. Auf 'raise' folgt ein direktes Objekt.

*Prices **rose** dramatically at the end of last year.*
*Could I **raise a question** here?*

IV. Look at these newspaper headlines. They all contain intransitive verbs. What sort of change do they indicate? Up or down?

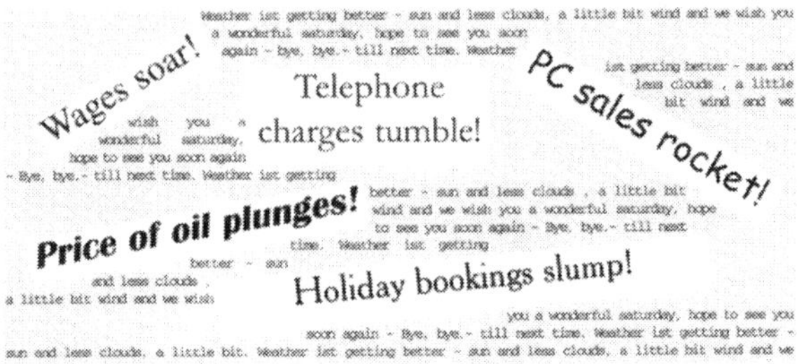

V. Use the correct form of 'raise' or 'rise' to complete these sentences.

1. Last year the price of petrol ... by 5%.
2. Can you ... your hand if you want to say something, please?
3. The sun ... in the east and sets in the west, doesn't it?
4. I'd like to ... an objection if I may.
5. It's still raining and the level of the rivers continue to ... .
6. Thanks for ... that problem. Shall we talk about it now?

VI. Read these two sentences out loud. What's the difference in meaning?

1. This month the number of unemployed people rose *to* 3,645,987.
2. This month the number of unemployed people rose *by* 3,645,987.

VII. Which word in the box describes the situation best?

encouraging • worrying • annoying • threatening • exciting • disappointing

1. Your mother fell over, broke her arm and had to be taken to hospital.
2. Your English is getting better and better!
3. You've been offered a new job.
4. You've had to cancel your summer holiday.
5. Your neighbour is getting angry and shouting at you.
6. Your computer won't work and you want to write an important letter.

VIII. Which of the following would you consider to be advertising?

1. A supermarket chain has cut all its prices. It advertises in the daily papers and on television to announce the cuts.
2. The Government has decided to start a new savings scheme. Advertisements in the daily papers explain the scheme and tell readers how to join.

3. A manufacturer has brought out a new improved product. He takes space in papers and buys time on television to tell people about it.
4. Summer is coming - the ice-cream season. An ice-cream company wants to remind people to ask for its products by name. There is a television campaign supported by poster advertising.
5. There has been an earthquake in South America. Emergency supplies are desperately needed. A charity advertises in the daily papers asking for money and explaining how it will be spent.

5C

Andrew Brown - heading the Advertising Association

I. As you listen to Andrew Brown, read and answer this question.

What one of these subjects does Andrew not talk about in the interview?

a) the role of the advertising industry in the UK economy
b) branding
c) the people in advertising
d) his own career in advertising
e) humour in advertising
f) tabloid newspapers
g) slogans

II. Listen to the interview again. Which is the correct answer? Tick it.

1. How much money is spent on advertising per year in the UK?
   a) £12 billion. b) £20 billion. c) £25 billion.
2. The largest advertising medium in the UK is ...
   a) television. b) posters. c) the press.
3. A 'brand' is ...
   a) a product that sells very well for a long time.
   b) a product that people recognize and believe in.
   c) a product with an interesting name.
4. The UK has ...
   a) a poor reputation for advertising.
   b) a good reputation for advertising.
   c) an excellent reputation for advertising.
5. Andrew Brown has been in advertising ...
   a) for ten years. b) for twenty years. c) all his working life.
6. Humour plays ...
   a) an insignificant part in TV advertising in Britain.
   b) a small part in TV advertising in Britain.
   c) an important part in TV advertising in Britain.

III. Explain the underlined parts of the text using your own words.

1. You need people who are interested in tackling a problem in an innovative way.
2. I worked my way up through the business.
3. He is responsible for managing a number of different accounts.
4. A slogan summarizes the proposition that the brand or service is making in a succinct way.
5. Some slogans are part of culture because they have been persevered with.

IV. Say these words.

1. attribute
2. curiosity
3. creativity
4. vignette
5. athleticism

V. Complete the grid.

	noun	adjective
1.	belief	...
2.	excellence	...
3.	curiosity	...
4.	creativity	...
5.	responsibility	...
6.	memory	...
7.	culture	...
8.	strategy	...

5D

Troubleshooter launches an advertising campaign

Troubleshooter is pleased with himself. He's just come out of a shop after speaking to another satisfied customer. Suddenly he has an idea for an advertising slogan: 'My success depends on yours.' The time has come for Troubleshooter to launch his own advertising campaign!

Troubleshooter carries out some market research

First he goes to a printer and shows him a design for a poster. The printer is sceptical. Has Troubleshooter done enough market research? In a flashback interview we see Troubleshooter talking to Mr Morrison, a toy shop owner. Mr Morrison is clearly very disappointed with Troubleshooter's services. Troubleshooter had told him that the point of sale was very important and had advised him to put his toy *bazookas* in the shop window. Mr Morrison did exactly as Troubleshooter had said but not one bazooka was sold.

Of course Troubleshooter doesn't want to tell the printer the truth about his market research so he tells him that Mr Morrison was particularly enthusiastic about his services. The printer seems to know Mr Morrison better than Troubleshooter thinks. "You must be joking," he laughs. "You're *having* me *on*."

The next day Troubleshooter picks up his posters and begins distributing them around the town. Unfortunately he doesn't realize that a group of children have discovered a different use for them. After buying bazookas and water pistols at Mr Morrison's shop, they've stuck the posters to the front of the printer's shop and are using them as targets.

The printer is extremely angry when he sees what has happened to his shop window. He's about to attack Troubleshooter when Mr Morrison comes up and intervenes. "You are a complete genius!" he says to Troubleshooter. "All my bazookas and all my water pistols have sold out completely! And all because of your poster campaign!"

bazooka	Panzerfaust
have sb on	jmdn. auf den Arm nehmen

I. Answer the questions.

1. What does Troubleshooter do at the printer's?
2. Is Troubleshooter's advertising campaign a success? Is his poster campaign a success?
3. How do you explain Mr Morrison's very different reactions at the beginning and end of the story?

II. What do these words and expressions mean? Tick one answer.

1. 'My success depends on yours' (line 3) means ...
   a) if you are successful then I will be successful.
   b) if you work with me then we will be successful.
   c) if you work hard you will be successful.

2. The 'point of sale' (line 9) is ...
   a) the reason for buying something.
   b) the place where a customer buys a product.
   c) the time of the day when most people go shopping.
3. 'You're having me on' (line 15) means ...
   a) you are not explaining everything clearly.
   b) you're not telling me the truth.
   c) you're not giving me a chance to say something.

III. Match the idiomatic expression (1-4) to its explanation (a-d).

1. He can't take a joke.
2. His behaviour has gone beyond a joke.
3. He made a joke of his new hairstyle.
4. The joke was on him, not you.

   a. He laughed about his own situation.
   b. He looked foolish. You didn't.
   c. He doesn't laugh when you play a trick on him.
   d. What he's doing is not funny. It's a bit worrying.

5E

Mineral water

TOURISM AND TRAVEL

6

6A

The hotel business

Kevin Poulter

Ettington Park is a luxury country hotel near Stratford-upon-Avon. Kevin Poulter is the General Manager. "Tourism is an important sector of the country's economy. It *accounts for* 25% of the United Kingdom's total export of services and is an important earner of foreign currency. Stratford-upon-Avon acts like a magnet for the tourist industry. This has come for a number of reasons, particularly the Royal Shakespeare Theatre, the five Shakespearean properties, including Anne Hatheway's cottage and Shakespeare's birthplace, together with Warwick Castle and the Cotswolds. Tourism is a *service industry*. Here at Ettington Park we provide services not just for tourists but for businesses. We offer conference facilities, *activity days* and *corporate team-building programmes* and special packages *tailored for* companies' needs. We are in fact part of a chain and that means although the hotel has its own very individual character, we are in fact part of a group which has hotels all over Britain."

Sheila Smith is the Reservations Manager. "The business at the hotel is divided between *corporate* and individuals and my role is to look after the reservations for the individual guests. Every year we *draw up* a budget and it sets targets in terms of *room occupancy*. In other words, we set a target for the number of visitors that we hope to attract. Although I'm not responsible for setting the budget, I am involved as part of the team in the discussions that *go ahead*. We aim to attract a variety of visitors, especially overseas visitors, including visitors from the United States, Japan, Europe - a lot from Germany. Although we have a large number of overseas visitors, most of our guests come from the United Kingdom. There are a number of hotels in the area and we compete fiercely against each other and when I get an inquiry, you have to be quick off the mark in order to get the reservation which is what we try to do. Many people coming here are coming here for a special occasion. It may be a birthday or a wedding anniversary and they're buying a dream, a complete experience. My job is to make sure that everything during their stay is absolutely perfect so that they will go away and recommend us to their friends."

Chris Olger is Food and Beverage Manager at the hotel. "I'm responsible for purchasing and stores. As far as buying the wines, I operate within the group's policy. We buy from nominated suppliers in order to benefit from the *economies of scale*. However, we can purchase from local wine *merchants* for the more specialist and local wines. The *chef* is responsible for the menu planning here at the hotel, and he has won some prestigious awards and he's been with us since 1990. When there's a conference to cater for I work very closely with the conference team. I need to know the special dietary requirements. The most common are vegetarians."

account for	ausmachen	corporate	*hier*: Geschäftsleute
service industry	Dienstleistungsbranche	draw up	festsetzen, aufstellen
activity day	Aktiv-, Erlebnistag	room occupancy	Zimmerbelegung
corporate team-building programme	Programm zur Steigerung der Teamfähigkeit, zur Integration von Mitarbeitern	go ahead	stattfinden
		economies of scale	*Vorteile durch hohe Stückzahl*
tailor for	zuschneiden, abstimmen auf	merchant	Händler(in)
		chef	Küchenchef(in), Koch, Köchin

■ Working with the text

I. What line(s) in the text show(s) you that ...

1. Ettington Park likes to attract business people?
2. many people staying at the hotel are British?
3. the food at Ettington Park must be very good?

II. Answer these questions.

1. What brings people to Stratford-upon-Avon?
2. What reasons do individual guests have for staying at Ettington Park?
3. What policy does Ettington Park operate regarding the purchase of wine?

III. Which is the correct answer? Tick it.

1. The expression 'Tourism is an important earner of foreign currency' (lines 3-4) means ...
   a) tourism helps British people to learn foreign languages.
   b) tourism attracts foreign people to Britain.
   c) tourism brings money from other countries into Britain.
2. The expression 'to be quick off the mark' (line 24) means ...
   a) to get up very early in the morning.
   b) to react quickly.
   c) to answer the phone as soon as it rings.
3. A 'nominated supplier' (line 32) is someone ...
   a) who has a good reputation in supplying wines.
   b) who has been asked by the chain to supply wine to all their hotels.
   c) who can supply wine more quickly than other people.
4. The expression 'economies of scale' (line 32) means ...
   a) buying products when they first come onto the market.
   b) buying products in different sizes.
   c) buying products cheaper because you have ordered them in large quantities.

5. The expression 'special dietary requirements' (line 37) means ...
   a) the special type of food people have to eat.
   b) the special time of day people have to eat.
   c) a certain amount of money people want to spend on food.

IV. Say these words out loud.

1. luxury hotel
2. Warwick
3. budget
4. award
5. vegetarian

V. Complete these definitions. Use your own words.

1. A vegetarian ... .
2. A chef ... .
3. A menu ... .
4. A beverage ... .

VI. Say the same thing but use different words for the underlined parts of the text.

1. 'Stratford-upon-Avon acts like a magnet for the tourist industry.' (lines 4-5)
2. 'We aim to attract a variety of visitors.' (lines 19-20)
3. 'My job is to make sure the guests go away and recommend us to their friends.' (lines 27-29)
4. 'I operate within the group's policy.' (line 31)

■ Exercises

Focus on → subclauses

Viele Nebensätze werden durch Konjunktionen eingeleitet, wie z.B. *after* (nachdem), *although* (obwohl), *because* (weil), *but* (aber), *if* (wenn, falls), *in order to* (um ... zu), *so* (daher), *so that* (damit), *unless* (wenn ... nicht), *until* (bis), *whereas* (wohingegen), *whether* (ob) und *while* (während).

Although the hotel has its own individual character, *we are part of a group.*
Although I'm not responsible for the budget, *I am involved in the discussions.*

I. Underline the most appropriate conjunction in the (brackets).

1. We arrived at the hotel (as/although/until) it was getting dark.
2. We got a room (because/in order to/although) there was a conference on.

3. We had to wait for a table in the restaurant (because/unless/if) it was so busy.
4. (If/While/After) we were waiting, we had a drink at the bar.

II. Make one sentence out of two by using the conjunction in the (brackets).

1. The hotel was successful. It was obvious it could have been even more successful. (but)
2. We advertised the hotel in the local and national press. It was not enough to increase room occupancy very significantly. (although)
3. We have a very flat hierarchy. We involved the staff in the discussions. (so)
4. Some of the staff's ideas were accepted. Others were rejected. (whereas)
5. We recognized the advantages of tailoring requirements to companies' needs. Then we began to offer conference facilities. (after)
6. The number of business guests increased rapidly. We started to offer corporate packages. (as soon as)

III. Add the correct form of the word in the (brackets).

1. We need the wine ... (urgent). Can you deliver it before tomorrow?
2. Your idea sounds ... (great). We'll get back to you as soon as possible.
3. Please contact us ... (immediate) with your latest offer.
4. The new software is ... (extreme) easy to use.
5. The staff work ... (hard) and earn ... (excellent) money.
6. The hotel gardens look ... (magnificent)! The gardeners have done a ... (marvellous) job.
7. The chef seems ... (happy) in his job but he ... (rare) smiles.
8. The work was completed ... (satisfactory) but not as ... (good) as we had expected.

IV. Mark the stressed syllable in these words.

1. exports
2. magnet
3. industry
4. supplier
5. comfortable
6. anniversary
7. requirement
8. advertisement

V. Complete the sentences.

1. The abbreviation PTO means ... ... You write it at the bottom of a piece of paper to tell the reader there is something on the other side.
2. The letters AGM stand for ... ... It is the time of the year when a company's shareholders find out how successful the company has been and what plans it has.
3. FOB is an Incoterm (international commercial term). It means ... ... 'Our prices are FOB Felixstowe' means the price of the goods includes the loading costs at the port of Felixstowe.

4. At the end of a letter you will often see the word 'Encl' or 'Enc', which is short for .... This tells the reader that something else has been sent with the letter.
5. You send an 'sae' or ... ... to a company or organization so that they can send you something without having to pay for the post.
6. VAT stands for ... ... and is a tax on goods and services.
7. If you want somebody to do something as quickly as they can you write 'asap' which means quite simply ... ...
8. Some English abbreviations come from Latin: 'eg' means 'exempli gratia' but people usually say ... .

VI. This is what David, a trainee, says about his job. Read the text and answer the questions below.

"With pre-dinner drinks, we sit them down, we offer them the menus and we give them pre-dinner drinks and then we show them through to the Oak Room Restaurant, and then afterwards, after they've dined, we come back here for coffee and offer them liqueurs and port."

1. What sort of work is David doing at Ettington at the moment?
2. He talks about 'them' and 'they'. Who does he mean?
3. What is a 'liqueur' /lɪˈkjʊə/? Is it the same as 'liquor' /ˈlɪkə/?

VII. Read about the facilities available at Ettington Park. Answer the questions.

HOTEL FACILITIES	48 bedrooms and suites	
	2 four-poster suites	
	Private dining rooms	
	Car parking	
	Gardens	
	Baby sitting service	
	Access for disabled guests	
THE OAK ROOM RESTAURANT	Traditional and modern English cuisine	
LEISURE FACILITIES	Indoor heated pool	
	Spa, sauna	
	All weather tennis courts	
	Horse riding	
	Fishing	
	Croquet	
	Laser/clay pigeon shooting (on request)	
CONFERENCE FACILITIES	5 conference rooms	
	Business centre	
	Largest room capacity - 65	
RAILWAY STATION	Stratford-upon-Avon	6 miles
AIRPORTS	Birmingham International	26 miles
	Heathrow	90 miles
MOTORWAY	M40, Junction 15	12 miles
DISTANCES	Stratford-upon-Avon	5 miles
	Warwick	12 miles
	Cotswolds	18 miles
	Coventry	20 miles
	NEC Birmingham	30 miles

1. What is the difference between a 'bedroom' and a 'suite'?
2. What is special about a 'four-poster suite'?
3. How do British people pronounce the word 'sauna' and 'croquet'?
4. What is the 'Cotswolds'?
5. What do the initials 'NEC' stand for?

6B

Booking a holiday

These two young people have come into a travel agency to make a reservation.

- We finally made up our minds. We've decided on Tenerife in early September.
- Have you decided on a hotel with meal arrangements or are you going *self-catering* in an apartment?
- We've decided to go for a hotel.
- With meal arrangements. It's my holiday as well!
- Right. Let me take some details then. The surname is ...?
- Jones.
- Right Mr Jones. And your initial?
- Is L.
- And Mrs Jones?
- Is H.
- And which date did you want to travel out?
- The 2nd September, please.
- Right. And how long for? Seven or fourteen nights?
- We want to go for a fortnight.

▸ Fourteen nights' duration.

▸ Which airport would you like to travel from?

▸ We'd like to fly from Gatwick, if possible.

▸ Now if Gatwick's not available would you consider our other local airport, Stanstead?

▸ Well, I suppose we could.

▸ So, Gatwick preferably. If not, Stanstead. Which hotel did you have in mind?

▸ We decided on the Jason Beach Hotel. What do you think?

▸ Let me have a look. Well, it looks very nice; excellent location, set round by the bay. And did you want a room with a sea view?

▸ Does it cost extra?

▸ There is a *supplement* for a sea view, but for £1 a day, just think, you have the privacy of sitting on your balcony looking out to sea.

▸ It's worth it, isn't it?

▸ Yes, we'll have a sea view.

▸ And did you want *full board* or *half board*? Half board is breakfast and evening meal ...

▸ Half board.

▸ Right, let me just check the availability for you. Right, we have availability at the Jason Beach Hotel for fourteen nights. You're lucky. There's a double room available with sea view. Uh, it doesn't have a bath. It has a shower. Is that all right?

▸ What do you think? OK? Yes, we'll go for it.

▸ Good! We'll just do a *full costing* then. Right, so we have a *basic cost* for each adult of £524 and then your sea view supplement which is £1 a night, making £14 per person. *Total cost* is £1,076. Then there's your insurance *on top of* £37.95 per person. Shall we *go ahead* and book that?

▸ Yes, go ahead!

self-catering	Selbstversorgung	basic cost	Grundpreis, -kosten
supplement	Zuschlag	total cost	Gesamtpreis, -kosten
full board	Vollpension	on top of	von zusätzlich
half board	Halbpension	go ahead	es machen
full costing	Gesamtkalkulation		

■ Working with the text

I. Complete the text below using the information in the dialogue.

This couple, Mr and Mrs ..., are going on holiday to ... for ... weeks. They are staying at the ... ... there. They have booked a ... room with a ... view and ... board. There's one small problem, however. The room doesn't have a ... . It only has a ... . The cost of the holiday is ... including insurance for both of them.

II. Questions on the text. Answer them.

1. Mrs Jones says 'It's my holiday as well' (line 6). What does she mean?
2. Why does having a sea view cost more?
3. The travel agent talks about insurance (lines 42-43). What sort of insurance does she mean?

III. Finish the definitions. Use your own words as far as possible.

1. A 'self-catering holiday' ... .
2. A 'fortnight' ... .
3. Somebody's 'surname' ... .
4. If you have 'full board' ... .
5. A 'sea view supplement' ... .

IV. Explain the difference in meaning between ...

1. to 'make up one's mind' (line 2) and to 'have in mind' (line 23).
2. to be 'lucky' and to be 'happy'.
3. a 'bath' and a 'bathroom'.

V. Further questions.

1. London has three main airports. Can you name them? (Two are in the text!)
2. Is going to a hotel in Tenerife your idea of a holiday? Say why or why not.

■ Exercises

Focus on ➔ 'have' + noun

Das Verb 'have' bedeutet in erster Linie ‚besitzen', ‚zur Vefügung haben'. 'Have' steht oft bei einem Substantiv, z.B. *to have a meeting* (= to meet). Diese Kombination 'have' + Substantiv kommt überwiegend in der gesprochenen Sprache vor.

*It doesn't **have a bath**. It **has a shower**.*
*Let me **have a look**.*

I. Rewrite these sentences using a 'have' + noun construction. (You will have to make another small change in sentence 6!)

1. We looked at some brochures.
2. They didn't swim in the sea.
3. She chatted to her friends.
4. Did you ride along the beach on a donkey?
5. We walk into the village nearly every evening.
6. They sat on the balcony and drank the local wine.

II. Make these sentences sound more natural by using the construction 'take' + noun. (You will need to make other small changes to your sentences!)

1. He showered before dinner.
2. She photographed the sun going down.
3. It was Christmas Eve last year when they decided to emigrate.
4. They've spent all day caring for the children.
5. She stood on the top of the hill and breathed in deeply.
6. She stepped towards him and slapped him in the face.

Focus on → prepositions at the end of questions

Präpositionen (z.B. *at, by, for, from, in, on, to, with*) können auch am Ende einer Frage stehen.

Which airport would you like to travel ***from?***
Which airline are you flying ***with?***

III. Ask for the information which is missing. Form questions with 'who', 'where' or 'what'.

1. At the airport I bumped into , an old school friend of mine.
2. During the flight I was sitting right next to the . It's the worst seat on the plane.
3. On the bus to the hotel I was talking to .
4. On the first night I got a phone call from .
5. One day while I was on the beach I came across . Do you know them?
6. On the last day I got bitten by a . It was terrible!

IV. Underline the stressed syllables in the following questions.

1. Which hotel did you have in mind? The Jason Beach Hotel or the White Sands Hotel?
2. Which airport would you like to travel from? Gatwick or Stanstead?

3. Was it seven or fourteen nights?
4. Did you want full board or half board?

V. Say these dates out loud.

1. 6 January	4. 1 July
2. 14 March	5. 30 September
3. 21 May	6. 8 November

VI. Write down a homophone (a word which is spelt differently but said in the same way).

1. board	4. sea
2. night	5. right
3. not	6. check

VII. Put the parts of the dialogue into the correct order. Start with sentence e.

a. ▸ A shower is fine. How much is the room?
b. ▸ Certainly. Single or double?
c. ▸ Does that include breakfast?
d. ▸ Fine. I'll take it.
e. ▸ Good evening. Can I help you?
f. ▸ It's £75.
g. ▸ Single, please.
h. ▸ Would you prefer a room with a bath or a shower?
i. ▸ Yes, it does.
j. ▸ Yes, please. I was wondering if you had a room for one night.

VIII. What do these symbols mean?

I'm only joking!

- Are you on a diet?
- Yes, I am. Sea food.
- What do you mean by 'sea food'?
- Every time I see food, I eat it!

6C

Kevin Poulter - managing the hotel staff

I. As you listen to Kevin Poulter, read and answer this question.

Kevin covers four main areas in his interview. Which are they? Mark them.

a) the organizational structure at Ettington Park Hotel
b) his own career in the tourism industry
c) the opportunities for young people in tourism
d) his objectives as General Manager at Ettington Park Hotel
e) Stratford-upon-Avon as a tourist centre

Shakespeare's Hamlet in Stratford

II. Listen to the interview again. Which is the correct answer? Tick it.

1. How many departmental managers are there at Ettington Park Hotel?
   a) 5. b) 6. c) 9.
2. What subject did Kevin study at college?
   a) Hotel and Catering Management.
   b) Business Management.
   c) Economics.
3. How close is the cooperation between Stratford and the city's hoteliers?
   a) Not very close.
   b) Quite close.
   c) Very close.

III. What does Kevin mean? Mark the appropriate sentence.

1. A 'graduate scheme within a hotel company' means …
   a) a foreign language seminar for everybody in the hotel's management team.
   b) a health and fitness course for all hotel employees.
   c) a training programme in hotel management for students organized by the hotel chain.
2. If a hotel is 'refurbished' it means …
   a) it has been decorated.
   b) it has been advertised in the local press.
   c) it has closed down.
3. The expression 'This hotel is show business' means …
   a) this hotel must offer tickets for theatre productions.
   b) this hotel must sell itself to the public.
   c) this hotel must make itself available for film productions.

IV. Kevin uses the abbreviations 'BA' and 'BSc'. What do these stand for and what do they mean?

6D

Troubleshooter gets all the credit

Troubleshooter has gone to Drusillas Park, the best small zoo in the country. The new manager comes out of his office. "Business is *brisk*," he says. "But it could be brisker." He is determined to *make* his *mark on* the place and would like Troubleshooter to suggest some improvements.

On his way around Drusillas Troubleshooter meets Kevin, whose father is the *headkeeper* at the zoo. Kevin gives Troubleshooter a lot of ideas for improving the zoo: a glass *dome* so that people can get nearer to the animals, a *ramp* for wheelchair users, signs near the railway line for the deaf and hard of hearing, a playground for small children, a glass wall to see the penguins catching fish, and new animals such as *porcupines* and pink flamingos.

Troubleshooter makes a note of Kevin's suggestions and soon finishes his report. A few weeks later he goes back to see what changes have been *implemented*. The manager is delighted. "It's an absolute miracle," he says. "Business is booming!"

Kevin is disappointed that Troubleshooter has been given all the credit for ideas that weren't his. He buys himself some cake and a biscuit and sits on a bench. "It was really difficult coming up with all those ideas," he says to himself. At that moment Troubleshooter comes up. "Not at all. It was a *piece of cake*," he says, taking the plate out of Kevin's hands. Kevin can't believe it. "That really *takes the biscuit*," he says. "Don't mind if I do!" says Troubleshooter disappearing with the biscuit as well.

Kevin is alone. "Adults! Businessmen!" he *moans*. "Who needs them?"

brisk	flott, forsch	porcupine	Stachelschwein
make one's mark on	seinen Stempel aufdrücken, sich profilieren	implement	durchführen
		piece of cake	Kinderspiel, Klacks
headkeeper	Oberwärter(in)	take the biscuit	alles übertreffen, das Höchste sein
dome	Kuppel		
ramp	Rampe	moan	schimpfen

I. Questions on the text. Answer them.

1. What job does Troubleshooter have to do at Drusillas?
2. Why is Kevin so important for Troubleshooter?
3. How does Kevin feel at the end of the story? Why?

II. What do these words and expressions mean? Mark the correct answer.

1. The expression 'Business is brisk' (line 2) means …
   a) business is going well.
   b) business is hard.
   c) business is unrewarding.
2. The expression 'to make one's mark' (line 3) means …
   a) to do something successfully.
   b) to work quickly.
   c) to change everything dramatically.
3. If you 'make a note of something' (line 11) you …
   a) give your opinion about something.
   b) copy something somebody else has written.
   c) write something down on a piece of paper.
4. If you 'give somebody credit for something' (line 14) you …
   a) say that they have done something well.
   b) say that they have made a mistake.
   c) say that they have earned too much money.
5. The expression 'It was a piece of cake' (line 17) means …
   a) it was difficult. b) it was easy. c) it was impossible.
6. The expression 'That takes the biscuit' (lines 18-19) means …
   a) that's remarkable. b) that's clever. c) that's stupid.

III. These words are often mispronounced. Can you see why?

1. biscuit /ˈbɪskɪt/
2. penguin /ˈpeŋgwɪn/

IV. Translate the <u>underlined</u> words into your first language.

1. Everybody turned to <u>the bench</u> when the verdict was about to be announced.
2. She was in the cabinet but now she's a <u>backbencher</u>.
3. He's an excellent footballer so he doesn't want to be sitting on the <u>bench</u> every week.

V. What do you think of zoos? Write a short comment in English (50 words).

6E

Which airport is it?

Figures on the flight path

■ Initial capacity of 35 million passengers and three million tons of cargo a year is projected to rise by 2040 to 85 million passengers and nine million tons.
■ A second runway is due to open next winter.
■ The airport is expected to generate £420 million in revenue in its first year against costs of half that amount. It expects to repay the development debt of nearly £1 billion by 2001.
■ It is expected to employ more than 45,000 staff.
■ The roof area is equivalent to London's Soho and its vaulted design is five times more energy-efficient than a flat roof.
■ Skylights and reflectors provide natural light.
■ The smart building shuts off lighting and air-conditioning in unoccupied areas and turns off travelators and escalators when not in use.
■ Glass walls offer panoramic and uninterrupted views of the runways, the South China Sea and the New Territories hills.
■ The two 4,000-yard runways are 80 yards wide.
■ The airport was built on a man-made island constructed by removing the peaks on two small islands, Chek Lap Kok and Lam Chau, and shovelling the landfill, augmented by hardcore, into the sea.
■ A rail link will enable passengers in the business district to be at the airport in 23 minutes.
■ The development has nine other elements, including a town of 25,000 people.
■ The Tsing Ma road and rail link is the world's longest two-tier suspension bridge.
■ The terminal has 80 departure gates, 12,500 seats, 2,000 display screens and 141 shops and restaurants.

It's Kansai International Airport, Japan.

HUMAN RESOURCES 7

7A

Job hunting

Marion Tracy

Adecco Alfred Marks is one of the largest and longest-established *recruitment agencies* in the United Kingdom. Marion Tracy is a *consultant* in one of their branches.

"We really deal in this branch with temporary and permanent staff on a commercial level. So we're looking for good quality *PA*s, secretaries, receptionists, telephonists, administrators and maybe occasionally *office juniors* and some account staff. These days we are looking for people with skills, people who have *IT* skills, either word packages, computer packages; and all of these things really are based on computers. Even if you *go along* as a telephonist, we're talking about a computerized *switchboard*. You must have a good telephone manner in practically every job you go for but of course these days you really have to *package* yourself. We have to sell you as a package to a prospective employer. Well, the applicant will come in and we'll basically do a very quick - what we call a doorstep - interview, have a little chat with them at the door in our reception and see what they're looking for.

No longer do we work with pieces of paper in boxes. Everything goes onto a computer and then it can be *drawn up* in front of each of the consultants in the branch here. We will then test their skills. This isn't an exam but it means that then we know what they can do when we're trying to sell them to a prospective employer and we will then interview them for about twenty minutes just to find out a little more about them."

Kirstin is looking for a new job. This is what Marion says to her.

▸ So what I'll do is I'll have a chat with him on the phone, I'll send him your *CV* and ask him to set up an interview for you tomorrow. You are free tomorrow?

▸ Yes, I am.

▸ Right, OK. I don't really need to tell you how to go to an interview but what you must realize is that these days you have got to sell yourself. You have got to package yourself so that this client wants to buy you. So, nice and enthusiastic, beautifully turned out.

▸ OK.

▸ OK? So, I'll talk to him this afternoon. Then I'll give you a buzz and we'll get all sorted for tomorrow.

recruitment agency	Personalagentur	go along	*hier*: sich bewerben
consultant	Berater(in)	switchboard	Vermittlung, Zentrale
PA	persönliche(r) Assistent(in)	package	präsentieren
		draw up	abrufen
office junior	Bürogehilfe, -gehilfin	CV	Lebenslauf
IT	Informationstechnik		

■ Working with the text

I. Complete these sentences using the information in the text.

1. Marion Tracy works in a recruitment agency. Her job involves ... .
2. Marion says that IT skills are very important today because ... .
3. Marion gives Kirstin some advice about ... .

II. Answer these questions.

1. How does Marion help Kirstin exactly?
2. In what respect does Marion not help Kirstin in her search for a new job?

III. What are the <u>underlined</u> words referring to in the text?

1. '<u>We</u> see what they're looking for.' (lines 14-15)
2. '<u>It</u> can be drawn up in front of each of the consultants.' (line 17)
3. '<u>This</u> isn't an exam.' (line 18)
4. 'I'll have a chat with <u>him</u>.' (line 23)

IV. Choose a suitable ending to the sentence.

1. A 'prospective employer' (line 12) is ...
   a) somebody who often applies for jobs.
   b) somebody who has offered you a job.
   c) somebody who may offer you a job.
2. A 'doorstep interview' (line 13) is ...
   a) an interview at home.
   b) a short informal interview.
   c) an interview in an office.
3. 'Beautifully turned out' (line 29) means ...
   a) clean and well dressed.
   b) wearing lots of jewellery and make-up.
   c) speaking slowly and clearly.
4. 'I'll give you a buzz' (line 31) means ...
   a) I'll phone you.
   b) I'll send you an e-mail.
   c) I'll write to you.
5. 'We'll get all sorted for tomorrow' (lines 31-32) means ...
   a) we'll get all your papers and documents in the right order for tomorrow.
   b) we'll send off your CV tomorrow.
   c) we'll get everything ready for your interview tomorrow.

V. What do the following abbreviations stand for?

1. PA (line 5) 2. IT (line 7) 3. CV (line 23)

VI. Further questions. Use your own words as far as possible.

1. What do you understand by a 'good telephone manner' (line 10)?
2. Marion says: 'We will then test their skills' (line 18). What skills do you think she means?
3. How would you describe the way Marion deals with Kirstin?
4. What other tips would you give somebody who is going to an interview?

■ Exercises

Focus on ➔ inversion

Auf negative Adverbialbestimmungen wie *under no circumstances, at no time, no longer* oder *not until much later* folgt, wie bei Fragen, die Satzstellung: Hilfsverb + Subjekt. Inversion kommt ebenfalls bei sog. restriktiven (einschränkenden) Begriffen vor, wie *hardly, seldom, rarely, little, only after* und *never.* Sätze mit Inversion haben meist einen formalen oder literarischen Klang.

***No longer** do we work with pieces of paper in boxes.*
***Only then** did I realize what he had said.*

I. Rewrite these sentences including the expressions in (brackets).

1. You are not allowed to park here. (under no circumstances)
2. The managing director was not informed of the union's decision. (at no time)
3. He did not find out who his boss was until a month later. (not until later)
4. She didn't know why she had been given the job until she had been with the company for six months. (not until)

II. Rewrite these sentences. Start with the words in (brackets). (You will have to make other changes to your sentence.)

1. She had just arrived at the office when the sun came out. (Hardly ...)
2. I've never been to such a wonderful concert. (Seldom ...)
3. They didn't appreciate the problems we were facing. (Little ...)
4. We lost our money. And we lost our credit cards. (Not only ...)

Focus on ➔ 'nice and' ...

Das Wort 'nice' wird im gesprochenen Englisch oft verwendet. Vor einem anderen Adjektiv dient 'nice and' zur Hervorhebung im Sinne von ‚sehr'.

*So, **nice and** enthusiastic, beautifully turned out.*
*The work was **nice and** easy.*

III. What does 'nice' mean in these sentences? Choose a word from the box.

attractive • charming • fine • friendly

1. They were so *nice* to us when we stayed with them at the weekend.
2. The weather's been *nice* lately, hasn't it?
3. You're so stupid! - Oh, that's *nice* of you!
4. What do you think of our new chair? - Oh, very *nice*.

IV. Rewrite the sentences using 'nice'.

1. It's so quiet here, isn't it?
2. We'll get back very early tomorrow morning.
3. Your car's very clean. Have you just washed it?
4. Wow! Your office is so tidy! What happened?

V. What's the difference between ...

1. 'temporary staff' and 'permanent staff'?
2. a 'secretary' and a 'receptionist'?
3. an 'employer' and an 'employee'?

VI. Hilary Woodland, in charge of Graduate Recruitment at Marks & Spencer, talks about recruitment procedures. Put the four sentences together to form a paragraph.

a. But we're also looking for people whose real interest lies in retail, who really get motivated by - and get a buzz from - working in retail and working with the customer."
b. So we shortlist those forms and we draw up the lists of people that we want to interview.
c. The interviewer is looking for evidence of five key skills: leadership, planning and organizing, assertiveness, analytical consideration and job motivation.
d. "We receive about seven, eight thousand application forms in the UK and we receive about two thousand application forms in Europe.

VII. Join the verbs (1-6) with the endings (a-f) to form a logical sequence of events.

1. to read	a. a letter of application and a CV
2. to write	b. the job
3. to ring and confirm	c. an advertisement in a newspaper
4. to go to	d. the offer
5. to be offered	e. the date of the interview
6. to accept	f. the interview

VIII. Tony Bailey talks about how he got a weekend job. Use seven words from exercise VII to complete the text.

"Last summer I applied for a part-time job in a supermarket near where we live. My brother saw the ... on the supermarket notice board. I ... the manager, Mr Poole, from home and he ... me to come to an ... the following week.

The interview lasted about half an hour. Mr Poole read through the ... I had brought along and asked me about school, what sort of things I did in my free time and what work experience I had. At the end he ... me the job and I ... immediately."

IX. Now complete the rest of the text by putting one word of your choice into each gap.

"I've been working at the supermarket ... two months now. I only do ten ... a week: six on Saturday and four on Sunday. I stack shelves, tidy up and help ... if they've got any problems. I enjoy the job and get on well with the other ... who work there.

The extra money is very useful. You see, I'm saving up to buy a new ... and a laser printer. Next year is my ... year at school so I don't know if I can carry on working then. It will be difficult without the extra money but I think it's ... to do well in my final ... . "

7B

Attending an interview

Kirstin has gone for an interview.

- I see you worked for Drake & Brown as a receptionist. Tell me what you did there.
- Well, it's quite a small firm so I did pretty well everything. I worked in the front office. I was on the switchboard, I had to deal with incoming calls, I had to use the fax machine, I dealt with the post, I had to *keep records* of the incoming and outgoing mail and I was supposed to keep a daily record of the *petty cash.*

▸ You were there four years. Why did you leave?

▸ I left because I wanted to travel.

▸ Excuse me, Mrs Skinner. I was wondering if I could have a word.

▸ Of course.

▸ I'm afraid I want to hand in my resignation.

▸ No. Really? Why is that? Is there a problem?

▸ Oh, no. I want to travel. I plan to go to Europe for a year to live and work.

▸ I see. Well, I don't suppose I can stop you so I must wish you good luck.

▸ I will give a month's *notice* so that will *take* me *up* to the end of July.

▸ Oh, we'll miss you. Oh, I'll have to advertise the *vacancy*.

▸ I was wondering. Could you write me a *testimonial*? It will help me when I'm applying for another job.

▸ Of course. And if you wish to use my name as a reference, you're very welcome to do so. Meantime I wish you the very best of luck.

▸ Now tell me. Why do you think you're suitable for this job?

▸ I think I've got all the skills you need. I've got IT skills, a good telephone manner and I've had five years' work experience in a similar environment. I know you're planning to *market* into Europe and I've got good language skills and I've lived and worked in Europe for a year.

▸ You certainly have the skills. It's not just skills we need. It's the personality as well. The work is demanding. There are *deadlines* to be *met* and some of the clients can be difficult. Do you think you could cope with all this?

▸ I feel sure I'll be able to cope with the pressures of the job. I'm quite used to working to deadlines and I don't mind staying late if there's work to be finished. And dealing with difficult clients: well, I know from experience that I can be tactful and diplomatic but I can also be quite firm when necessary.

▸ You sound too good to be true.

▸ I wouldn't say that. I've had my fair share of disasters but I don't let them *get on top* of me.

keep records	aufzeichnen, dokumentieren
petty cash	Portokasse
notice	Kündigung
take up	weitermachen, -arbeiten
vacancy	offene Stelle
testimonial	Referenz
market	Absatzmärkte erschließen, vertreiben
meet deadlines	Termine einhalten
get on top	*hier*: negativ beeinflussen

■ Working with the text

I. Which lines in the text show you that Kirstin ...

1. had a lot of different duties in her previous job?
2. had a good relationship with her previous employer?
3. is an optimistic sort of person?

II. Questions on the text. Answer them.

1. What was Kirstin's last job and how long did she work in it?
2. Why did she resign from the job?
3. What two areas does the interviewer ask Kirstin about?

III. Choose a suitable ending to these sentences.

1. 'Petty cash' (line 8) is ...
   a) money which can only be used in emergencies.
   b) money which is used for buying presents.
   c) money which is used for small payments.
2. 'I was wondering if I could have a word' (line 11) means ...
   a) Can I borrow your dictionary?
   b) Can I speak to you?
   c) Can I have some new software?
3. 'I will give a month's notice' (line 17) means ...
   a) I will hand in my resignation a month before I leave.
   b) I will hand in my resignation in a month's time.
   c) I will hand in my resignation every month.

4. A 'testimonial' (line 19) is ...
   a) a short CV.
   b) a job description.
   c) a written statement about a person's character and abilities.
5. 'Do you think you could cope with all this?' (line 30) means ...
   a) Will you be polite all the time?
   b) Will you be able to manage all these things successfully?
   c) Will you be able to make all the photocopies we need?
6. 'You sound too good to be true' (line 35) means ...
   a) you seem to be the perfect person for the job.
   b) you seem very well behaved.
   c) you seem to be telling the truth.
7. 'I've had my fair share of disasters' (line 36) means ...
   a) too many bad things have happened to me.
   b) enough bad things have happened to me.
   c) not enough bad things have happened to me.

IV. Give a German equivalent for the following.

1. 'I was on the switchboard.' (line 5)
2. 'I'll have to advertise the vacancy.' (line 18)
3. 'I'm used to working to deadlines.' (lines 31-32)
4. 'I can also be quite firm when necessary.' (line 34)

V. Further questions. Write three or four sentences for each answer.

1. What do you think of Kirstin's performance at the interview? Do you think she got the job?
2. What do you think about working abroad? Is it a useful experience? Would you like to do it? Say why or why not.

■ Exercises

Focus on ➔ gerund or infinitive after verbs

Es gibt Verben, nach denen das Gerund - die -ing-Form des Verbs - steht, z.B. *avoid, enjoy, mind, postpone* oder *suggest.* Es gibt aber auch Verben, z.B. *decide, hope, plan, promise* oder *want,* nach denen der Infinitiv mit 'to' steht. Das Gerund ist jedoch die einzig mögliche Verbform nach einer Präposition. (s. auch Unit 8, Focus on, S. 135)

*I **plan to go** to Europe for a year.*
*I don't **mind staying** late.*
*I'm quite **used to working** to deadlines.*

I. Join the sentences together using a gerund or infinitive construction. You may have to add a word (eg a preposition) or make other changes.

1. He works shifts. He dislikes it.
2. I lost the money. I admit it.
3. Did you bring the magazine? Or did you forget it?
4. They want to go to the party. In fact they are looking forward to it.
5. You have been very helpful. Thank you.
6. Having coffee in a smoky café is terrible. I object to it.
7. I ordered the books last week. I didn't forget.
8. She thinks we could have the meeting later. It was her suggestion.

Focus on ➔ reported speech

Bei Aufforderungen oder Bitten wird die indirekte Rede oft durch die Konstruktion Verb + Objekt + Infinitiv wiedergegeben.

*She **told me to package** myself.*
*She **advised me to sell** myself.*

II. You've been given this advice by Marion Tracy. Now you're telling a friend what she told you. Put the sentences below into reported speech. Start with 'She told me ...' or 'She advised me ...'. (Be careful with sentence 6!)

1. 'Read all the local papers.'
2. 'Apply for as many jobs as possible.'
3. 'Be polite on the phone.'
4. 'Arrive for the interview on time.'
5. 'Smile at the interviewer.'
6. 'Don't worry if you are not successful the first time.'

III. What's the difference between ...

1. 'keeping records of the mail' and 'keeping copies of the mail'?
2. a 'testimonial' and a 'reference'?
3. an 'interviewer' and an 'interviewee'?
4. 'staying late' and 'staying up late'?

IV. Complete the text using the correct forms of the verbs in (brackets).

Interviewer: Please come in and have a seat. Now, where ... (you, hear) about the possibility of ... (do) an apprenticeship at Meason's?
Applicant: We ... (tell) about it by our careers advisor, Mr Price.
Interviewer: I see. And what ... (attract) you to the work of a mechanic?

Applicant:	I ... (be interested) in cars and engines ever since I ... (be) a small boy. I suppose you could say it's my hobby.
Interviewer:	Would you mind ... (tell) me something about your work experience?
Applicant:	Well, last summer I ... (have) a job in a shop which ... (sell) spare parts.
Interviewer:	And have you stopped ... (work) there?
Applicant:	Unfortunately it ... (be) a temporary job. If I ... (have) the opportunity I would have stayed there longer.
Interviewer:	I understand. And now? What ... (you, do) at the moment?
Applicant:	I ... (work) in a supermarket and ... (apply) for jobs.

V. *What sort of job is the right one for you? To find out read through this list and tick the statements you agree with.*

a I'm interested in meeting new people.
b I go red when I say something in front of other people.
c I'd love to live in a foreign country.
d I don't like making decisions by myself.
e I don't mind doing what my friends do.
f I wouldn't mind bungee jumping off a high bridge.
g I enjoy being alone.
h I enjoy working together with other people.
i I like team games rather than individual sports.
j I don't mind telling other people what to do.
k I enjoy wearing the latest fashions.
l I often ask my friends for advice or help.
m I don't have many friends.
n I want to be responsible for anything I do.
o I don't like to go to parties.
p I like doing things I've never done before.
q I don't like being in situations I cannot control.
r I don't like telling jokes.
s I enjoy showing people what I know and can do.
t I like being the centre of attraction.

Now see if you have more than three ticks in any of the four groups and read what it says below about what sort of job you could do.

Group 1	b	g	m	o	r
Group 2	t	j	s	q	n
Group 3	d	l	e	i	h
Group 4	c	f	k	p	a

Group 1: *Backseat worker*. You are the sort of person who works well on your own. You don't find it easy to mix with other people so working in a laboratory or a in a small office may suit you.

Group 2: *Decision maker*. You're more the type of person who likes to be in the middle of the action. You enjoy having people around you and making decisions so working in management or sales may be what you'll find most interesting.

Group 3: *Team player*. You prefer to be a member of a team and not always decide things on your own. Since you like being with other people nursing, the police force or banking may be what you'd like to do.

Group 4: *Risk taker*. You're a person who likes a challenge and is not afraid of taking risks. Perhaps you should start up your own business or go into advertising.

7C

Chris Brown - training to be a manager

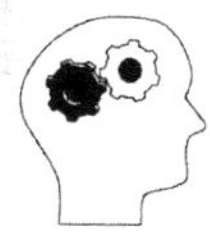

I. As you listen to the interview, read and answer these questions.

1. All three people in this interview work for Marks and Spencer. What are their jobs? Mark the correct answer.

Chris Brown is	a. in charge of recruitment.
Gail Hovey is	b. a deputy manager.
Hilary Woodland is	c. a management trainee

2. What do they talk about in the interview? Mark the correct answer.

Chris Brown talks about	a. applying for a job.
Gail Hovey talks about	b. finding shop staff.
Hilary Woodland talks about	c. interviewing graduates.

II. Listen again. Which is the correct answer? Tick it.

1. Chris Brown says that filling in an application form was ...
   a) a chance to show how good his English was.
   b) a chance to sell himself and get an interview.
   c) a chance to write about his childhood.
2. Chris Brown says the first interview he had at M&S lasted ...
   a) one hour. b) four hours. c) all day.
3. Hilary Woodland says that after the first interview successful candidates ...
   a) get a job offer in writing.
   b) attend an assessment centre.
   c) begin a management training course.
4. Hilary Woodland says that management training for graduates takes on average ...
   a) one month. b) six months. c) one year.

5. Part of Gail Hovey's job is ...
   a) to find Chris Brown his first job as Deputy Manager.
   b) to tell Chris Brown what to wear at work.
   c) to monitor Chris Brown's progress.

6. Gail Hovey talks about the good reputation M&S has. Why does Gail think it is so good?
   a) Because of the company's advertisements.
   b) Because of the company's emphasis on customer care.
   c) Because of the company's friendly customers.

III. Which is the correct answer? Tick it.

1. If work is 'gruelling' it is ...
   a) interesting. b) good fun. c) demanding.
2. If you do 'seasonal work' you work ...
   a) in the summer.
   b) at certain busy times of the year.
   c) when you have got enough time.
3. If a company's reputation is gained through 'word of mouth' it is gained ...
   a) through people talking to their friends about the company.
   b) through the company advertising on the radio.
   c) through the company making announcements outside its stores.

IV. Would you like to work in the retail business? Say why or why not. Write 30 to 40 words.

7D

Troubleshooter seeks secretary

Troubleshooter has placed an advertisement for a secretary/PA with excellent word processing skills and a good telephone manner.

Six applicants arrive. They sit outside Troubleshooter's van waiting to be interviewed. The first candidate always takes her cat out with her wherever she goes but Troubleshooter says there's *no room* in his van *to swing a cat* so she won't do. The second candidate is scratching himself so much that Troubleshooter begins to scratch himself as well. He won't do. The third candidate can't stop *sneezing*. She won't do, either. The fourth candidate has some very good references but her perfume is overpowering. She certainly won't do. The fifth candidate has no dress sense at all. He won't do. Troubleshooter has strong words for the last candidate. "Do you always wear so much make-up?" he asks. "I can hardly see you, my dear!" Suddenly she bursts into tears. Clearly she won't do.

Eventually Troubleshooter makes up his mind. "I'm not going to employ a personal assistant. They'll be very upset but what shall I say to them?" he remarks. He climbs out of his van to announce his decision. "Ladies and ..." Suddenly he stops in his tracks. All the candidates have left. Troubleshooter turns to the camera again. "It's true what they say. It's lonely at the top."

no room to swing a cat	sich (vor Enge) nicht rühren können
sneeze	niesen

I. Answer the questions.

1. Why is Troubleshooter talking to so many people?
2. Does he manage to do what he intended to do by the end of the story?

II. Identify the correct ending for the sentence.

1. When Troubleshooter says 'She won't do' (line 5) he means …
   a) the woman doesn't work hard enough.
   b) the woman won't do what he says.
   c) the woman is not suitable for the job.
2. If somebody's perfume is 'overpowering' (line 9) it …
   a) smells very good.
   b) is too strong.
   c) can't be bought in supermarkets.
3. If you say somebody has 'no dress sense' (lines 9-10) you mean they don't know …
   a) which clothes suit them.
   b) which dress to wear for special occasions.
   c) how to address people.

4. If you have 'strong words' (line 10) for somebody you say something which …
   a) could make them laugh.
   b) could make them angry.
   c) could make them fall asleep.

5. If you 'stop in your tracks' (line 16) you stop …
   a) talking. b) walking. c) sneezing.

III. Match the underlined idiomatic expression (1-3) with its explanation (a-c).

1. I wanted the party to be a secret but my brother <u>let the cat out of the bag</u>.
2. He was <u>like a cat on hot bricks</u> before his final examination.
3. You <u>haven't got a cat in hell's chance</u> of winning the football pools!

   a. have no possibility
   b. revealed the secret
   c. very nervous

IV. What does the expression 'Curiosity killed the cat' mean? When would you say it?

7E

Reading job advertisements

REVLON

European Regional Director

Travel Retail

London **£ Excellent Package**

With products sold in over 175 countries, Revlon is one of the most recognised brand names in the world. A world leader in colour cosmetics, Revlon holds the number one position in mass cosmetics in the United States. Committed to innovation and growth for the future, Revlon is now leveraging its cosmetic expertise in markets all over the world, with the Travel Retail division becoming an increasingly significant sector.

As Regional Director, you will be responsible for business development and strategy implementation for the Travel Retail sector across all European markets. Accountabilities including planning and managing sales efforts, executing incentives, negotiating and implementing the marketing calendar, putting price guidelines into place and evaluating new distribution opportunities. Working closely with the worldwide department, this role will play a key part in helping formulate global initiatives from a European perspective.

The position is a key leadership role and as such, competitive candidates will be graduates with at least five years' blue-chip FMCG experience gained within the travel retail sector. Knowledge of international markets coupled with strong sales/marketing skills is essential, and European language ability a distinct advantage.

Interested candidates should write enclosing a full curriculum vitae to our retained consultant Kevin Dunbar at Michael Page Sales & Marketing, Savannah House, 11 Charles II Street, London, SW1Y 4QZ, quoting reference 430893. Fax 0171 839 8086, e-mail: kevindunbar@michaelpage.com

Registered No: 0058

Michael Page
SALES & MARKETING

Registered No: 0065

Australia · China · France · Germany · Hong Kong · Italy · Netherlands · New Zealand · Singapore · Spain · UK · USA

COMMUNICATIONS 8

8A

Handling information ●●

Chris Holmes is Head of Human Resources at Marley Floors & Waterproofing. "About three years ago we reviewed our communications and decided that we needed to put in place communication structures which more directly communicated with our employees. The first initiative that we decided to implement was called team *briefing*. This is the *backbone* of our communication strategy. Essentially it starts with the Board and *cascades down* through the organization, through managers, supervisors, to the shop floor. The beauty of team briefing is not only does it give us the opportunity to communicate a management message but also the ability to gain feedback from our *workforce* on the way in which they react to particular issues. Therefore it's a sort of two-way traffic."

Clare Kelly is Marketing Services Assistant. Electronic communications are central to the work of her department. "We have a *web site* on the Internet where we display information about our products and services. People send us requests for information via the e-mail service, where we can either respond by e-mail or we can send them information in the post. We used to have quite a lot of difficulty

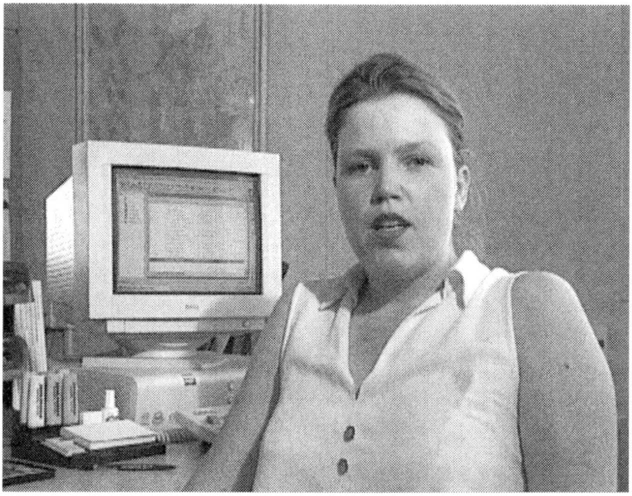

keeping in contact with our agents in America because they are not office based and it was often hard to get hold of them. Whereas now, when we can send them an e-mail message, they can pick it up on their laptop regardless of whether they're in the office or not."

Loreena Wright is a secretary at Marley. "As well as being the *Manufacturing Director*'s secretary, I do a lot of work for the personnel department which means I deal with a lot of letters, good old-fashioned letters. I'm not a traditional secretary, as I don't do *shorthand*, but I do do Teeline which is a form of speedwriting.

I sometimes have to use a typewriter because we have some pre-printed forms that cannot be printed on a laser printer. Therefore I have to photocopy the forms and then type in the information that is needed."

briefing	Informationsgespräch	web site	Website (*Onlineangebot*)
backbone	Rückgrat	manufacturing director	Produktionsleiter(in)
cascade down	stufenförmig nach unten führen	shorthand	Kurzschrift, Stenografie
workforce	Arbeiter-, Belegschaft		

■ Working with the text

I. What do the three people talk about? Select an answer.

1. Chris Holmes talks about ...
   a) Marley's homepage.
   b) Marley's in-company communication strategy.
   c) Marley's computer systems.
2. Clare Kelly talks about ...
   a) keeping in contact with customers using modern communication systems.
   b) having language problems with her boss.
   c) transporting laptop computers from one office to another.
3. Loreena Wright talks about ...
   a) how much photocopying she does.
   b) how much tea she makes.
   c) the work she does.

II. Questions on the text. Answer them.

1. What is team briefing and why is Chris so enthusiastic about it?
2. What means of communication does Clare use nowadays to keep in touch with Marley's agents or customers?
3. In what sense is Loreena not a traditional secretary?

III. Which answer is correct? Mark it.

1. The 'shop floor' (line 7) refers to ...
   a) the factory workers.
   b) the reception area.
   c) the place where meetings are held.

2. If you are 'not office based' (line 16) you probably ...
   a) work on the telephone.
   b) don't have a job.
   c) travel a lot in your job.

3. A 'personnel department' (line 21) deals with ...
   a) a company's employees.
   b) a company's communication networks.
   c) a company's secretaries.

IV. What is the underlined word referring to?

1. 'Essentially it starts with the Board.' (line 6)
2. 'We can send them an e-mail message.' (lines 17-18)
3. 'We have some pre-printed forms that cannot be printed on a laser printer.' (lines 24-25)

V. Express the underlined parts of the text in your own words.

1. 'We reviewed our communications.' (line 2)
2. 'This is the backbone of our communication strategy.' (line 5)
3. 'We used to have a lot of difficulty keeping in contact with our agents.' (lines 16-17)
4. 'They can pick it up on their laptop regardless of whether they're in the office or not.' (lines 19-20)

VI. Further questions.

1. Do you agree with Chris Holmes when he says team briefing is 'a sort of two-way traffic' (line 10)?
2. What is your feeling about the Internet? Do you use it? Do you think it is useful? Give some reasons for your opinion.

■ Exercises

Focus on ➔ past tense and perfect forms

Die einfache Vergangenheit (past tense) wird in Erzählungen und Berichten verwendet. Das Present Perfect dagegen ist keine reine Vergangenheitsform. Es verbindet die Vergangenheit mit der Gegenwart.

*About three years ago we **reviewed** our communications.*
*We **have capitalized** on the emerging technology.*

I. Put the verbs in (brackets) into the past tense.

The first videophones ... (be) Japanese and ... (appear) in the late 1980s. They ... (be, not) very sophisticated devices. Whenever callers ... (want, send) an image of themselves, they ... (must, interrupt) their call for six seconds so that the black-and-white picture ... (can, transmit). Later, in the early 1990s, an American company ... (bring out) a videophone which ... (can, send) colour images. It ... (be) an expensive product, however, and ... (turn out) to be a flop. Mobile phones ... (be) also costly when they first ... (come out). They ... (have) poor voice quality, too. Nevertheless people ... (buy) them because they ... (want, make) calls while moving. Technology ... (improve) rapidly to meet the demands of the customers and the mobile communications market ... (boom). Why ... (the same, not, happen) with the videophone?

II. Combine the pairs of sentences to make one sentence. Use the present perfect.

1. I live in Dublin. (I came here three years ago.)
2. I have a new car. (I bought it six months ago.)
3. I live in my own flat. (I moved into it three weeks ago.)
4. My brother lives in Canada. (He went there in 1995.)
5. John is a software engineer. (He became a software engineer five years ago.)
6. He is not in the office again today. (The last time he came was two weeks ago.)

III. Present perfect or past simple? Use the correct form of the words in (brackets) to complete the sentences.

1. How long ... (you, live) in New York before you moved to Seattle?
2. ... (you, buy) a new computer last month?
3. Can you imagine it? My sister ... (buy) herself a videophone!
4. They ... (not, be) to the cinema once this year. They prefer the theatre.
5. I ... (not, see) John this morning. Have you?
6. Rebecca ... (have) three job interviews so far this month but she ... (not, hear) whether she ... (be successful) yet.

IV. Complete these mini-dialogues by using the expressions in the box.

already • before • just • last week • recently • yet

1. Can I get you a cup of coffee? - No, thanks. I've ... had one.
2. Have you seen Tom ...? - Yes, he was here yesterday, I think.
3. Can I borrow your newspaper? - In a minute. I haven't finished with it ... .
4. What an incredible CD! - I know. I've never heard anything like it ..., either.

5. Have you been to the bank ...? - Yes, I was quick, wasn't I?
6. My parents both had their birthdays ... . - Really? Are they the same age?

Focus on ➔ 'to be used to' + -ing and 'used to' + infinitive

Auf das Vollverb 'to be used to' folgt ein Gerund oder Substantiv. Auf das Hilfsverb 'used to' folgt der Infinitiv.

*I'm quite **used to working** to deadlines.*
*We **used to have** quite a lot of difficulty keeping in contact with our agents.*

V. Complete the sentences. Use the correct form of the words in (brackets).

1. He … (used to, work) freelance but now he prefers to be employed.
2. She … (be used to, speak) English because her husband is English.
3. When we were young we … (used to, write) everything by hand. We didn't have computers.
4. When my children were young they … (be used to, look) after themselves. We didn't have any money for an au pair.

VI. Complete these sentences. Use a preposition from the box.

about (x2) • for • from • in (x2) • to • with

1. We apologized ... being late.
2. Do you believe ... ghosts?
3. Do you know if she agrees ... us?
4. They succeeded ... changing their boss's mind.
5. What were you talking to Karen ...?
6. What part of the US do you come ...?
7. Please don't worry ... us while we're away.
8. I listen ... music every day. Don't you?

VII. What are emoticons?

An emoticon (also known as a 'smiley') is a symbol which adds extra meaning to a message. For example, an emoticon may be used at the end of a comment to show that the comment was not intended to be taken seriously. Most emoticons are designed to be interpreted with the viewer's head tilted over (*geneigt*) to the left.

:-) Your basic smiley. This smiley is used to show joking statement since we can't hear voice inflection over e-mail.
;-) Winky (*zuzwinkernd*) smiley. User just made a sarcastic remark.
:-(Frowning (*finster*) smiley. User did not like the last statement or is upset or depressed about something.

Match the smiley with an explanation.

1.	**(-:**	a. User is a smoker.
2.	**8-)**	b. User has a broken nose.
3.	**:-***	c. User wears braces (*Hosenträger*).
4.	**:-~)**	d. User is yawning (*gähnt*).
5.	**:-#**	e. User is left handed.
6.	**:^)**	f. User just ate something sour.
7.	**I-O**	g. User is a chef.
8.	**:-Q**	h. User has a cold.
9.	**C=:-)**	i. User is wearing sunglasses.

What does this smiley mean? Have a guess! It's not difficult.

10.	**[:-)**	...

8B

Meeting customers face to face

‣ Charlie Chaplin is Brand Manager at Woofwear, a manufacturer of clothes for the *equestrian* and country clothing trades. This years Woofwear has gone to a trade fair at Birmingham's National Exhibition Centre. One afternoon Charlie takes two advertising executives for a coffee.

‣ What would you like to drink?

‣ Um, I'd like an apple juice, I think.

‣ Katrina?

‣ Oh, I'll just have a cup of coffee actually.

‣ And would you like something to eat?

Charlie Chaplin (right) meets two advertising executives

- Um ...
- I've heard the muffin's quite good.
- Here we are.
- Oh, good!
- Well, the main things we want to advertise are going to be the clothing.
- Right. Well, I've got a features list here. If we look at the rates here, at the back of the magazine, you can see here that according to the number of ads that you do ...
- We need to confirm things with you in writing.
- Yup. Please do.
- I'll give you a call in the week so that we can *firm* things *up* there.
- Right. OK. I'm in the office on Wednesday but after that you can contact me on my mobile.
- Right. That'd be fine!
- OK?
- Lovely!
- We look forward to seeing you again soon.
- Yup. Thank you very much.
- Take care.
- Nice to meet you again, Charlie.
- See you soon.
- Keep in touch, won't you?

equestrian	Reit-, Reiter-
firm up	unter Dach und Fach bringen

■ Working with the text

I. Tick the most appropriate answer to the question.

1. It is clear from the conversation that ...
   a) the three ladies are meeting for the first time.
   b) the three ladies have met quite often before.
   c) the three ladies have met only once or twice before.
2. During the conversation the two advertising executives want Charlie to ...
   a) advertise Woofwear's products in their magazine.
   b) show them Woofwear's stand at the trade fair.
   c) tell them about the best food at the café.
3. It is clear from the conversation that ...
   a) the advertising executives are buying the food and drink.
   b) Charlie is buying the food and drink.
   c) each person is buying her own food and drink.
4. The conversation ends with ...
   a) the advertising executives promising to phone Charlie.
   b) Charlie promising to call the advertising executives.
   c) the advertising executives promising to meet Charlie the following day.

II. Look at these phrases from the text. What do they mean? Tick the correct answer.

1. 'I've heard the muffin's quite good' (line 11) means ...
   a) the muffins will be sold out if we don't eat one soon.
   b) they make fresh muffins every day.
   c) why don't you try a muffin?
2. Charlie says 'Here we are' (line 12) when ...
   a) she puts the food and drink on the table.
   b) she gives the other ladies the bill.
   c) she shows the other ladies her card.
3. When the advertising executive says she wants to 'firm things up' (line 20) she means ...
   a) she would like to try on some of the company's clothes.
   b) she would like to make the agreement more concrete.
   c) she would like to go to a fitness studio.

4. A 'mobile' (line 22) is ...
   a) a small office in the back of a car.
   b) a type of telephone.
   c) a new kind of toy.
5. Another expression for 'Take care' (line 28) is ...
   a) Be careful. b) Look after yourself. c) Enjoy yourself.

III. Further questions. Answer them.

1. Are trade fairs important for business? Give a reason for your opinion.
2. Do you think that good personal relations with customers are important for business? Say why or why not.

■ Exercises

Focus on → the gerund after 'to'

Die einzig mögliche Verbform nach einer Präposition ist das Gerund. Aber Vorsicht - auch 'to' kann eine Präposition sein!

*The staff are used **to attending** trade fairs.*
*We look forward **to seeing** you again soon.*

I. Complete these sentences. Use the correct form of the word in (brackets).

1. I object to ... (wait) so long to be served.
2. He wants to ... (leave) now.
3. We look forward to ... (meet) you next week.
4. She's not used to ... (get) up early.
5. They're not accustomed to ... (be) invited to parties.

II. Look at these uses of the word 'actually'. Link them to sentences 1-4.

a. when you're giving an opinion
b. when you're correcting something somebody said
c. when you feel worried about what you're saying
d. when you're giving advice/instructions

1. He doesn't play tennis. He plays squash *actually*.
2. I think the coffee is really nice *actually*.
3. *Actually*, Tom, we usually have a short nap after lunch.
4. I'm sorry. I don't *actually* eat meat.

Focus on → question tags after imperatives

Nach einer Aufforderung steht oft ein Frageanhängsel: *won't you?* steht normalerweise nach einer Einladung, *will you?, would you?, can you?* und *can't you?* nach einer Bitte. Bei einer verneinten Befehlsform steht immer nur *will you?*

Keep in touch, ***won't you?***
Don't be late, ***will you?***

III. Add the tags.

1. Do sit down, ...
2. Help me, ...
3. Call us, ...
4. Don't forget, ...
5. Open a window, ...
6. Don't do that, ...

IV. Which small word is missing? Put it in the gap.

1. I would be grateful ... you could send me an application form.
2. Would you ... staying a bit later tonight?
3. I was wondering if you ... help me with the computer.
4. Would you be so kind ... to post this letter for me?
5. Thank you for your letter ... 25 April.
6. I look forward ... meeting you next week.
7. Can we pay ... cheque or do you insist on cash?
8. Further to my letter ... 4 December ...
9. We have pleasure ... enclosing some brochures.
10. We would like to have the goods ... Friday at the latest.

V. Complete the text using the correct forms of the verbs in (brackets).

Receptionist:	Woofwear. Good morning.
Kammerloher:	Hello. This is Mr Kammerloher in Würzburg, Germany ... (speak). I ... (wonder) if I could talk to Charlie Chaplin, please?
Receptionist:	I'm afraid she ... (just, go out) for lunch.
Kammerloher:	I see. ... (you, know) when she'll be back exactly?
Receptionist:	I'm not sure but if you call in an hour she ... (definitely, be) at the stand. Can I take a message?
Kammerloher:	We ... (meet) in Birmingham last week and yesterday she ... (send) a quotation by fax. There ... (seem, be) a discrepancy between the prices in her fax and the catalogue.
Receptionist:	I think it'd be better if you ... (ring) again later, Mr Kammerloher.
Kammerloher:	I understand. Look, I ... (try) again tomorrow morning.

Receptionist: Fine. Thank you for ... (call).
Kammerloher: Thank you.

VI. Put in the American English words for the British English words in (brackets). (The first letter of the word is given.)

1. When you write down an address the most important thing to remember is the z... (postcode).
2. Waiter! Could you bring us the c... (bill), please?
3. Are most of your staff on v... (holiday) over Christmas?
4. They live in a small a... (flat) in center city Philadelphia.
5. She's starting a new job in the f... (autumn).

VII. Put in the British English words for the American English words in (brackets). (The first letter of the word is given.)

1. It is not unusual to see people in London standing on the p... (sidewalk) and asking for money.
2. How many p... (students) are there at your school?
3. Is there a speed limit on British m... (freeways)?
4. When we arrived at the airport we took a t... (cab) to the hotel.
5. You jump in the car and I'll put the suitcases in the b... (trunk).

It's only a joke!

- Have you heard about the cheapest Christmas present for a person who's got everything?
- No, I haven't. What is it?
- The phoneless cord!

8C

Linda Metcalfe - organizing trade fairs

I. Listen to the two parts of the interview in which Linda Metcalfe speaks. Read and answer this question by marking the two correct answers.

1. Linda talks about ...
   a) the National Exhibition Centre in Birmingham.
   b) Birmingham Airport.
   c) the communication between organizers and exhibitors at the trade fair.
   d) German manufacturers at the fair.
2. Listen to the whole interview again. Who else speaks during the interview?
   a) Two manufacturers and one retailer.
   b) Two retailers and one manufacturer.
   c) Three retailers.

II. Listen again. Which is the correct answer? Tick it.

1. According to Linda Metcalfe, what three main reasons do the exhibitors have for attending the trade fair in Birmingham?
   a) They speak to customers, they display their goods and they meet nice people.
   b) They speak to customers, they display their goods and they look at the competitors.
   c) They speak to customers, they display their goods and they get to know England.

2. How many different countries do the exhibitors come from?
   a) 20. b) 44. c) 63.
3. What does Charlie 'take one step further'?
   a) A message from a manufacturer.
   b) A complaint from a customer.
   c) A competitor's idea.
4. Why does the German manufacturer think the trade fair in Birmingham is important for her?
   a) Because it's a truly international fair.
   b) Because it's close to Germany.
   c) Because all the people are so friendly to her.
5. What does the American woman think of the trade fair?
   a) She's not happy with it.
   b) She's very pleased with it.
   c) She thinks it is a bit too big.

III. What do the underlined expressions mean? Explain them in English.

1. a venue for an exhibition
2. exhibitors have a shop window
3. to eye up the competition
4. a firm's entry in the trade fair catalogue
5. we are the bit manufacturer in Germany

IV. Complete the sentences.

1. 'BETA' means the 'British … Trade Association'.
2. The letters 'NEC' stand for the 'National … Centre'.

8D

Troubleshooter keeps in touch

Troubleshooter likes to be reachable during his lunch hour. "You never know when some important client might need my services," he says. Before he goes to the pub, he switches on his answerphone, leaves a note - Gone to Lunch - under his windscreen wiper and sets his mobile phone.

At the pub Troubleshooter notices that the only other guest is using a mobile phone. This makes him angry. He can't stand people using mobile phones in public places. He writes a message on a piece of paper and asks the waiter to *convey* it to the man. The message is short: 'Please be quiet!' The man reads the message but is not impressed. He *scribbles* MYOB on it and sends it back. Troubleshooter decides he has no alternative but to ring the man on his mobile phone. His voice gets louder and louder. "I wonder whether you would be as good as to make all these phone calls outside in the street," he says, "where they won't be disturbing quite so many people!" The man refuses and just before a fight breaks out Troubleshooter is ejected from the pub.

Back at his van Troubleshooter listens to the messages on his answering machine. He immediately recognizes the caller's number. It is the man who was in the pub! The second message sounds promising. "I'll bring the details over now," says the man, "and leave them with your secretary." This gives Troubleshooter an idea.

Troubleshooter changes into a secretary. A few minutes later the man drives up, winds down his window and gives the secretary some documents. The secretary assures the man that Troubleshooter will be in touch as soon as he gets back. "Troubleshooter is very keen on daily communication with all his clients," she says. "By phone or by fax." The man sees a chance to *extend* an invitation to the young lady. "I say. Have you eaten?" he asks. "Why don't I take you to lunch? Hop in."

The secretary gets into the man's car. He turns to her and looks her straight in the eyes. "I know just the spot for a spot of face-to-face communication," he says.

convey	übermitteln, -bringen	extend	*hier*: aussprechen
scribble	kritzeln		

I. Answer the questions.

1. Why does Troubleshooter get so angry in the pub?
2. Why does he 'turn into' a secretary at the end of the story?

II. Identify the correct ending for the sentence.

1. You usually use your car's 'windscreen wipers' (lines 3-4) when it is …
   a) raining. b) sunny. c) dark.
2. If you are 'ejected' (line 14) from a place like a pub you …
   a) are invited to leave the pub.
   b) are thrown out of the pub.
   c) are asked to go to the next pub.
3. If you are 'in touch' (line 21) with somebody you …
   a) sit next to them frequently.
   b) contact them frequently.
   c) work with them frequently.
4. The expression 'Hop in' (line 24) means …
   a) walk towards my car. b) drive my car. c) get into my car.
5. If you know 'just the spot' (line 26) for something, you know …
   a) where to do something.
   b) how to do something.
   c) why to do something.

III. What's the difference between …

1. 'I've been to lunch' and 'I've gone to lunch'?
2. to 'leave a note' and to 'make a note'?
3. to 'take somebody to lunch' and to 'take lunch to somebody'?

IV. What do these abbreviations mean?

1. MYOB
2. B&B
3. R&D
4. MP
5. mph
6. GNP

8E

Working on a PC

DISTRIBUTION 9

9A

A distribution centre

Paddock Wood is a distribution centre for a number of importers and distributors. One of the distribution companies there is Coolchain.

Roy Hook, Business Development Director at Coolchain, talks about how the distribution business works. "It's all about logistics. In other words it's about good organization. Our job is to deliver a product to the people, and people are a very vital element in this. The other key elements are vehicles, *warehouses*, and absolutely vital, good communications. Coolchain handles all types of fruit, vegetables and salads. From the moment we receive the produce to the moment we deliver it to the supermarket depot, it remains in temperature-controlled conditions all along the chain, *hence* the name Coolchain. We have two types of clients. We have the importer of produce who will bring in fruits and veg from all parts of the world. Some of these importers use our warehouses, our *packhouses* and distribution vehicles. Some of them have their own warehousing and packing facilities and simply use us for distribution. The second kind of client is the UK grower, who grows his own produce and usually packs it on the farm. We deliver to the retailers' depot, the RDC or 'regional distribution centre'. We do not deliver to the high-street shops."

Alex Hunt

Alexander Hunt is a grower. His main *crops* are *raspberries* and other soft fruit. "We here at Boundary Farm are members of Kentish Garden. That is a grower-owned cooperative of some sixty-five members throughout the UK providing soft fruits for the *multiples* and the wholesale markets. And it is a very professional operation based here at Paddock Wood, close to the farm, where we have a full team that organize all the marketing and distribution for us. We pick here daily and we receive our instructions from the Kentish Garden Marketing Office over fax, phone and our modem link into our computer into the farm office. We react to that on the farm by picking daily into the suitable *punnets* and trays, and pick and pack according to orders and distribute daily. Soft fruit is very delicate and its shelf life is limited and we here at the farm start the *coolchain* process off by picking and packing in a temperature-controlled environment."

warehouse	Lager(haus)	raspberry	Himbeere
hence	also	multiple	Ladenkette
packhouse	Abpackhalle	punnet	Körbchen
crop	Ernte	coolchain	Kühl(ungs)kette

■ Working with the text

I. Answer the questions about Roy Hook's part of the text.

1. According to Roy Hook, what four elements are involved in the distribution business?
2. What is Coolchain? What does the company do exactly?
3. Coolchain has two types of clients. Can you name them?
4. Coolchain deals with two types of importers. What's the difference between them?

II. Answer the questions about Alexander Hunt's part of the text.

1. What does Alexander Hunt grow on Boundary Farm?
2. Which services, if any, does he make use of at Paddock Wood?
3. To what extent are efficient communications important for Alexander Hunt's business?
4. Why is a temperature-controlled environment so important for the work at Boundary Farm?

III. Find the word in Roy Hook's part of the text which means ...

1. the organizing of people, systems and equipment in an efficient way.
2. cars, buses and lorries.
3. a company with shops in most large cities.
4. a person who sells goods to the general public.

IV. Do the same for Alexander Hook's part. Find the word which means ...

1. a type of business which is owned by the people who run it.
2. fruit that cannot be keep for long periods of time.
3. a device which changes an analogue signal into a digital one.
4. a small, light box in which raspberries and similar fruits are sold.

V. Say these words out loud. Pronounce them correctly.

1. logistics
2. produce (*noun*)
3. vehicle
4. fruit
5. raspberry

VI. Complete the grid.

	noun	**verb**
1.	distribution	...
2.	facilities	...
3.	...	deliver
4.	communications	...
5.	...	process
6.	importer	...
7.	operation	...
8.	...	order

VII. Use your own words. Say what the difference is between ...

1. a 'warehouse' and a 'packhouse'.
2. a 'retailer' and an 'importer'.
3. a 'fax link' and a 'modem link'.
4. 'picking' and 'packing'.

Exercises

Focus on ➔ 'according to'

Die Präposition 'according to' hat mehrere Bedeutungen. Sie betont u.a., dass Informationen nicht vom Sprechenden, sondern aus einer anderen Quelle stammen. Deshalb sagt man nicht ~~*according to me*~~ oder ~~*according to my opinion*~~, sondern *in my opinion/view.*

***According to** environmental experts more goods are ...*	(laut)
*We pick and pack **according to** orders.*	(nach)
***According to** Article 45 ...*	(gemäß)

I. Join up the beginning and end of the sentences.

1. According to the latest figures released	a. according to plan.
2. There are six classes divided up	b. I owe him £20.
3. Every person will be given a task	c. according to age.
4. According to Mike	d. according to their skills.
5. Everything went	e. the company is doing very well.

II. Continue these sentences using your own words.

1. According to the weather forecast it's ... .
2. According to my train timetable the next ... .
3. The salary for the new position is negotiable and according to the candidate's ... .

III. Now translate these sentences into German.

1. According to our records he's been in prison three times.
2. The work was carried out according to her instructions.
3. Can you arrange the shoes according to size?

Focus on ➔ parts of the year

Neben den Jahreszeiten, Monaten und Wochentagen gibt es im Kalender eine Reihe anderer Tage und Zeiten, die eine besondere Bedeutung haben. Der Begriff *bank holiday* z.B. besagt nicht nur, dass die Banken geschlossen haben, sondern auch, dass es sich um einen gesetzlichen Feiertag handelt (z.B. Ostermontag, 1. Weihnachtstag usw.).

IV. Answer the questions.

1. Name the four seasons.
2. Name the twelve months of the year.
3. Name the seven days of the week.

V. Give the German for the following. (Use a dictionary if you wish.)

VI. What do British people associate with the following? Add three more things to each list.

1. Christmas:	tree, ..., ..., ...
2. Easter:	church, ..., ..., ...
3. New Year:	parties, ..., ..., ...
4. Boxing Day:	sport, ..., ..., ...

VII. Match a word in the box to an object.

jar • tray • punnet • pallet • box • glass • tin

1. 
2. 
3. 
4. 
5. 
6. 
7. 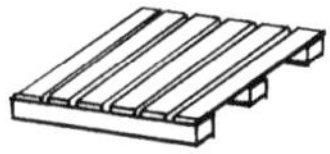

VIII. Emma Sheen is a Produce Technologist at Paddock Wood. Complete her text. Use the words in the box.

bays • consignment • coolchain • environment • load • pallets

"When a lorry arrives with a ..., it backs up onto one of the ... . The door opens automatically and the ... can be off-loaded on ... using fork-lift trucks. In this way the fruit remains in the same temperature-controlled ... and the ... isn't broken."

IX. What form of the words in (brackets) are needed to complete the sentences?

1. We have pleasure in ... (acknowledge) the receipt of your order.
2. We have not yet received ... (confirm) of your booking.
3. After a day of hard but fair ... (negotiate) the participants shook hands and congratulated each other on the compromise they had reached.
4. With the EU ... (expand) to the east other languages apart from English will become increasingly important in business and commerce.
5. A freight ... (forward) transports goods from the seller to the buyer.
6. The ... (agree) has been drawn up but not signed.
7. Our main ... (compete) are in Japan and Taiwan.
8. The material you sent us is very ... (inform).

9B

Buying produce at the farm shop

The farm shop opens each year in June in time to sell the local fruit: strawberries, cherries, raspberries and other soft fruit. *Free-range* eggs and honey from the farm are also on sale. Local people can buy their produce here where it is grown. The service is friendly and it's an opportunity to meet friends and have a chat.

Assistant: Shall I *pop* the eggs *in* your basket?

Mary: Oh, lovely! I want some raspberries at the weekend. Will you have plenty?

Assistant: I'm sure we'll have plenty but I can certainly put some aside for you if you'd like.

Mary: That's a good idea. I've got the family coming for the weekend. I've got ten for lunch on Sunday!

1 lady: Hello, Mary! Congratulations on your new grandchild. I've just heard.

Mary: Thank you. It's a boy. We're delighted! Now we've got one of each.

2 lady: Congratulations, Mary! Wonderful news.

Mary: Thank you. And here he is. A few hours old.

1 lady: He's lovely. Who do you think he's like?

2 lady: Oh, I think Jane.

1 lady: And Jane's fine, is she?

Mary: She's fine! She's going home tomorrow.

1 lady: Good. Give her my love.
2 lady: And mine, too - and to the proud father!

One of the customers is hoping to see the owner of the shop.

2 lady: Do you think Mr Williams is going to be in, dear? I was hoping to see him about a holiday job for my son.
Assistant: I'm not sure. He said he'd be here at about ten o'clock. I think he must have been delayed.
2 lady: Do you think he'll be coming in? Shall I wait?
Assistant Oh yes. He's definitely coming. (To another assistant in the shop:) Mr Williams is definitely coming in this morning, isn't he, Rachel?
Rachel: Oh yes. He's certainly coming in but I couldn't say exactly when. He should be here quite soon I think, hopefully in about half an hour.
Assistant: Would you like these in a tray?
2 lady: Yes, please.
Assistant: We'd like the tray back next time you come.
2 lady: Yes, of course. I won't hang around any longer for Mr Williams. Perhaps you could tell him I'll pop in tomorrow morning.
Assistant: I'll do that. See you soon.

pop in	hineintun
free-range	von freilaufenden Hühnern

■ Working with the text

I. Use the information in the first part of the text to choose the correct ending for the sentence.

1. The customer, Mary, wants to buy a lot of raspberries because ...
   a) her grandson eats nothing but raspberries.
   b) she has invited ten people to lunch on Sunday.
   c) it's the end of the raspberry season soon.
2. The customer has got ...
   a) one grandchild. b) two grandchildren. c) three grandchildren.
3. The other ladies in the shop ...
   a) know the customer well.
   b) don't know the customer at all.
   c) have met the customer only one or two times before.

4. Jane is probably ...
   a) the customer's daughter.
   b) the customer's sister.
   c) the customer's best friend.

II. What do these sentences mean? Explain them in English.

1. 'Now we've got one of each.' (line 13)
2. 'And here he is.' (line 15)
3 'Who do you think he's like?' (line 16)
4. 'She's going home tomorrow.' (line 19)

III. Translate these sentences from the first part of the text into German.

1. 'Who do you think he's like?' (line 16)
2. 'Give her my love.' (line 20)

IV. Use the information in the second part of the text to choose the correct ending for the sentence.

1. The customer wants to see the shop owner because ...
   a) she's unhappy about the service at the shop.
   b) she would like her son to work at the shop.
   c) she has lost a tray somewhere in the shop.
2. The shop owner, Mr Williams, ...
   a) might come in later. b) can't come in later. c) will come in later.
3. The customer ...
   a) is going to ring Mr Williams the next morning.
   b) is going to come into the shop the next morning.
   c) is going to wait in the shop all morning.

V. Questions on the second part of the text. Answer them.

1. Can you see from what the assistant says what time of day it is?
2. Why does the shop assistant want the customer to bring the tray back?

VI. All these words have three syllables. Which syllable takes the main stress?

1. definitely 5. certainly
2. holiday 6. family
3. tomorrow 7. delighted
4. strawberries 8. wonderful

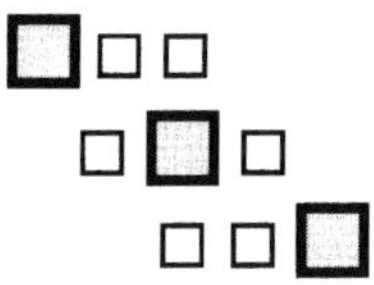

VII. Write down the homophones.

1. sale	3. here	5. son
2. meet	4. see	6. would

VIII. Further questions. Write two or three sentences for each answer.

1. Why do people like to buy fruit and vegetables where they are grown?
2. Could you imagine working on a farm? What would attract (or not attract) you to the work?

■ Exercises

Focus on → the verb 'pop'

Das Verb 'pop' wird verwendet, wenn man etwas schnell, unerwartet oder ohne große Mühe macht.

*I'll **pop** the eggs in your basket.*
*I'll **pop** in tomorrow morning.*

I. Rewrite the sentences using the verb 'pop'.

1. She often comes in here for half an hour and has a cup of coffee.
2. He's just driven over to the next village to see his mother for half an hour.
3. They've walked down the road to get something from the shops.
4. I am just going out for five minutes.

II. Translate into German.

1. He popped his head into the room.
2. She popped a letter through the letterbox.
3. I'll pop this cake in the oven.

Focus on ➔ 'sale' / 'sales'

Das Substantiv 'sale' / 'sales' hat verschiedene Bedeutungen:

*They are negotiating the **sale** of their US subsidiary.*	(Verkauf)
***Sales** have risen by 10% this month.*	(Umsätze)
*In many shops the **January sales** begin in December.*	(Winterschlussverkauf)
*The new computer will not be **on sale** until next year.*	(zum Verkauf, geschäftlich)
*Is your house **for sale**?*	(zum Verkauf, privat)

III. Complete these sentences. You will need one - or sometimes two - words.

1. The law forbids the ... of alcohol to people under eighteen.
2. The latest digital camera is now ... in all our shops.
3. Have the summer ... started yet?
4. ... of new cars have risen dramatically in the last six months.
5. I'm sorry but this picture is not ... .

IV. Explain these words and expressions. (Use a dictionary if you wish.)

1. sales talk
2. a car-boot sale
3. a sales representative

V. How would you respond to the following? Write down your reactions.

1. How are you?
2. Congratulations.
3. Here you are.
4. Bless you!
5. Thanks for all your help.
6. How do you do.
7. Can I disturb you for a second?
8. I must be going.
9. Give my love to Frank.
10. Good luck.

VI. Match the question (1-3) with its answer (a-c).

1. What's he like?
2. What does he look like?
3. What does he like?

a. He's tall and he's got dark hair.
b. Music and sport, especially running.
c. He's very friendly.

VII. Complete this interview with the owner of a farm shop. Use the correct form of the words in (brackets). (If there is a question mark in brackets, think of a word yourself!)

- How long ... (you, have) your shop?
- ... (?) about two years now.
- And how do you succeed in ... (attract) so many customers?
- We make sure that we have good quality ... (?). And we see that our prices are ... (slight, low) than those in other shops.
- And what about staff? Is it easy ... (find) people?
- No, it isn't. I'm sure that most shop owners ... (tell) you how ... (?) it is to get good staff. Most young people are not interested in ... (apply) for vacant jobs in this line of ... (?). They ... (not, want, do) this sort of work. They'd rather ... (be) unemployed.

VIII. Describing people. Complete the sentences using a word from the box below.

greedy • impatient • lazy • materialistic • mean • rude • selfish • wasteful

1. People who throw away food they can't eat are ... .
2. People who push in front of others in queues are ... .
3. People who want more money all the time are ... .
4. People who play their music loudly are ... .
5. People who don't let you borrow something from them are ... .
6. People who drive everywhere instead of walking are ... .
7. People who buy things they don't really need are ... .
8. People who never say hello when you say hello are ... .

Two men in a balloon.

Two men are flying in a hot-air balloon. The wind is strong and they come away from their course. They go down to 20m above ground and see a passer-by. 'Could you tell us where we are?' they ask. 'You're in a balloon,' says the passer-by. The men turn to each other. 'The answer is perfectly right and absolutely useless. He must be an economist.' The passer-by hears them and replies. 'Then you two must be businessmen.' 'That's right!' say the men. 'How did you know?' The passer-by smiles. 'You have such a good view from up there and yet you don't know where you are!'

9C ●●

Brian Nixon and Carol Bushen - distributing stock

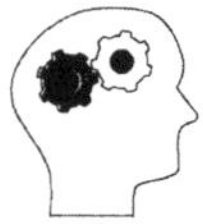

I. Listen to Brian Nixon and Carol Bushen talking about their work at a distribution centre. As you listen, answer this question.

What aspects of their work do Brain and Carol talk about? Mark four items.

a) how big the distribution centre is
b) their competitors
c) the warehouse
d) seasonal work
e) the product lines
f) the computer system

II. Listen again. Identify the correct ending to the sentence.

1. As a distribution centre, Tibb & Britain is quite special because ...
   a) it is the biggest in Europe.
   b) it serves only one supermarket chain.
   c) its warehouses are completely computerized.
2. Tibb & Britain delivers to ...
   a) 56 stores. b) 65 stores. c) 84 stores.

3. There are two sections in the company's warehouse. They are ...
   a) one for hot food and one for cold food.
   b) one which is at a normal temperature and one which is temperature-controlled.
   c) one for British products and one for products from other European countries.

4. The number of product lines is growing by ...
   a) 2% per year. b) 20% per year. c) 52% per year.

5. The abbreviation **DISCO** stands for ...
   a) **D**on't **I**nterfere **S**uddenly **C**ausing **O**ffence.
   b) **D**istribute **I**nteresting **S**tock **CO**nstantly.
   c) **DIS**tribution within Stock **CO**ntrol and distribution of goods.

6. DISCO helps ...
   a) to regulate the flow of goods through the distribution system.
   b) to regulate the sort of music the lorry drivers listen.
   c) to regulate how much data is transmitted to the computers in the warehouse.

III. Match the expressions (1-5) with their definitions (a-e).

1. fleet size	a. a vehicle which lifts and moves pallets
2. line growth	b. products which have to be kept cool
3. chilled lines	c. a group of lorries
4. bar code	d. an increase in the number of different products
5. fork-lift truck	e. thick and thin lines which can be read by a computer

IV. Look at the underlined words. What do they mean? Give the German.

1. This shop has got an excellent <u>stock</u> of wine. That's why it's always so busy.
2. Have you got this television <u>in stock</u>? It's not available in your other shops.
3. I'm sorry. We haven't got the shoes you want. We're <u>out of stock</u> of them.

Look up other meanings of the word 'stock' in your dictionary.

9D

Troubleshooter knows when he's not wanted

Troubleshooter has set up a new *subsidiary* company: Troubleshooter Courier Services. The front of his new brochure shows the high standards he has set himself: 'Delivery before midday - any time, any place.' Fortunately Troubleshooter has got a young man to help him. A schoolboy on work experience will be with him for two weeks.

Troubleshooter gives the young man a short test. He asks him what the four elements in a distribution network are. They young man hasn't forgotten. "Items to be delivered, vehicles, warehousing facility or depot and an up-to-the-minute communications network." Troubleshooter is impressed. Now the young man has a question. "The business is a bit small, isn't it?" he asks. Troubleshooter smiles. He is confident that things can develop. Not for the first time he quotes his old professor: "From tiny *acorns* mighty oak trees grow."

The young man has been given the job of sorting, *coding* and preparing the parcels for *onward* delivery. Troubleshooter reminds him of the company's guarantee: delivery before midday the next day. "Off you go!" he says. The boy sets off on his bike and begins to deliver the parcels. In the meantime Troubleshooter *mans* the phone and has a *nap*.

Soon, however, it becomes clear that time is *running out*. The parcels are *piling up* and it's nearly midday. Troubleshooter decides that he will have to deliver while the young man looks after the phone.

Troubleshooter quickly puts the remaining parcels into his van and drives off. But he has not been concentrating. He delivers the parcels to the wrong addresses. Soon a crowd of angry customers has gathered around the young man demanding their money back.

Troubleshooter drives up and sees what is happening. "Oh dear!" he says. "I know when I'm not wanted. But that young man seems to be *coping* admirably. I think I'll leave it to him. It'll be good work experience for him dealing with dissatisfied customers!"

subsidiary	Tochter-	nap	Nickerchen
acorn	Eichel	run out	(*Zeit*) davonlaufen
code	*hier*: adressieren	pile up	sich stapeln
onward	weiter	cope	zurechtkommen
man	besetzen		

I. Answer these questions.

1. What new business has Troubleshooter set up?
2. Is the business doing well?
3. Does the young man help Troubleshooter. If so, how?

II. Identify the correct ending for the sentence.

1. Things begin to go wrong for Troubleshooter when …
   a) the young man delivers the parcels.
   b) Troubleshooter falls asleep.
   c) there are too many parcels and not enough time.
2. Troubleshooter makes a mistake by …
   a) delivering parcels to the wrong addresses.
   b) asking the young man to help him.
   c) driving too dangerously.
3. At the end of the story Troubleshooter …
   a) sorts out all the problems.
   b) drives away from a difficult situation.
   c) is pleased that business is going so well.

III. Explain these expressions. Use your own words.

1. from tiny acorns mighty oak trees grow (line 12)
2. to man the phone (lines 16-17)
3. to have a nap (line 17)
4. to cope admirably (line 26)
5. dissatisfied customers (lines 27-28)

IV. Link the underlined idiom (1-4) to its meaning (a-d).

1. I think you're barking up the wrong tree if you think he can help.
2. Money doesn't grow on trees, you know.

3. He told her a lie and then she found out the truth. He's really up a gum tree now.
4. She's worked very hard over many years and now she's at the top of the tree.

   a. to be difficult to get
   b. to be in an impossible position
   c. to direct your attention at the wrong person
   d. to reach the highest position in your profession

V. Match the English (1-7) with the German equivalents (a-g).

1. This side up	a. Zerbrechlich
2. Use no hooks	b. Feuergefährlich
3. Lift here	c. Gift
4. Inflammable	d. Oben
5. Fragile	e. Vor Nässe schützen
6. Poison	f. Hier anheben
7. Keep dry	g. Keine Haken gebrauchen

9E

English tomatoes

EXPORT AND IMPORT 10

10A

Exporting porcelain

Jacqui Irons is Export *Sales Manager* at Royal Worcester, a famous British porcelain manufacturer. Jacqui talks about the export business. "Within the export department we have sales managers for various areas and I'm actually the Export Sales Manager for Italy, Germany and France. I speak Italian, French and German which is probably the reason why I'm responsible for those countries. In my three markets in Europe I work with agents, commercial agents. That means that the commercial agents have a team of representatives who sell Royal Worcester and we pay the agent *commission* on the sales that they make. In countries further *afield* like Japan and America and Korea, we use a distributor rather than an agent. A distributor is a company that actually buys the product from us, stores it in their warehouse and then they sell to the customer. An important part of my role is market research. In other words, it's testing new ideas and new product designs with my customers, with our retailers, in Germany, Italy and France. So when I go on a trip to these countries I'll take a design *portfolio* with me. This is actually the design portfolio I took on a recent trip. So in here we have future designs, ideas for designs that we launch next year and I would take these and ask customers their opinion on them because each of the countries in Europe has very different tastes regarding *tableware*."

Ros Whitfield is the Customer Service Manager at Royal Worcester. "When we receive an order, perhaps by fax or by telephone, we have to put the order onto our own order forms and use our own product codes. The order is then sent to another department who put the order onto the computer and give it a computerized order number. Every order is sent to the production manager who gives the order a *lead time* or sometimes this is called a schedule date. This is the date when we expect to dispatch the goods to the customer. The lead time is usually four to six weeks. The goods for that order are manufactured in the factory and they are then packed in the warehouse in special strong cartons to insure that the goods are not sent out and received broken. An invoice is raised in the shipping department and this is sent out to the customer. Most customers have an *open account* or credit facility. This means that they can pay for their goods within thirty or sixty days of the date of the invoice. In some countries such as Italy and Germany, customers pay into a Royal Worcester bank in their country. In some countries outside Europe where payment is less certain it is necessary for the customers to pay by a *letter of credit*. This means a payment is very sure."

sales manager	Verkaufsleiter(in)	tableware	Tafelgeschirr, -besteck
commission	Provision	lead time	Liefer-, Produktionszeit
afield	entfernt	open account	Barkonto
portfolio	(Akten)mappe	letter of credit	Kreditbrief, Akkreditiv

■ Working with the text

I. Continue these sentences using the information in Jacqui's part of the text.

1. Jacqui works for a company which ... .
2. Jacqui is an export sales manager with responsibility for ... .
3. Royal Worcester works with two types of people in foreign countries. They are ... .
4. There is a clear difference between the work these two types of people do. An ... .
5. One of the most important aspects of Jacqui's job is ... .
6. When she travels to Europe Jacqui often takes a design portfolio with her. This is ... .

II. Identify the word in Jacqui's part of the text. Which word means ...

1. money which is paid to a person for selling goods and which is related to the value of those goods?
2. the process of collecting information about what people buy and why?

3. what somebody likes?
4. plates, cups, glasses etc?

III. Use a preposition to complete these sentences.

1. She's one of the sales managers ... Europe.
2. The company pays commission ... everything the agents sell.
3. A distributor buys the product ... the manufacturer.
4. They store the goods ... their own warehouses.
5. When she goes ... a trip, she usually takes a portfolio with her.

Manufacturing plates

IV. Read Ros's part of the text. Complete the diagram below showing the manufacturing process. (Some of it has been done for you.)

1 The order is received.	➔	2 The order ... computer.	➔	3 The order ... production department.
				↓
6 The goods	←	5 The goods	←	4 The order is given ... .
↓				
7 The goods are dispatched.	➔	8 An invoice		

V. Find the expressions in Ros's text which mean ...

1. the time between receiving an order and dispatching the goods.
2. a strong box made from paper.
3. a piece of paper which lists what work has been done and what it costs.
4. a document from a bank which allows somebody to take money from another bank.

VI. Answer these questions on both parts of the text.

1. Why is it difficult for Royal Worcester to design porcelain that will sell all over the world?
2. Why is the packing of the product so important at Royal Worcester?
3. Why do some customers have open credit facilities while others have to pay by letter of credit?

■ Exercises

Focus on → 'pay' / 'pay for'

Das Englische unterscheidet zwischen den Verben 'pay for sth' und 'pay sth'. Das Verb 'pay for' benutzt man für konkrete Gegenstände, die man kauft (z.B. *pay for a meal*). Das Verb 'pay' dagegen verwendet man für Dienstleistungen, die man in Anspruch nimmt (z.B. *pay a bill, pay rent* usw.). Es gibt darüber hinaus eine Reihe von zusammengesetzten Verben mit 'pay', z.B. *pay sb back* (zurückzahlen), *pay sth off* (abzahlen), *pay sth into* (einzahlen).

I. Which of the nouns can follow the verb 'pay for'? Which nouns can't?

They paid *for*	a) their parking fine. b) their car. c) the milkman. d) the lunch. e) the shoes.

II. Which of the nouns can follow the verb 'pay'? Which nouns can't?

They paid	a) the electricity bill. b) their debts. c) the meal. d) the school fees. e) their taxes.

III. Add the correct preposition to complete these questions.

1. Is it OK if I pay … cheque?
2. Could you pay … cash, please?
3. Do you get paid … the hour in your job?
4. How much interest does your bank pay … savings?

IV. Add a particle to make these sentences complete.

back • into • off • up

1. I'd like to pay this cheque … my current account, please.
2. We're paying … the mortgage on our house over 25 years.
3. She had to pay … £500 to have her car repaired!
4. He can't remember if you have paid … the money you owe him.

V. Look at the underlined verbs. What does the speaker mean exactly?

1. 'Let me get you a drink.'
2. 'I'd like to treat you to a meal one evening.'

VI. Complete this grid.

	Country	Adjective	People
1.	Austria	Austrian	the Austrians
2.	China	…	…
3.	France	…	…
4.	Germany	…	…
5.	Greece	…	…
6.	India	…	…
7.	Italy	…	…
8.	Japan	…	…
9.	Spain	…	…
10.	Turkey	…	…

VII. Choose a country from the list above which you have been to. Write a short paragraph (80 to 100 words) about your visit. Say when you were there, what you did there and whether you enjoyed it or not.

VIII. Parts of a letter. Join the two halves of the sentences to make up a letter. What is missing to complete it?

1. Thank you very much
2. We are pleased that
3. Please find our order
4. Since there is a great demand for the goods
5. Payment will be effected
6. Should this order be carried out to our satisfaction

   a. detailing the plates, cups and saucers we require.
   b. for your letter of 20 June.
   c. prompt delivery is extremely important.
   d. we will be placing further orders with you in the future.
   e. within 30 days from date of invoice.
   f. you are able to grant us 10% discount on our initial order.

10B

Importing tea

A trainee at Twinings, the well-known British tea producers, is meeting John Scarhill, the company's Import Administrator. John is explaining to the trainee how tea is imported.

▸ First we receive a contract from our agent for the teas we purchased the previous week. This one is from a company in Sri Lanka and shows a number of different tea standards at different prices.

▸ Who is responsible for shipping and *consignment*?

▸ Our supplier or agent. He must see that everything is in order and send us the necessary documents.

▸ So, all of this happens in India or China or wherever?

▸ That's right. Once the tea's been bought and shipped and just before the ship arrives, we receive the documentation.

▸ I'll never remember what all of these are!

▸ You'll get used to them fairly quickly. The most important is the *bill of lading*. It's a receipt for the container by the shipping company, an identification for *cargo* and a document of *entitlement* to collect the container at the port. In other words, if you have this document, you can collect our consignment of tea, whoever you are. So we keep this in a safe place until the ship arrives.

▸ OK. What else?

▸ There's a certificate of insurance. We generally raise that here. And, of course, we've got the invoice from the supplier.

▸ Right. How do you pay?

▸ If it's an overseas agent, we usually pay by a *bill of exchange*, sometimes called a bank *draft*.

▸ What's this one for?

▸ That's a certificate of *origin*. It shows details of the consignment, the exporter's name, the importer's name, that's us, Twinings. There's no import duty, no tax, on tea these days so a certificate of origin is not strictly necessary. It's still sent to us as a kind of tradition but we don't use it anymore.

consignment	Ladung	bill of exchange	Wechsel
bill of lading	Seefrachtbrief	draft	Wechsel
cargo	(Schiffs)fracht, -ladung	origin	Herkunft
entitlement	Berechtigung		

■ Working with the text

I. Which sentence best finishes the statement? Mark it.

1. After Twinings have bought tea abroad, their agent sends them ...
   a) the tea. b) a contract. c) the paperwork.
2. Before the ship with the tea arrives in England, Twinings get ...
   a) the necessary documents. b) a new trainee. c) another contract.

3. The ‘bill of lading’ (line 14) is an important document because with it Twinings can ...
   a) pay for the consignment.
   b) store the consignment.
   c) collect the consignment.
4. The other two important documents Twinings need are ...
   a) a certificate of insurance and a certificate of origin.
   b) a certificate of insurance and the supplier’s invoice.
   c) a certificate of insurance and the tea grower’s passport.

II. What do you think? Mark the correct answer.

1. A ‘bill of lading’ (line 14) is sent to the importers by ...
   a) the exporters. b) the shipping company. c) the importer’s agent.
2. If you ‘raise’ a certificate of insurance (line 20) you ...
   a) obtain it. b) issue it. c) destroy it.
3. A ‘bill of exchange’ (line 23) is a promise ...
   a) to repay a debt on a fixed date.
   b) to purchase more goods in the future.
   c) to pay for goods in another currency.
4. Another word for ‘tax’ (line 28) is ...
   a) duty. b) draft. c) cargo.

III. Answer these questions.

1. What three functions does a bill of lading have?
2. Why do Twinings need a certificate of insurance?
3. What is the purpose of a certificate of origin?

IV. Say the same thing but use different words for the underlined parts of the text.

1. 'These are the teas we purchased the previous week.' (lines 4-5)
2. 'He must see that everything is in order.' (line 8)
3. 'Once the tea's been shipped, we receive the documentation.' (lines 11-12)
4. 'It shows details of the consignment.' (line 26)

V. What do the underlined words refer back to in the text?

1. 'This one is from a company in Sri Lanka.' (line 5)
2. 'All of this happens in India or China or wherever?' (line 10)
3. 'You'll get used to them fairly quickly.' (line 14)
4. 'We generally raise that here.' (line 20)
5. 'It's still sent to us as a kind of tradition.' (line 29)

■ Exercises

Focus on → verbs with two objects

Es gibt eine Reihe von Verben mit zwei Objekten: einem direkten und einem indirekten. Das indirekte Objekt ist in der Regel eine Person und steht normalerweise an erster Stelle nach dem Verb. Kommen beide Objekte in Form von Pronomen vor, steht üblicherweise das direkte Objekt an erster Stelle. In Passivsätzen wird die Person vom Objekt zum Subjekt des Satzes (‚persönliches Passiv').

John showed the ***trainee*** *(*indirect*) the different* ***forms*** *(*direct*).*
John showed ***them*** *(*direct*) to* ***him*** *(*indirect*).*
The ***trainee*** *(*personal passive*) was shown the forms.*

I. Rewrite these sentences by putting the indirect object after the verb.

1. Can I make some tea for you?
2. We showed our passports to the customs officer.
3. They offered their seats to the elderly couple.
4. He bought a necklace for his girlfriend.

II. Change the direct and indirect objects into pronouns. Rewrite the sentences.

Example: *Give the woman the book.* ⇒ *Give it to her.*

1. Send your grandmother some flowers.
2. Lend the children your football.
3. Give the policewoman your address.
4. Teach the boys a song!

III. Turn these sentences into personal passive forms.

1. The secretary met the guests at the airport.
2. The company thanked the agent for his help.
3. The export manager asked the distributor to place an order.
4. The personnel department offered both candidates a job.

Focus on ➔ 'explain', 'suggest', 'describe'

Auf die Verben 'explain', 'suggest' und 'describe' folgt immer zuerst das direkte Objekt. Das indirekte Objekt verlangt die Präposition 'to'.

*He explained the **documentation** (*direct*) **to** the new **trainee** (*indirect*).*
*He explained it **to him** (*indirect*).*
~~*He explained the trainee the documentation.*~~

IV. Translate these sentences into English. Use the verbs from above.

1. Beschreiben Sie uns Ihre jetzige Tätigkeit.
2. Kannst du mir vorschlagen, wen ich zum Essen einladen soll?
3. Sie hat ihren Kollegen den Unterschied zwischen 'buy' und 'purchase' erklärt.

V. Which verb from the box can replace the verb 'get' in the sentences below?

annoy • arrive at • become • buy • catch • prepare • receive • understand

1. Which ferry shall we *get*? The one at 6.30?
2. Can you *get* some tea bags for me on the way back from the shops?
3. Sorry. I didn't *get* the joke. Say it again, will you?
4. We *got to* the airport just as the plane was leaving.
5. His stupid remarks really *get* me sometimes!
6. Did you really *get* the e-mail I sent you last night?
7. We're *getting* older. But are we getting wiser?
8. I'll *get* dinner tonight if you wash up afterwards.

VI. What form of the words in (brackets) is needed to complete the sentences?

1. The ... (consign) will be forwarded to your address by our agent.
2. We work closely with our ... (distribute) throughout Europe.
3. A group of management ... (consult) were asked to analyse the company's working methods.
4. Over the last ten years the ... (consume) of tea has risen by over 10%.
5. There were over forty ... (apply) for the vacant post.
6. Flight ... (cancel) at Heathrow brought chaos to London's major airport.
7. The ... (divide) of Germany ended in 1989 with the fall of the Berlin Wall.
8. She handed in her ... (resign) after she had been offered a new job at a different company.

VII. Everyday language. Find an appropriate response (a-h) to the sentences (1-8).

1. What can I get you?
2. Would you mind if I open the window?
3. Haven't I met you somewhere before?
4. I'll see you at seven then.
5. Oh no. I've forgotten the CD!
6. How was the meeting?
7. You haven't got her fax number, have you?
8. How long have you been here for?

a. Never mind. Next time.
b. Oh, for about an hour.
c. Could it be a bit later?
d. I don't think so.
e. A pint of bitter, please.
f. No, I haven't I'm afraid.
g. No, go ahead.
h. Oh, don't remind me!

VIII. Read about Incoterms and answer the question below.

Prices for exports include the terms of delivery. These are often one of the following:

- **CIF**: The price covers **C**ost, **I**nsurance and **F**reight to a port in the buyer's country.
- **FOB**: The price includes all costs **F**ree **O**n **B**oard a ship. (The buyer pays for shipment and insurance.)
- **EXW**: This price is the **EX-W**orks cost of the goods. (The buyer pays for freight and insurance from the supplier's factory.)

An Israeli company is doing business with an English firm. Which of its prices would be the highest? Say why.

a) EXW Tel Aviv b) FOB Haifa c) CIF Felixstowe

Ordering a pizza

A leading management consultant walks into a pizzeria and orders a pizza. When the pizza is done, the man at the counter asks him: 'Shall I cut it into six pieces or eight pieces?' The management consultant replies: 'I'm feeling quite hungry. You'd better cut it into eight pieces.'

10C

Sam Twining and Rachel John - working for reputable companies

I. Listen to Sam Twining and Rachel John talking about the companies they work for. As you listen, answer these questions.

1. Sam Twining talks about three main things. Which are they? Mark them.
   a) how Thomas Twining established Twinings nearly 300 years ago
   b) which countries Twinings imports from and which countries it exports to
   c) how to drink tea
   d) why tea is good for you
2. Rachel John talks about two main areas. Which are they? Mark them.
   a) why Royal Worcester has got the word 'Royal' in its name
   b) why good porcelain is so expensive
   c) the different markets for porcelain

II. Listen again to Sam Twining. Tick the correct ending for the sentence.

1. As a young man Thomas Twining once worked for ...
   a) an importer. b) a Chinese businessman. c) an apprentice.
2. In the eighteenth century tea was drunk only by ...
   a) the Chinese. b) the rich. c) business people.
3. When he was 31, Thomas Twining bought a coffee house and began to sell ...
   a) tea. b) cakes. c) cigars and cigarettes.

4. Today Twinings export to ...
   a) 88 countries. b) 90 countries. c) 76 countries.
5. Sam Twining thinks tea tastes better if you drink it ...
   a) with milk. b) out of bone china cups. c) in large quantities.

III. Listen again to Rachel John. Tick the correct ending for the sentence.

1. When King George came to Worcester in 1788 he visited the porcelain factory and asked if he could ...
   a) have a service made for himself. b) drink tea. c) stay a whole week.
2. In 1789 the king ...
   a) visited Worcester again.
   b) granted the company a royal warrant.
   c) was no longer interested in porcelain.
3. Two Royal Worcester products which have been made for special markets are ...
   a) a side plate for Japan and a tea cup for China.
   b) a plate for Germany and a salad bowl for Saudi Arabia.
   c) a dish for Japan and a coffee cup for Saudi Arabia.
4. Rachel tells the viewer that ...
   a) Japanese brides drink strong coffee.
   b) Japanese brides give their wedding guests presents.
   c) Japanese brides go to Saudi Arabia for their honeymoon.

IV. Pronounce these words properly.

1. monopoly	4. porcelain
2. aristocracy	5. warrant
3. bone china	6. bride

10D

Troubleshooter goes to France

Troubleshooter is in Dover. He's off to France to export some English wine. After collecting his documentation he drives through customs. He stops briefly to show the customs officer his papers but the officer does not seem very interested and waves him through.

On the ferry Troubleshooter tries to get into conversation with two men. He asks the first man how many *gallons* of wine Britain imports each year. He invites the second man to be his sales representative. Then he wants to know how the French will pay him for his wine: by letter of credit, by bank draft, in Sterling or in euros? Finally Troubleshooter announces that he is intending to maximize his *revenue* by importing cheese into Britain on his way back.

The ferry arrives in France and Troubleshooter drives to a nearby restaurant to introduce his wine to the guests there. Although a bottle costs £4 in England, Troubleshooter offers it to the French for £10. However, he's obviously been too greedy since the French show no interest. Troubleshooter doesn't give up. He decides to put Plan 2 into action. He buys some cheese and returns to England.

At Dover the customs officer is waiting. Troubleshooter is worried because he's left all his paperwork in France. The customs officer stops him and asks him to open the back of his van. Fortunately there's no duty to pay on the wine but the officer would like to know what is in Troubleshooter's briefcase. He leans forward and opens it. The smell of cheese is overpowering. Now he's had enough. "Right you!" he says angrily. "On your way. And don't let me catch you here again. I don't know - wasting Her Majesty's customs officers' time!"

gallon	Gallone (*ca. 4,5 Liter*)
revenue	Einnahmen, Einkünfte

I. Answer the questions.

1. Why is Troubleshooter going to France?
2. Is his trip successful? Say why/why not.
3. What problem does he have when he returns to England?

II. Complete these sentences using your own words.

1. If you work on a commission basis, you ... .
2. The 'euro' (line 8) is ... .
3. If you are 'greedy' (line 14) ... .
4. You pay 'duty' (line 18) ... .
5. You use a 'briefcase' (line 19) ... .

III. What's the German for the verb 'catch' in these sentences?

1. The dog *caught* the ball.
2. The police *caught* the man shoplifting.
3. We had to run to *catch* the train.
4. The idea *caught* my attention.
5. We *caught sight of* them in the crowd.
6. He *caught* his trousers in the barbed wire.
7. I didn't quite *catch* your last point. Could you say it again?
8. The house *caught* fire and burned down in twenty minutes.

IV. Going through customs.

10E

How to make tea

TEN TIPS FOR A PERFECT POT OF TEA

1. Only use fresh, high quality tea
Tea should be kept in airtight containers, away from strong smelling items.

2. Use fresh water
Always empty the kettle, and fill it with freshly drawn cold water. Hot or reheated water contains less oxygen and gives a flat, stale taste.

3. Ensure the teapot is clean
A layer of tannin does not improve flavour – it just makes the tea bitter! Two dessert spoonfuls of bicarbonate of soda and boiling water will remove the staining in about two to three hours.

4. Warm your pot
Rinse it with hot water. This ensures the water stays at boiling point when it touches the tea.

5. Use the right amount of tea
One teaspoonful per person, plus 'one for the pot' is a good guide. When using tea bags the same rules apply.

6. Brewing time is critical
Pour in the boiling water and let the tea brew for three to five minutes, depending on the size of tea-leaf being used. If the strength is not to your liking adjust the amount of tea used, not the brewing time.

7. Stir before serving
Some people turn the pot three times one way and three the other, which does the same job!

8. Serve straight away
Tea will taste stewed if left in the pot for more than ten minutes. Do not use a tea cosy as this simply speeds up the stewing process.

9. Rinse your teapot
Use cold water and never put it in the dishwasher, and never use a detergent.

10. Experiment with your own special blend
Use loose tea or tea bags. A blend of Earl Grey and Assam will allow the delicate flavour of the Earl Grey to come through the stronger, malty Assam. There are endless permutations!

TWININGS

R. TWINING AND COMPANY LIMITED,
SOUTH WAY, ANDOVER, HANTS SP10 5AQ

THE TRANSPORTATION OF GOODS 11

11A

Carrying goods by road and rail

Alan Bennett is the Commercial Director of Rail *Freight* Distribution Ltd, based at the Wilsden Euro Terminal in London.

"*Intermodal transport* is about moving freight from a factory where it's produced to a warehouse or shop where the freight is required, in a container, without having to pack and repack the freight *en route*, using a combination of transport modes; road and rail and perhaps sea. Intermodal transport is, above all, a partnership between the public sector, that's governments and local authorities, who invest in roads, who will invest in new freight terminals, and the private sector, that's freight *forwarders*, that's road transport *operators*. Our network links the regions of Great Britain, the north of Scotland, the West Country, Wales to the railways of continental Europe via the Channel Tunnel."

What, in Alan Bennett's view, are the environmental advantages of moving freight by rail rather than road?

"A recent report has shown that by 2010 road *congestion* will have increased by fifty per cent if nothing is done to *shift* freight from road to rail. One of our freight trains can take up to fifty lorries off the road. That means less road traffic, which means less road congestion, it means less *exhaust* emissions. But customer choice is based on economic criteria. We can offer faster transit times than road transport and we can offer greater load security. Let me give you an example. If a load leaves Wilsden London at ten o'clock tonight, Wednesday, it will have arrived in Milan at six o'clock on Friday morning."

freight	Fracht(gut)	forwarder	Spediteur(in)
intermodal transport	Transport auf verschiedenen Verkehrsmitteln	operater	Unternehmer(in)
		congestion	Stau
		shift	verlagern
en route	unterwegs	exhaust	Auspuff

■ Working with the text

I. Are the following statements true or false according to the first part of the text? If any statements are false, correct them.

	true	false
1. Intermodal transport means moving freight by train.		
2. One of the advantages of intermodal transport is that you do not repack the freight.		
3. Intermodal transport is part of public-sector industry.		
4. Rail Freight Distribution Ltd operates in Britain and continental Europe.		

II. Using the information in the second part of the text, choose the correct ending for each sentence below.

1. An environmental report has shown that ...
   a) drivers will drive more dangerously in the future.
   b) roads will become busier in the future.
   c) trains will be more comfortable in the future.
2. If more freight can be transported by train, there will be ...
   a) less money for lorry drivers.
   b) fewer customers in the supermarkets.
   c) less air pollution.
3. Another aspect of rail freight is that ...
   a) it is quicker and safer than road freight.
   b) it is cheaper and more reliable than road freight.
   c) it is more convenient for supermarket chains than road freight.

III. Find the words in the text which mean ...

1. goods which are carried by ship, train, lorry or aeroplane.
2. industries and services which are owned by the state.
3. a company which transports goods from one place to another.
4. the south-west of England.
5. the rail link between England and France.
6. the situation when roads become very crowded.

IV. Now define or explain the following expressions. Use your own words.

1. the private sector (line 8)
2. Great Britain (line 10)
3. exhaust emissions (line 17)
4. customer (line 17)

V. Explain these sentences from the text. Use your own words.

1. 'Our network links the regions of Great Britain.' (lines 9-10)
2. 'Our freight trains can take up to fifty lorries off the road.' (lines 15-16)
3. 'Customer choice is based on economic criteria.' (lines 17-18)

VI. Pronounce these words.

1. freight
2. en route
3. congestion
4. exhaust emission
5. economic criteria

VII. Further questions.

1. Do you think more freight will be transported by rail in the future? Give some reasons for your opinion.
2. Do you feel enough is being done to protect the environment?

■ Exercises

Focus on ➔ simple perfect forms

Mit dem Hilfsverb 'have' bzw. 'has' kann man die zusammengesetzten Zeiten Present Perfect, Past Perfect und Future Perfect bilden. Bei Past Perfect Simple interessiert uns das Geschehen *vor* der Vergangenheit. Bei Future Perfect Simple geht es um eine in der Zukunft abgeschlossene Handlung. Dabei wird oft der genaue Zeitpunkt genannt.

The consignment arrived in Milan two days after it ***had left*** *London.*
By 2010 *road congestion* ***will have increased*** *by fifty per cent.*

I. Complete the sentences. Use the past perfect simple form of the verb in (brackets).

1. My boss wasn't in her office when I arrived. She ... (go) out for lunch.
2. I got to work half an hour late. The meeting ... (already, begin).
3. It was my first journey to England by car. I ... (never, be) through the Channel Tunnel before.
4. We sent the consignment by road because we ... (not, have) the time to organize rail transport.

II. Use the future perfect simple form of the verb in (brackets) to complete these sentences. ●●

1. The load ... (reach) the south of France by the weekend.
2. In twenty years the number of cars on the road ... (double).
3. In two months' time the new terminal ... (be) in operation for over a year.
4. Mr Bennett hopes that in the next decade rail ... (increase) its share of the freight market.

Focus on ➔ 'by' and 'until'

Das Wort 'until' wird verwendet, wenn man den Abschluss einer noch andauernden Handlung bzw. eines noch andauernden Zustandes betonen möchte. Das Wort 'by' dagegen wird benutzt, wenn eine Handlung vor einem bestimmten Zeitpunkt in der Zukunft stattfinden soll. Beide Präpositionen kommen häufig mit Zukunftsformen vor. Das deutsche Wort ‚erst' wird mit 'not ... until' wiedergegeben.

We will be working ***until*** *ten o'clock tonight.* (ununterbrochen bis)
The consignment will have arrived ***by*** *3pm.* (Terminerfüllung bis)

III. Is it 'by' or 'until'? (Translate sentence 4 into German.)

1. Can you repair my car ... Monday morning?
2. Is it OK if I stay with you ... the weekend?
3. I'd like you to give me back the book ... Friday lunchtime if possible.
4. We won't arrive in England ... late afternoon.

Focus on ➔ telling the time

Man fragt nach der Zeit mit den Formulierungen *What's the time?* oder *What time is it?* oder *Have you got the time?* Normalerweise wird die *12-hour clock* benutzt. Im britischen Englisch sagt man 'past' (nach) und 'to' (vor). In den USA bevorzugt man 'after' und 'of'. Um deutlich zu machen, dass Vormittag, Nachmittag oder Abend gemeint ist, fügt man 'in the morning', 'in the afternoon' oder 'in the evening' hinzu. Die Abkürzungen 'am' und 'pm' werden lediglich in der Schriftsprache verwendet.

IV. What's wrong with the sentences? Correct them.*

1. *The meeting begins at 9am in the morning.
2. *Shall we book a table for 21.00 hours?

V. Say the times out loud.

1.

2.

3.

4.

5.

VI. Gareth Lesley is part of the management team at Rail Freight Distribution. Complete his text. Use the words in the box.

dangerous • explosive • for • furniture • goods • machines • since • white

"We've been in operation ... around about three years, ... the Channel Tunnel opened, and we carry all sorts of ..., which can be anything from foodstuffs and fish and meats, through to your everyday products which are used in the home such as ... goods - washing ..., tumble dryers and so forth - through to people's ... and basically anything that is not ... or is going to be ... to the Channel Tunnel."

VII. Read this article from a newspaper and answer the question below.

New Rail Freight Terminal an 'instant success'

Commercial services started in May at the £250 million Daventry International Rail Freight Terminal. The rail port is now moving 300 containers per week, with the capacity to handle 165,000 containers annually. Welcoming the formal opening of the new terminal as 'good news for the environment, good news for the economy and good news for the East Midlands', Glenda Jackson made it clear that the government intends to see rail freight at the heart of Britain's rail industry. 'We have already made it quite clear that we wish to see rail increase its share of the freight market. We are pursuing a number of initiatives to encourage future growth of rail freight.'

What initiatives do you think the British government is encouraging? Write a short paragraph (40 to 50 words) outlining your ideas.

What's a meeting?

▸ What's a meeting?

▸ It's a group of people who take minutes but waste hours.

11B

Moving house

▸ Katie and ▸ Joe have just bought a house. They want to move their belongings from their flat to their new home.

Deciding whether to use a *removals company*

▸ Let's make up our minds. Are we going to get a removals company to do the move for us? Or are we going to do it ourselves?

▸ It depends on costs. What will it cost us?

▸ I've got *quotations* from three different companies here. Two of them are very similar. One is quite a lot more expensive.

▸ Hmm, I see what you mean. I wonder why that one's more expensive than the others.

- You see, if we pack everything ourselves, the glass and china and the kitchen equipment, it will cost us that much. If we get them to pack as well as move the furniture, it will cost us this much. And if they unpack at the other end, it will cost this much.
- Let's get them to do everything. I hate packing and unpacking.
- Or we could hire a van for the day and do everything ourselves. It really would be much cheaper. I'm sure we could manage.
- Oh, no. It's *dreadfully* hard work.
- Look. If we hire a van for the day it would cost us this much. That's a *fraction* of what it would cost to have a removals firm.
- But how are we going to move all this stuff and have you ever driven a van like that?
- I wonder if Frank is free that day. I'm sure he would help us. He could help move the furniture.
- No, really. It's not a good idea.

Getting lost

- So where the hell are we exactly?
- Well, we should have turned off further back.
- Yes, we should have turned off back there! Give me the map! Here it is! Here it is! If you hadn't been listening to the radio then maybe you would've seen it. Maybe you would've ... But no. It's always my fault, isn't it?

(They arrive at the house and open the back of the lorry.)

- Oh no! God, no. Oh, look, who put that in there?
- Ah, yes. It's all my fault! I should have known!

Unpacking at the new house

- I am totally exhausted. I told you. We should have got the removals company to do it.
- But you saw the cost of it, too.
- They wouldn't have dropped the television set and broken a leg of the table. Think what that's going to cost us!
- Well, you're always right.
- You should listen to me. If you had listened to me, we wouldn't have taken the wrong *turning* and we wouldn't have got lost in the middle of nowhere. I can't believe it. Look at this! Half the dinner service is broken.
- What a mess!
- You see. I told you. This is what happens when you do it yourself. Oh, we shouldn't have packed this ourselves. Now I'm going to have to get it replaced. I just hope it's covered by the insurance.
- What a day! Well, we did save some money.
- Yes, but was it worth it?
- Let's spend some of it on a meal out. I think we deserve it.

removals company	Umzugsfirma	dreadful	schrecklich
quotation	(Preis)angebot, Kostenvoranschlag	fraction	Bruchteil
		turning	Abzweigung

■ Working with the text

I. Complete these sentences using the information in the first part of the text.

1. Katie and Joe have bought a house and now they want to ... .
2. They have got to decide whether ... .
3. Katie would like to ... .
4. But Joe would prefer to ... .

II. Now answer these questions about the second part of the text.

1. Why do Katie and Joe have an argument in the van?
2. What do the couple discover when they arrive at their new house and open the back of the van?

III. Read the third part of the text. Choose the most appropriate ending to the sentence.

1. Katie is upset because ...
   a) Joe always drives too quickly.
   b) so many things have broken during the move.
   c) Frank doesn't want to help them any longer.
2. Katie hopes that they will get some money from ...
   a) their insurance company.
   b) their parents.
   c) Frank.
3. Joe tries to make the best out of a difficult situation by suggesting that they ...
   a) buy a new television set.
   b) go out for something to eat.
   c) ring their insurance company.

IV. Which word in the text is being described?

1. what a piece of work will probably cost
2. plates, cups, bowls with the same design
3. a very small piece or amount
4. a small lorry
5. very tired

V. Finish these sentences in a logical way.

1. A removals company will help you ... .
2. When you hire a van or a car you ... .
3. You use a map when ... .
4. You say 'What a day!' when ... .

VI. What's the opposite of the underlined expression?

1. This quotation is more expensive than the other.
2. Let's pack. It won't take long.
3. I wonder if Frank is free that day?
4. Did we take the wrong turning?
5. How much money did we save?

Exercises

Focus on → 'I wonder if ...'

Die oft verwendete Struktur 'I wonder if ...' bedeutet soviel wie ‚Ich würde gerne wissen, ob ...'. Die Vergangenheitsformen 'I wondered if ...' oder 'I was wondering if ...' werden verwendet, um eine Bitte besonders zuvorkommend zu formulieren. Weitere höfliche Ausdrücke im Englischen sind *I'm afraid ...*, *Excuse me, ...* und *I'm sorry but ...* Auf *Would you mind if ...* folgt eine Vergangenheitsform.

I wonder *why that one's more expensive than the others.*
I was wondering if *I could disturb you for a second?*
I'm afraid *I can't come to the party.*
Would you mind if *I left a bit earlier today?*

I. Rewrite the sentences. Use 'I wondered' or 'I was wondering' in your request.

1. You want to send a fax from your neighbour's fax machine.
2. You would like to make a quick call from your friend's mobile phone.
3. You're hoping to borrow your boss's dictionaries.
4. You wish to have your friend's car for an evening.

II. Which word is missing from these sentences?

1. Excuse me! Hello! I'm ... but do you think you could move your car?
2. Are you Mrs Gordon? I'm ... there's been a terrible accident at the bottom of the road.
3. I was ... if I could use your phone for a minute. It's urgent.
4. Would you ... if I didn't stay until the end?

Focus on → present tense after conjunctions of time

Bei if-Sätzen steht normalerweise kein *will* oder *would* nach dem *if*, sondern eine Gegenwarts- oder Vergangenheitsform: Diese Regel gilt auch für eine Reihe von Konjunktionen, z.B. *after, before, as soon as, until* und *when.*

Before *they* ***arrive****, I'll make some tea.*
We can't wait here ***until*** *he* ***comes****.*

III. Complete these sentences. Use the correct form of the word in (brackets).

1. I ... (tell) you as soon as I know.
2. We'll ring you before we ... (leave).
3. She ... (see) us when she ... (arrive).
4. He ... (hear) us if we ... (talk) loudly!

Focus on ➔ modal auxiliary + 'have' + past participle

In der Kombination Hilfsverb + 'have' + Partizip wird das modale Hilfsverb stark betont. Das Wort 'have' wird normalerweise in der gesprochenen Sprache auf ein schwaches /əv/ reduziert.

*We **wouldn't have*** /ˈwʊdəntəv/ ***taken** the wrong turning.*
*They **should have*** /ˈʃʊdəv/ ***packed** this.*

IV. Form perfect forms with modal auxiliaries. Then find the sentence (a-e) which best follows on.

1. You (should, tell) me!
2. You (must, hear) me!
3. You (might, warn) me!
4. You (could, phone) me!
5. You (may, hurt) me!

a. I didn't expect you today!
b. Now I'm in a terrible position!
c. That knife's really sharp!
d. Then I could have helped you!
e. I shouted as loudly as I could!

Now say sentences 1-5 out loud using a weak form of 'have'.

V. Complete the text. Use the words from the two boxes.

airport • bag • boarding pass • check-in desk • Gate • hand luggage • luggage
suitcase • Terminal • ticket • Underground

After Deborah had got off the ... at Heathrow ... she walked to ... One. At the British Airways ... she handed over her ... to the flight attendant. She had one ... and a small shoulder ... . 'How many items of ... have you got?' the flight attendant asked. 'Just one,' Deborah replied. 'This is ... .' The flight attendant gave Deborah her ... . 'Your plane's boarding at ... Fourteen at 12.15. Have a pleasant flight.'

baggage reclaim • conveyor belt • customs • flight • departure lounge
duty-free shop • friends • screen • passport control • security check • took off

After passing through a ..., where someone looked at her bag, and ..., Deborah could go into the ... . The first thing she did was to buy some perfume in the ... . Then she sat down near a television ... and waited for her ... to be called. Fortunately the plane ... on time and an hour and a half later Deborah was back in Germany. She went to the ... area and waited for her suitcase. After a few minutes her case appeared on the ... . She picked it up, passed quickly through ..., went outside and met her ... who had been waiting for her.

On top of it!

A party of businessmen went out climbing. After several hours they got hopelessly lost. One of them studied the map, looked at distant landmarks and consulted his compass. After ten minutes he turned to the rest of the group. 'OK,' he said. 'See that big mountain over there? Well, according to the map, we're standing on top of it!'

11C

Andy Ingleston - enjoying the challenge

Having a look at the tachograph

I. As you listen to Andy Ingleston talk about Dockspeed, read and answer this question.

What four things does Andy talk about? Mark them.

a) the work of Dockspeed
b) how many hours a week he works
c) what happens in the control room
d) the training programme for drivers
e) the importance of the tachograph
f) the success of Dockspeed

II. Now listen again. Identify the correct ending to the sentence.

1. How many lorries does Dockspeed have today?
   a) 12. b) 27. c) 62.
2. What is Dockspeed's turnover?
   a) £7 million. b) £17 million. c) £70 million.
3. What does Dockspeed do?
   a) It delivers goods to British ports.
   b) It delivers goods throughout Europe.
   c) It delivers goods to British supermarkets.
4. Why is route planning so important for Dockspeed?
   a) Because empty lorries cost a lot of money.
   b) Because Europe's roads are very congested.
   c) Because the control rooms closes at midnight every night.
5. How many hours per day can a lorry driver from Britain work?
   a) 8. b) 9. c) 10.
6. What is the purpose of a tachograph?
   a) It shows how long and how fast a driver has been driving.
   b) It shows how much freight the driver is carrying.
   c) It shows how much overtime a driver has done.
7. What three reasons does Andy give for Dockspeed's success?
   a) Fast lorries, a good computer system and careful drivers.
   b) Hard work, well-paid staff and teamwork.
   c) Good organisation, lean management and modern technology.

III. Select the correct definition.

1. 'Refrigerated products' are products ...
   a) that must be eaten cold.
   b) that must be stored cold.
   c) that must be grown in cold climates.
2. 'Annual turnover' means ...
   a) how much business a company does in a year.
   b) how much tax a company pays in a year.
   c) how much profit a company makes in a year.
3. The word 'groupage' is ...
   a) the bringing together of several freight forwarders to one distribution centre.
   b) the bringing together of several drivers to one warehouse.
   c) the bringing together of several consignments to make into a full vehicle.

4. 'Perishable products' are products which ...
   a) can be bought all over Europe.
   b) are only available in the summer.
   c) have a short shelf life.

IV. Explain these expressions from the interview using your own words.

1. 'We made a conscious decision to position this company in an area of the marketplace which was not of interest to the larger companies within this sector.'
2. 'We like to think that we can triumph in the face of adversity.'

11D

Troubleshooter earns some free samples

Troubleshooter has a sweet tooth so he's looking forward to his next *assignment*: transporting a box of marshmallows to the Grand *Duchy* of Luxembourg. "This is an urgent consignment and a very important one," says the lady outside the sweet-shop. She hands him the box of marshmallows. "They must be there by five o'clock this afternoon." Troubleshooter wants to know if there are any free samples. "Yes, yes," says the lady. "As many as you want!"

Without a moment to lose Troubleshooter heads off for Luxembourg. A few miles down the road, however, his van breaks down. In the distance he hears a train and paddles across a lake in a small boat to get nearer to it. He arrives at the station and - after paying for his freight - jumps on the next train. The miniature steam train takes him to a few miles away from a small airport.

At the airport Troubleshooter has to *clear* customs. He shows the customs official the documentation: the airway bill, *packing list*, invoice, certificate of origin and certificate of insurance. There's one problem, though. None of the planes fly to Luxembourg.

There's only one chance for Troubleshooter to get his free samples. He'll have to charter a plane. "But it'll cost the earth!" he exclaims. At the same moment his mouth begins to water at the thought of the marshmallows. "All right. I'll do it," he announces. "Whatever the price!"

As the plane takes off for Luxembourg, Troubleshooter can be seen heating marshmallows over a small fire. "Was it worth it?" he asks. He pops a warm marshmallow into his mouth and closes his eyes. "*Yummy*!"

assignment	Aufgabe, Auftrag	packing list	Packliste
duchy	Herzogtum	yummy	jamjam, lecker
clear	(*Zoll*) passieren		

I. Answer the questions.

1. What has the owner of the sweetshop asked Troubleshooter to do?
2. Why is her assignment such an attractive one for Troubleshooter?
3. What price does Troubleshooter have to pay for getting some free samples?

II. Identify the correct ending to the sentence.

1. If you 'have a sweet tooth' (line 1) ...
   a) you like going to the dentist.
   b) you like to eat sweet food.
   c) you like being polite and friendly to everyone.
2. If something you have to do is 'urgent' (line 3) it ...
   a) is very delicate. b) is very expensive. c) is very important.
3. If your 'mouth waters' (line 18) ...
   a) you are very thirsty.
   b) you want to eat something.
   c) you have said something rude.
4. You say 'yummy!' (line 22) when ...
   a) you have eaten something which tastes very nice.
   b) you have completed a job successfully.
   c) you are feeling warm and cosy.

III. Link the idiom (1-4) to its meaning (a-d).

1. We fought tooth and nail to get our plan accepted.
2. We ran for the train and caught it by the skin of our teeth.
3. I'm fed up to the back teeth with my job.
4. When he smiles like that I know he's lying through his back teeth.

a. to be very bored
b. with very little time to spare
c. with great determination
d. to deliberately not tell the truth

11E

Handling perishables

INSURANCE

12

12A

Insurance for personal and business needs

Sue Rawlings works for Guardian Insurance. "Guardian Insurance provides a very wide range of insurance - or *cover* as it is known - for personal needs. In Britain sixty-six per cent of the population own their own homes and this means that they need insurance. We offer buildings and *contents insurance* for home owners. Buildings insurance provides cover against the risk of fire, flood, storm damage and a number of other risks to the house or building. It is important to have adequate cover and not be under-insured. For this reason we make an adjustment every year to the *premium* levels and cover to act against the effects of inflation. We also provide cover for many other person insurance needs such as your boat, your caravan, even your *grand piano*. It's also possible to insure your pets against illness, or against damage or injury they may cause to other people or their property. We can even cover a garden party against the risk of bad weather. You name it, the insurance market can cover it."

David Ross talks about the special insurance needs businesses have. "*Corporate* insurance is the insurance we offer to companies of all kinds. Quite often companies will come to us with a variety of insurance needs and we will offer them a package which is tailor made to their requirements. Take a pub, for example. They would need insurance for liability, both employers' and public, as well as cover for stock and buildings. We can provide business interruption cover. In other words if your premises are burnt down the insurance pays for temporary premises in order that the business can go on as usual and work is uninterrupted. The second element in a corporate package of insurance is liability. Liability basically means responsibility in a legal and financial sense. So there is employers' liability which is a legal requirement in the UK, that is to say, you're obliged by law to have it. If an employee is injured through employer's negligence, then the employer is liable. He is legally obliged to pay financial compensation to the injured employee. Then there's public liability. That's liability with respect to the general public. For example, if someone has just washed the floor, if a customer slips and breaks a leg then you are liable. You are obliged to pay financial compensation and you must *pay up*. Then there's products liability. If any of your products cause illness or injury to a customer then as a manufacturer you are liable and must pay compensation to the injured party."

cover	(Versicherungs)schutz; Deckung	grand piano	Flügel
contents insurance	Hausratversicherung	corporate	Firmen-, Unternehmens-
premium	Prämie	pay up	(be)zahlen

■ Working with the text

I. Are these statements true or false according to Sue Rawlings' part of the text? Tick the appropriate box.

	true	false
1. Another word for insurance is 'cover'.		
2. Buildings and contents insurance is a popular type of insurance in Britain.		
3. At Guardian Insurance premiums go up every year.		
4. At Guardian you can even insure your pet dog against bad health.		

II. Explain the difference between ...

1. 'buildings insurance' and 'contents insurance'.
2. a 'storm' and a 'flood'.
3. being 'under-insured' and being 'over-insured'.
4. 'damage' and 'injury'.

III. List the five types of insurance (or 'cover') which David Ross talks about in his part of the text.

IV. Imagine you run a business. Say which type of insurance you would need if ...

1. an employee injured himself?
2. a customer hurt himself?

3. one of your products harmed somebody?
4. your business was flooded and you needed new premises?

V. Find the word in the text. The first letter is given. Which word means ...

1. that you are responsible by law for something? l...
2. that you did not do something which you were supposed to do? n...
3. the money you receive from somebody who is responsible for harming you? c...
4. a person who is involved, for example, in signing a legal document? p...

VI. Put the words from exercise V in their correct form into the following sentences.

1. There are problems when one of the ... does not fulfil the requirements of the contract.
2. The company did not check that the lift was working properly so when two employees had an accident the company was ... .
3. If he's not careful, he will become ... for all the debts the company has.
4. Workers who are unfairly dismissed may be able to claim ... from the employers.

VII. Further questions. Write two or three sentences for each answer.

1. In Britain 66% of the population own their own homes. In Germany there are fewer home owners. Why do you think this is so?
2. What is your experience with insurance companies? What sort of cover do you need for the life you lead?

■ Exercises

Focus on → word partnerships

Wörter gehen Verbindungen mit anderen Wörtern ein, z.B. Verben mit Substantiven oder Verben mit Präpositionen. Der Wortschatz lässt sich effektiver ausbauen, wenn man sich solche ‚Wortpartnerschaften' einprägt.

*You must **pay compensation** to the injured party.*
*We **provide cover** for many other insurance needs.*
*It's possible to **insure** your pets **against** illness.*

I. Which prepositions are needed to complete these sentences?

1. Two students have been accused … cheating in the exam.
2. Can you explain the meaning of this sentence … me, please?
3. We'd like to invite you … our garden party next weekend.
4. He wants to borrow some money … his parents.

5. Does she prefer her present job … the one she had before?
6. The college congratulated the students … their success.
7. You can't insure yourself … everything!
8. Do you spend much money … food and drink?

II. Which verb (1-5) goes with which noun (a-e)?

1. to apologize for	a. a new job
2. to apply for	b. a silly joke
3. to believe in	c. a mistake
4. to depend on	d. ghosts
5. to laugh at	e. somebody's help

III. Complete these sentences. Use a verb in its correct form from exercise II.

1. He said he was sorry and … his behaviour.
2. She's unemployed at the moment so she … as many jobs as she can.
3. We spend a lot of time sitting at our desks so we … getting a lot of exercise.
4. Everyone … the children when they said something funny.

IV. Put the verbs in their correct form into the sentences below.

belong to • happen to • listen to • speak to

1. Do you like … music?
2. Excuse me. Can I … Michael, please?
3. We found this bag. Do you know who it … by any chance?
4. A strange thing … me yesterday. Shall I tell you?

concentrate on • insist on • live on • rely on

5. It was his fault. That's why he … paying for the damage.
6. She finds it difficult to … her work.
7. You know you can … me if you need any help.
8. Is it true that some people have so little money that they have to … bread and water?

V. What's the difference? Translate into German.

1. We looked for my keys.
2. We looked at the photograph.
3. We looked after the baby.

VI. Which verb below does not go together with the noun 'compensation'?

1. to ask for
2. to offer
3. to claim
4. to suffer
5. to pay

compensation

VII. Which noun does not follow the noun 'insurance'?

insurance

1. premium
2. market
3. needs
4. manufacturer
5. policy

VIII. Which word does not precede the noun 'requirement'?

1. a legal
2. an uninterrupted
3. a basic
4. a financial
5. an immediate

requirement

IX. Sue Rawlings explains what 'insurance' is. Put the words in the box into her text.

claim • compensation • contract • contributions • document • misfortunes • premium

"The basic concept of insurance is that the ... of the many compensate for the ... of the few. Insurance is a pooling of risks. This means that the money paid by each person or company, the ..., goes into a pool. This pool is then invested and used to pay out when a misfortune occurs to a person or company and they feel the need to make a ... . That is, they call on their insurance company to pay out ... for the loss they've suffered. Your insurance policy is a ... with your insurance company. It's an important ... and you should keep it in a safe place."

A change?

'The only good change is a change for dinner.'

12B

Enquiring about motor insurance

▸ Phil Hickley is going to give some advice to ▸ Simon and ▸ Louise on insurance matters.

▸ Hello there.

▸ Hello, I'm Phil Hickley from Guardian Insurance. We have an appointment.

▸ Yes, come in.

▸ How can I be of assistance?

▸ We've got a number of things to sort out for insurance.

▸ We've got a number of questions to ask, too.

▸ OK, fire away.

▸ Well, first it's car insurance. We're taking delivery of a new car on Monday and we'd like to *fix up* some insurance.

▸ No problem. Have you insured a car before?

▸ I haven't.

▸ I have but it was a number of years ago and I have no *record* of the insurance.

▸ So you won't have any *no-claims discount* that we can use.

▸ Unfortunately not, no.

▸ Do you want *fully-comprehensive insurance* or *third-party, fire and theft*?

▸ Mmm, what's the difference as far as cost is concerned?

▸ The premiums for third-party, fire and theft are likely to be about half the premium for fully comprehensive. But is it a new car or a second-hand car?

▸ Well, it's a brand new car so I think we should go for comprehensive insurance.

▸ Yes, I agree. And also, with a new car, if the car is stolen within the first year or if it's a *write-off* then we'll replace it with a brand new car of the same *make* and the same model.

▸ Hm, that's good.

▸ All the details are enclosed in this *policy booklet* here, which you need to read carefully. Now what we're going to need to get you to do now is complete a proposal form which is included in the back of this brochure here. If that's acceptable to us we will *issue* you *with* a *cover note* which you get the following day, and then you'll get the policy and the certificate of motor insurance very soon afterwards.

▸ What about the premium? What would that be?

▸ Well, that's going to depend on a number of factors, some of which you can choose to help reduce the premium. For example, if you choose a higher voluntary *excess* - that's the amount that you pay in the event of a claim - that would help to reduce the premium. And also, if you restrict driving to just the two of you, both of those factors will help to reduce the premium.

▸ That sounds good.

fix up	(*Versicherung*) abschließen	write-off	Totalschaden
record	Dokument, Unterlage	make	Marke, Fabrikat
no-claims discount	Schadenfreiheitsrabatt	policy	Versicherungsschein, Police
fully-comprehensive insurance	Vollkaskoversicherung	booklet	Broschüre
		issue with	ausstellen
		cover note	vorläufiger Versicherungsschein
third-party, fire and theft	Teilkasko(versicherung)	excess	Selbstbeteiligung

■ Working with the text

I. Are these statements true or false according to the text? Or does the text not say?

1. Simon and Louise have bought a second-hand car.
2. They want to insure their car.
3. It's an expensive car.
4. Simon has insured a car before but Louise hasn't.
5. Phil Hickley advises the couple to take out fully-comprehensive insurance.

6. The couple must fill in a cover note and then they will receive their insurance.
7. There are five factors that effect the premium the couple must pay.

II. Further questions. Answer them.

1. Do you think the couple will take out insurance with Guardian Insurance? Give some reasons for your opinion.
2. Do Simon and Louise seem to know much about insurance? How do you know?

III. Which is the right answer? Mark it.

1. The expression 'Fire away' (line 9) means ...
   a) ask me your questions.
   b) wait a minute.
   c) speak more quickly, please.
2. When you have a 'no-claims discount' (line 15) ...
   a) you cannot receive compensation after you have had an accident.
   b) you pay a smaller premium than you did before.
   c) you cannot be made liable for an accident.
3. If a car is a 'write-off' (line 23) it is ...
   a) rusty. b) badly damaged. c) too slow.
4. A 'cover note' (line 29) is a ...
   a) list of instructions.
   b) temporary document.
   c) letter from your insurance company.
5. If something you do is 'voluntary' (line 35) you do it ...
   a) because you want to.
   b) because you have to.
   c) because you should do.

IV. Explain the difference between ...

1. 'third-party, fire and theft insurance' and 'fully-comprehensive insurance'.
2. the 'make' of a car and the 'model' of a car.
3. a 'cover note' and an 'insurance policy'.
4. a 'claim' and a 'premium'.

■ Exercises

Focus on ➔ confusable words

Manche Wörter kann man leicht verwechseln, z.B. *form* (Formular) und *formula* (Formel) oder *appointment* (Termin) und *date* (Datum, Rendezvous).

I. Complete the sentences using the correct word from the box.

account • bill

1. He asked the waiter for the … .
2. Can I withdraw £200 from my deposit …, please?

diary • agenda

3. She wrote down the appointment for 12.30 in her … .
4. Please find enclosed the … for tomorrow's meeting.

lonely • alone

5. We need to do more to help … people.
6. Do you like being … sometimes?

assurance • insurance

7. Could you give me some information on travel …, please?
8. I must read through my life … policies again.

borrow • lend

9. Banks will … you as much money as you want as long as you can pay it back.
10. She doesn't like it when people … her books.

woman • wife

11. A tall, dark-eyed … walked into the room.
12. He has moved to London but his … and children are still in the USA.

II. Use these words in sentences to illustrate their meaning. (Use a dictionary.)

1. politics ⇔ policy
2. to control ⇔ to check
3. to design ⇔ to construct
4. homework ⇔ housework
5. price ⇔ prize

III. Complete this grid.

	verb	noun
1.	reduce	...
2.	assist	...
3.	deliver	...
4.	enclose	...
5.	choose	...
6.	restrict	...
7.	advise	...
8.	agree	...

IV. Put this conversation into the correct order (1-6).

a. ▸ Mr Butterworth. Yes, of course. Ms Summerfield will be with you in a few minutes.
b. ▸ Oh yes, please. White, no sugar.
c. ▸ Good morning. Can I help you?
d. ▸ Thank you.
e. ▸ Please have a seat. Can I get you some coffee?
f. ▸ Yes. My name's Mark Butterworth of RJP Productions. I've got an appointment with Katie Summerfield at 2.30.

V. Look at the dialogue below and put the words in the correct order.

Receptionist:	you • good • help • I • can • afternoon
John:	an • got • Mrs Summerfield • four • I've • at • yes • half • appointment • past • with
Receptionist:	you • your • give • please • could • me • name
John:	Sweeney • Infotech • it's • John • from
Receptionist:	long • Mr Sweeney • be • won't • she
John:	much • thanks • very • OK

VI. Use the words in the box to complete the dialogue.

waiting • appointment • would • somebody • see • afraid • kind • sorry

Receptionist:	Good morning.
Jennifer:	Good morning. I've come to … Mrs Summerfield.
Receptionist:	Have you got an …?
Jennifer:	…?
Receptionist:	Have you arranged to see Mrs Summerfield?
Jennifer:	No, I'm … not. Is it inconvenient?

Receptionist: Well, she's with … else at the moment. If you don't mind … I'll ask her if she can see you.
Jennifer: That's very … of you.
Receptionist: … you like something to drink while you wait?

Entering a partnership.

A man went into business with a friend. 'Let's form a partnership,' he explained. 'We can run the business together for five years. You put in the capital and I'll put in the experience.' The man's friend thought for a moment. 'And what happens after five years?' he asked. 'It's very easy,' the man replied. 'You'll have the experience and I'll have the capital!'

12C

Phil Hickley - dealing with marine insurance

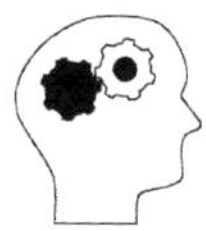

I. As you listen to Phil Hickley talk about insurance at Felixstowe Docks, read and answer this question.

Which type of insurance does Phil not talk about? Mark it.

a) insurance for port employees
b) public liability insurance
c) insurance against theft

d) life assurance
e) vehicle insurance
f) ship insurance
g) cargo insurance

II. Now listen again. Identify the correct ending to the sentence.

1. Many people working at Felixstowe Docks need to be protected against the risk of being injured or harmed by …
   a) the sea water. b) the heavy machinery. c) the stormy weather.
2. Although Felixstowe is a container port …
   a) there is still a need for public liability insurance.
   b) members of the public do make use of the passenger ferries there.
   c) it also has a maritime museum which is open to the general public.
3. The risk of theft is high at Felixstowe Docks because …
   a) there is no police station at the port.
   b) there is a prison nearby.
   c) many of the ships in the port carry valuable cargoes.
4. The two types of motor insurance required at Felixstowe are for …
   a) private cars and private motorbikes.
   b) private cars and commercial vehicles.
   c) buses and vans.
5. Another word for 'ship insurance' is …
   a) boat insurance. b) freight insurance. c) hull insurance.
6. 'Cargo insurance' is insurance of …
   a) the containers on the ships.
   b) the cars transported on the ships.
   c) the people working on the ships.
7. An 'accountant' is a person who …
   a) deals in foreign currencies.
   b) keeps and checks financial accounts.
   c) advises ship owners on questions of insurance.

III. Select the correct definition.

1. The 'Americas' are …
   a) the United States of America.
   b) North America and South America.
   c) Latin America.
2. The 'Far East' refers to countries like …
   a) Australia and New Zealand.
   b) China and Japan.
   c) Egypt and Iran.

3. The English equivalent for the German 'im Nahen Osten' is …
   a) in the Middle East.
   b) in the Near East.
   c) in the Centre East.
4. The 'United Kingdom' refers to …
   a) England.
   b) England, Scotland and Wales.
   c) England, Scotland, Wales and Northern Ireland.

IV. Explain the meaning of the underlined word by completing the sentence.

1. A ferry is … .
2. Electrical goods are … .
3. If you are a customs officer your job … .
4. When a ship capsizes it … .
5. An oil spillage happens … .

Say this tongue twister!

'Which switch, Miss, is the switch, Miss, for Ipswich, Miss?'

12D

Troubleshooter is made liable

There are six people involved in this episode of Troubleshooter. They are: the owner of a building materials shop, a young man who is cleaning the shop sign, a woman who is working in a nearby garden, a woman who is walking her dog, a man who has bought a *drainpipe* from the shop and, finally, Troubleshooter himself.

Troubleshooter tells the viewer that he is very careful with his insurance. He knows it's better to be safe than sorry. That's why he's got motor insurance and *public liability insurance*. But he is also a professional and as a professional, Troubleshooter assures us, he doesn't have accidents - touch wood!

And now something strange happens. Troubleshooter stands up and by mistake knocks over a row of pallets. The pallets hit some pieces of wood. The wood flies into a pile of boxes. The boxes knock over the cleaner on his step ladder. The cleaner's bucket of water falls on the lady's dog. The dog runs between the legs of the man with the drainpipe. The mans falls over. The drainpipe flies into the lady's garden and smashes her greenhouse.

All of a sudden four people are claiming compensation. Troubleshooter tries to establish liability. Who can be held responsible for the accident? The man with the drainpipe? The dog owner? The cleaner standing on the step ladder? The shop owner for allowing the boxes to be piled up so high?

The shopowner comes out of his shop. He has recorded the whole chain of events on his security camera and can prove that it was in fact Troubleshooter who is to blame for the accident. Troubleshooter is horrified. Will he go bankrupt? Will it mean the end of his business? Will it mean the end of Troubleshooter in fact?

Troubleshooter smiles. Of course! He has got his own insurance! All claims can be paid! Everybody can go home. What a relief! As he drives away from the scene of the accident, he stops for a moment. "But did I pay the premium?" he asks.

drainpipe	Abflussrohr
public liability insurance	Haftpflichtversicherung

I. Answer these questions.

1. What chain of events took place outside a buildings material shop?
2. To what extent was Troubleshooter involved in these events?
3. Does the story have a happy end for Troubleshooter?

II. Identify the correct end to the sentence.

1. The expression 'It's better to be safe than sorry' (line 7) means ...
   a) spend as much money as you can on insurance.
   b) say sorry when you make a mistake.
   c) take care before an accident happens rather than risk losses after it.
2. If you say 'touch wood' (line 9) you hope ...
   a) that the weather will get better.
   b) that bad luck will stay away.
   c) that you won't have an accident.
3. If you do something 'by mistake' (line 10) you do it ...
   a) with force.
   b) without wanting to do it.
   c) without noticing you've done it.
4. If you 'blame' (line 22) somebody for an accident then you ...
   a) say that they are responsible for it.
   b) say that they must pay for it.
   c) say that they tried to run away from it.

III. Match the underlined idiom (1-4) to its meaning (a-d).

1. Are your children <u>in safe hands</u> when they go away on their adventure holiday?
2. The roads could be busy so let's <u>play it safe</u> and leave very early in the morning.
3. Don't worry. Your job is <u>as safe as houses</u>. It's jobs like mine that are in danger.
4. It's <u>a safe bet</u> that as soon as you put up the sunshade it begins to cloud over.

   a. avoid risks
   b. very safe
   c. looked after and not in danger
   d. certain to happen

12E

A letter from an insurance company

SAGA
Services Ltd

Customer Reference: 777056/TH1913
Quotation Number: 2748236/996
Date: 21 March

Mr A PARK
Clovelly
Pretoria Road
High Wycombe
Buckinghamshire
HP13 6QW

Dear Mr Park

SAGA HOUSEHOLD INSURANCE

Thank you for your recent enquiry for Saga Homecare. I have pleasure in attaching your personalised quotation, together with a detailed guide to the comprehensive benefits available under this policy. Provided your circumstances do not change, this quotation is guaranteed for cover starting within sixty days from the date of this letter.

By offering insurance exclusively to people aged over 50, we can keep premiums low and give you substantial savings over comparable policies. In fact, more than 250,000 policy holders now enjoy comprehensive, value for money household insurance from Saga.

To start your cover, first check all the details on the quotation and ensure that all the information in the boxes is correct; then simply complete the Proposal Form and "Easy Payment Methods" form enclosed and return it to us in the freepost envelope provided. You can pay by cheque, credit card or direct debit.

If you prefer to pay by direct debit, please enclose a cheque for your first month's premium with your completed direct debit instruction. Your monthly premium is calculated by taking the premium plus a £12 administration charge and dividing the total by 12.

You don't even have to wait until your existing insurance is due for renewal. By switching to Saga now you could start saving money straight away - and most insurers will refund your remaining premium.

I very much hope that I will soon be able to welcome you as a new Saga Homecare Customer. And don't forget, if you find a policy giving you the same cover at a lower price within 2 months of taking out Saga Homecare, we will refund the difference.

If you have any questions or require immediate cover, please telephone us free on 0800 126 127, where one of our trained staff will be pleased to help. Our lines are open Monday to Friday 9.00 a.m. to 5.30 p.m. and Saturday 9.00 a.m. to 1.00 p.m.

Yours sincerely,

Simon Waugh
Managing Director

P.S. **Save 30% on worldwide flights**
Saga can also make air travel much easier on your budget. When you take out a policy with Saga, you will be entitled to a 30% discount on British Airways flights. Details are enclosed.

Company registration number 732602. Registered in England. Registered Office: The Saga Building, Middelburg Square, Folkestone, Kent CT20 1AZ

THE CITY AND INTERNATIONAL TRADE

13

13A

Insurance and investment banking

Nick Doak is the Manager of Media Relations at Lloyd's of London. "Lloyd's origins go back over three hundred years to a time when the only established form of insurance in the world anywhere was marine insurance. It was the insurance of ships and their cargoes on what were often very dangerous journeys around the world. Lloyd's List is the oldest newspaper in the world. Its origins were those of a *newssheet* that was put out at the time of Edward Lloyd's coffeehouse, the beginning of Lloyd's itself. Lloyd's started as a market of individuals offering insurance, there were no insurance companies at that time, and from that it has grown into the very sophisticated market that it is today.

Invisible exports are all about international trade. They move the money round which makes international trade possible: currency transactions, *futures* transactions, the purchase of insurance to protect international trade, and also, of course, the banking transactions which pay the money for goods and services. Between 1985 until 1995, in those ten years, Lloyd's alone contributed eighteen billion pounds to Britain's *balance of payments* and the rest of the insurance industry in

London probably contributed about the same. Many things in insurance can be predicted. From the records you can get a fairly accurate idea of how many cars are going to crash, how many houses are going to catch fire and the average length of a person's life. You cannot predict a catastrophe. If you could predict it, it wouldn't be one."

Jes Farr is the Communications Manager at Deutsche Morgan Grenfall, a major City investment bank. "Investment banking is for companies, usually international companies, companies that wish to borrow large amounts of money. Foreign exchange is essentially moving money around the world, changing it into various currencies and is probably the largest, the highest-volume business in investment banking. When a company wants to go public that means it's listing its shares on a stock exchange, and those shares are freely available to anybody who cares to buy them. Futures and *options* are used in the foreign exchange markets when a company needs to borrow money or is expecting to receive payment, for example, in a currency other than its own. To ensure that it doesn't lose money from when the deal is completed to when the payment is made, an option would be putting down a small amount of money to buy the option which would entitle them to buy a currency at a certain exchange rate. A future is similar except they must buy the currency at an agreed future exchange rate. There are also other investors who play the foreign currency market and sometimes these people are called speculators because they do not have a traditional corporate need for the currency. They are playing the currency markets."

newssheet	Informationsblatt	balance of payments	Zahlungsbilanz
future	Future, Termingeschäft	option	Optionsschein

■ Working with the text

Lloyd's of London

I. Using the information in Nick Doak's part of the text, identify the correct ending for the sentence.

1. Nick Doak talks about ...
   a) Lloyd's of London, the euro and the London Stock Exchange.
   b) Lloyd's of London, the insurance industry and invisible exports.
   c) Lloyd's of London, futures and options and investment banking.
2. Lloyd's of London is ...
   a) an insurance company.
   b) an insurance market.
   c) a merchant bank.
3. Lloyd's List is ...
   a) a list of insurance brokers.
   b) a newspaper.
   c) a record of the world's worst disasters and catastrophes.
4. The insurance industry is part of a country's ...
   a) invisible exports.
   b) futures transactions.
   c) currency markets.

II. Find the word or expression in Nick Doak's part of the text which means ...

1. the difference between the amount of money coming into a country and the amount going out.

2. the money used for everyday purchases in a particular country.
3. 1,000,000,000.

III. Using the information in Jes Farr's part of the text, identify the correct ending for the sentence.

1. Jes Farr talks about ...
   a) why there are so many investment banks in the City of London.
   b) how much profit investment banks make.
   c) what sort of business investment banks are involved in.
2. Investment banks' most important business is ...
   a) shares. b) foreign exchange. c) insurance
3. If a company goes public, ...
   a) members of the public can buy its shares.
   b) it must give a press conference every week.
   c) it is open to the public.
4. Dealing in futures and options is a good way of ...
   a) reducing your risks when you are buying foreign currencies.
   b) finding the cheapest insurance premiums.
   c) buying a lot of shares in a number of different companies.
5. The difference between futures and options is that ...
   a) with a future you must buy the foreign currency, with an option you can.
   b) with a future you can buy the foreign currency, with an option you must.
   c) with a future you shouldn't buy the foreign currency, with an option you should.

IV. Explain the difference between ...

1. a country's 'balance of payments' and a country's 'balance of trade'.
2. a 'million' and a 'billion'.
3. 'insurance' and 'assurance'.
4. the 'City of London' and the 'centre of London'.

V. What do the underlined words in Jes Farr's text refer back to?

1. 'Foreign exchange is essentially moving money around the world, changing it into various currencies.' (lines 23-25)
2. 'Those shares are freely available to anybody who cares to buy them.' (lines 27-28)
3. 'To ensure that it doesn't lose money from when the deal is completed to when the payment is made ...' (lines 30-31)
4. 'A future is similar except they must buy the currency at an agreed future exchange rate.' (lines 33-34)
5. 'They are playing the currency markets.' (lines 36-37)

VI. Say these words out loud.

1. invisible
2. billion
3. catastrophe
4. merchant
5. speculator

■ Exercises

Focus on ➔ reduced relative clauses

Das Partizip Präsens und das Partizip Perfekt können Relativsätze verkürzen. Das Partizip Präsens verkürzt einen aktiven, das Partizip Perfekt einen passiven Relativsatz.

Lloyd's started as a market of individuals ***offering (= which offered)*** *insurance. The money* ***paid (= which is paid)*** *by each person is called the premium.*

I. Identify the reduced relative clauses in this short text. How many are there?

The term 'risk' means a hazard against which the individual insures himself, such as a personal accident. But 'risk' is also used to describe a person or object insured. An individual is a bad life risk if he is suffering from a chronic disease. A building made of wood is a bad fire risk. Bad risks like these are covered at a higher premium.

II. Shorten these texts by using reduced relative clauses where possible.

1. The world's largest cigar, which weighed 110 kg, was insured for nearly £18 million. The cigar, which was rolled to celebrate the launch of a new brand, took 315 hours to make.
2. In 1901 the first car which was insured at Lloyd's was covered by a marine policy. Cars were such a novelty at the time that the underwriters wrote a policy on the basis that the car was a ship which was navigating on dry land.
3. A killer whale which was captured off the Canadian Pacific coast and which was towed to an aquarium in Seattle was insured for $8,000 against various emergencies, which included rescue attempts by other whales.

III. More information on famous or unusual risks can be found at Lloyd's website - www.lloydsoflondon.co.uk. Have a look!

Focus on ➔ abbreviations and acronyms

Bei Abkürzungen wird jeder einzelne Buchstabe gelesen, z.B. *BBC* /bi: bi: ˈsi:/ = *British Broadcasting Corporation.* Akronyme werden als ganze Wörter gelesen, z.B. *AIDS* or *Aids* /eɪdz/ = *Acquired immune deficiency syndrome.* Es gibt viele Abkürzungen und Akronyme im Geschäftsleben, z.B. *PDQ* /ˈpi: di: kju:/ = *pretty damn quick.*

IV. Test yourself! How many of these abbreviations and acronyms do you know?

1. AGM	6. cc	11. misc	16. PA	21. VAT
2. approx	7. CV	12. NATO	17. PIN	22. VIP
3. asap	8. EU	13. NB	18. PTO	23. wef
4. BA	9. GMT	14. ono	19. RSVP	24. WHO
5. BSc	10. MBA	15. OPEC	20. sae	25. wpm

V. Human qualities. Do you know what these adjectives mean? Categorize them into two groups: positive qualities and negative qualities.

affable, aggressive, alert, ambitious, artistically-minded, bashful, bloody-minded, bold, brave, callous, caring, cautious, committed, conscientious, considerate, cooperative, courageous, courteous, creative, critically-minded, cruel, determined, diplomatic, easy-going, enterprising, evasive, fair, firm, full of drive, generous

VI. Homonyms are two words that are spelt the same way and pronounced the same way as each other but which have different meanings. What do the underlined words in these sentences mean?

1. My brother's in the army. He's on leave at the moment.
2. She gave me some sound advice. I'll certainly follow it.
3. Who won the match? - Nobody. It was a draw.
4. I'm going away on business. I'm going to a trade fair in Birmingham.
5. We have to transport a lot of plant around the factory.
6. I had to buy a special saw to cut through the pipe.

*VII. Can you spot the *errors in these sentences?*

1. *The most people prefer more freetime to more money.
2. *We discussed about the facts and figures.
3. *The answer depends from a lot of factors.
4. *Our prices are not so high as our competitors'.
5. *We need more informations before reaching a decision.
6. *How do you call this part of the machine in English?

7. *The technician he spoke to told he didn't know the answer.
8. *Thank you very much for your order. I send the goods today.
9. *Retailers have often problems manufacturers don't understand.
10. *Sales have fallen down by 15%.
11. *In former times we manufactured photocopiers.
12. *Here is the menu. What do you like?
13. *Yes, I agree with you, Simon. What's your meaning, Susan?
14. *He suggested to advertise the post in the local paper.
15. *Fifty persons work in the office here.
16. *Can you say me something about your distribution policy?
17. *Would you explain me how the machining centre works, please?
18. *We'll see us again tomorrow, John. Bye.
19. *Please read our conditions on the backside carefully.
20. *We don't want that you have difficulties with your payment.
21. *If the goods are faulty bring them back to the shop where you bought them.
22. *Please let us have your order until next Friday.
23. *Mr Epson is used to repair these printers.
24. *I'm not interesting in your excuses. Tell me what happened.
25. *She doesn't smoke and I don't too.

13B

Finding out more about the export business

▸ Peter Bishop is Head of the International Trade Department at the London Chamber of Commerce. Today he is meeting a businessman, ▸ John Reid, who is new to the export business.

▸ It's our first major export order and I need to take advice on how to handle it. I was told that you could help.

▸ And where are you exporting to?

▸ Well, to the USA. We were at the New York Gift Show recently and there was a lot of interest shown in our products. So now we have a distributor based in Boston who will import directly from us.

▸ First you have got to know the US regulations with regards to your product. There are very strict health and safety standards there, so much so that if you don't *comply* with them completely your goods will get turned back at customs.

▸ And where can I get hold of the regulations?

▸ We can supply you with a copy or you can get a copy at our bookshop downstairs.

▸ With regard to the Made In Britain label, I understand that there are regulations concerning this, but I'm not at all clear about it.

▸ There are a number of issues here. Firstly, are the materials sourced in the UK or do you buy in from abroad? If you buy in from abroad, what manufacturing process has been undertaken before you re-export the goods? You'll find these useful regarding US regulations. Let's move on to financial matters. You need to do a credit report on the company you're selling to, your distributor.

▸ Can you help us there?

▸ It's a large order. You're probably going to need pre-shipment finance. Have you thought about that?

▸ I have thought of approaching my bank for an *overdraft.*

▸ Well, there are many alternatives. One that you should think about is *factoring*, which could take a load off your shoulders. It's when a firm of factors takes over your invoices. You pay them a fee which represents a percentage of the invoice value but you get paid straightaway.

▸ I need to know which currency to invoice in - pounds Sterling or US dollars. Should I sell forward? What does that mean?

▸ It's to do with currency *fluctuations.* It's a question of whether the pound will go up or down against the dollar and obviously there is a potential risk for you here. Selling forward means that you're not at risk when exchange rates fluctuates.

▸ As regards payment mechanisms, you could choose the collection method which involves bills of exchange, but the documentary letter of credit is the most secure form of payment.

▸ Could you explain how it works?

‣ Basically a letter of credit enables you to draw payment through a bank provided *stipulated* documents are produced. For example, bills of lading, certificates of origin and certificates of insurance as well as your invoice.

‣ I see.

comply	einwilligen, erfüllen	fluctuation	Schwankung
overdraft	Überziehung	stipulate	verlangen, vorschreiben
factoring	Finanzierung offener Buchforderungen		

■ Working with the text

I. Are these statements true or false according to the text? Or does the text not say? Tick the appropriate box.

	true	false	not say
1. John Reid wants to export teddy bears to the US.			
2. John would like to know about US import regulations.			
3. One main problem John has is choosing a name for his product.			
4. John is going to invoice his US distributor in Sterling.			
5. John is going to give his US distributor open credit facilities.			

II. Complete these sentences using the information in the text.

1. John Reid has found a distributor in Boston so now he ... .
2. If John doesn't comply to the US health and safety standards, ...
3. As the order from the distributor is a large one, John ... .
4. The best method of payment for John is a letter of credit because ... .

III. Identify the correct ending for the sentence.

1. If you 'comply' (line 12) with health standards, you ...
   a) ignore them. b) follow them. c) misinterpret them.
2. If goods are 'sourced' (line 17) in the UK ...
   a) they are bought in the UK.
   b) they are manufactured in the UK.
   c) they are sold in the UK.
3. If you get an 'overdraft' (line 25) from your bank you can ...
   a) withdraw more money than you have on your account.
   b) borrow money for a short period of time.
   c) get a loan at a special rate of interest.

4. If somebody takes a 'load off your shoulders' (line 27), they ...
   a) distribute your goods for you.
   b) store your goods for you.
   c) take care of a problem for you.
5. If you are paid 'straightaway' (line 29) you get your money ...
   a) immediately.
   b) in cash.
   c) in whatever currency you would like.
6. If you 'sell forward' (line 31) you sell your product ...
   a) at a certain date in the future.
   b) for an uncertain price at a certain date in the future.
   c) for an agreed price at a certain date in the future.
7. A 'letter of credit' (line 36) is ...
   a) a letter from one bank to another bank which guarantees payment to an exporter.
   b) an insurance certificate.
   c) a letter from the importer to the exporter promising payment.

IV. Explain these expressions using your own words. Use a dictionary if you wish.

1. to do a credit report on a company (line 21)
2. factoring (line 26)
3. an invoice (line 28)
4. currency fluctuations (line 32)
5. bill of exchange (line 36)

■ Exercises

Focus on ➔ talking about conditions

Es gibt viele Möglichkeiten, über Bedingungen zu sprechen. Zu den wichtigsten Verbindungswörtern bei Bedingungssätzen gehören *as long as* (solange), *if* (wenn), *in case* (falls), *on condition that* (unter der Bedingung, dass), *provided* (vorausgesetzt), *supposing* (angenommen), *unless* (es sei denn) und *whether* (ob). Auch Begriffe mit dem Suffix '-ever', z.B. *however, whichever, whoever* und *wherever*, können Bedingungen einleiten.

You can draw payment through a bank ***provided*** *the documents are produced.*
If *you don't comply with them your goods will get turned back at customs.*
It's a question of ***whether*** *the pound will go up or down against the dollar.*

I. Complete the sentences using an expression from the box.

as long as • provided that • supposing • unless

1. You can't come in … you've been invited.
2. You can borrow our car … you bring it back by tomorrow evening.
3. You can stay with us all week … you help with the housework.
4. … they don't ring. What are we going to do then?

II. Complete the sentences using an expression from the box.

however • wherever • whichever • whoever

1. … you do it, it's going to take you three years to complete it.
2. You'll find our house, … bus you take.
3. … becomes managing director, nothing's going to happen to our jobs, is it?
4. His new jacket is so bright people will notice him … he is!

III. Translate these sentences into German.

1. What are the entry requirements for joining the diplomatic service?
2. All the trade union's conditions must be met.
3. I wouldn't live in California under any circumstances. Would you?
4. A high standard of English is a prerequisite for studying for an MBA.

Focus on ➔ proverbs

Obwohl man viele Sprichwörter kennt, verwendet man sie selten. Auch englische Sprichwörter sollte man nicht überstrapazieren.

Absence makes the heart grow fonder.	(Die Liebe wächst mit der Entfernung.)
Familiarity breeds contempt.	(Allzu große Vertrautheit erzeugt Verachtung.)

IV. Match the proverb to its explanation.

1. Don't count your chickens before they're hatched.
2. Don't put all your eggs in one basket.
3. Never judge a book by its cover.
4. Never look a gift horse in the mouth.
5. There's no smoke without fire.
6. Too many cooks spoil the broth.
7. People who live in glass houses shouldn't throw stones.
8. Many hands make light work.

a. If a lot of people work together it makes a job easier.
b. Don't anticipate the future too much.
c. Don't criticize others people's faults if you have them yourself.
d. Don't invest all your efforts or attention in just one thing.
e. Don't judge people or things by their outward appearance.
f. Never refuse good fortune when it is there in front of you.
g. Rumours are usually based on some degree of truth.
h. Too many people interfering is not a good way of doing things.

Focus on ➔ language and humour

Humor spielt eine wichtige Rolle im täglichen Umgang mit Menschen, privat wie beruflich. Humor ist von Land zu Land unterschiedlich. Bei der von den Briten besonders geschätzten Ironie beispielsweise kommt es nicht nur auf den Gehalt, sondern auch auf die Wahl der richtigen Tonlage an.

V. Match the feature of language with its example (a-g).

1. *Homonyms* - words with the same spelling but different meaning
2. *Homophones* - words with the same pronunciation but different spelling and meaning
3. *Multi-word verbs* - verbs with various meanings
4. *Epigrams* - short witty sayings
5. *Spoonerism* - confusion of words by incorrect placing of first sound
6. *Hyperbole* - exaggerated statements made for effect
7. *Euphemism* - a polite way of expressing something which is unpleasant

a. eg 'If I said you had a beautiful body would you hold it against me?'
b. eg 'There is only one thing worse than being talked about, and that is not being talked about.'
c. eg 'You have hissed the mystery lectures!'
d. eg a parking fine / the weather's fine
e. eg this is a nice place / this plaice is nice
f. eg 'After a long illness he passed away in his sleep.'
g. eg waves as big as Everest

On a desert island.

A scientist, a lawyer and a businessman are stranded on a desert island with nothing to eat. One day a tin of soup washes ashore. The scientist says: 'Great! Let's smash the tin open with a rock.' The lawyer says: 'One second! The soup belongs to all of us so we must share it equally.' The businessman says: 'I've got an idea! Let's all sit down and have a meeting to discuss what we should do!'

13C

Roger Miles - feeling positive about the City

I. As you listen to Roger Miles talk about the City of London, read and answer this question.

Roger Miles explains why London is one of the world's financial centres. Which of the following reasons does he not give?

a) England's history as a trading nation
b) the concentration of financial activity in the City
c) the international nature of the financial markets in London
d) the English language as the language of business
e) other professional support in the City
f) the excellent infrastructure

II. Now listen again. Identify the correct answer to the question.

1. Approximately how many foreign banks are there in London?
   a) 50. b) 500. c) 5,000.
2. What is one of the main differences between the London, New York and Tokyo stock exchanges?
   a) London is an international share market. The other two are more local.
   b) New York is an international share market. The other two are more local.
   c) Tokyo is an international share market. The other two are more local.

Share prices are rising

3. What kind of professional support is available to the financial service industries located in the City?
   a) There are plenty of pubs and restaurants.
   b) There are numerous law firms and accountants, for example.
   c) There is a good selection of theatres and cinemas.
4. What development in the City's infrastructure has had the biggest impact on the money markets?
   a) The introduction of fibre optic communications.
   b) The construction of pedestrianized shopping areas.
   c) The opening of an international railway station.

III. Identify the correct ending to the sentence.

1. The 'Square Mile' is …
   a) the centre of London.
   b) the name of a pub next to the Bank of England.
   c) another name for the City of London.
2. The word 'equities' means the same as …
   a) shares. b) foreign currencies. c) marine insurance.
3. If you 'deregulate' a business activity, you …
   a) stop doing it.
   b) free it from certain rules and controls.
   c) make it available to a small group of people.

4. One ‘trillion’ dollars is …
   a) $1,000,000,000.
   b) $1,000,000,000,000.
   c) $1,000,000,000,000,000.
5. If you work in ‘public relations’ (PR) then your job involves …
   a) presenting a good image of your company to the public.
   b) making your company’s accounts available to the public.
   c) searching for smaller firms which your company can buy.

IV. Say these words out loud. 

1. equities
2. strength
3. expertise
4. infrastructure
5. volume

V. Find out more about the Bank of England by visiting www.bankofengland.co.uk.

VI. Could you imagine working in a bank in the City? Would that sort of work attract you? Write a text (60 to 80 words) outlining your point of view.

13D

Troubleshooter makes a name for himself in the City!

Troubleshooter has been invited to attend a meeting in London. As he comes out of Cannon Street Underground Station a young lady is there to meet him. Just as she sees Troubleshooter her mobile phone rings. She is informed that the meeting has been delayed for two hours. Troubleshooter is not at all disappointed. He suggests using the time to show the young woman around the City.

First they go to the Old Lady of Threadneedle Street - otherwise known as the Bank of England. “The City is my natural home. It is where I belong,” Troubleshooter says proudly. “In fact I am your original City Slicker.” Next Troubleshooter takes the young lady past Lloyd’s. “The building looks to me like the inside of my old mother’s gas boiler,” he remarks. The young lady is horrified. “It’s an award-winning piece of architecture!” she replies. Troubleshooter is quick to change the subject. “Would you care for a spot of *luncheon*?” The young lady agrees. The lunch is very good and when the bill comes Troubleshooter realizes that it's a good opportunity to make up for the bad impression he made in the morning. "This one's on me," he says.

In front of the Bank of England

In the afternoon, during a sightseeing tour on an open double-decker bus, the young lady and Troubleshooter get into another argument. Troubleshooter seems to mix up Westminster Abbey with St Paul's Cathedral and London Bridge with Tower Bridge. After two hours with Troubleshooter the young lady has had enough. She turns to him. "You're arrogant, ignorant and ridiculous!" She calls her boss on her mobile phone. "Kevin? Are you sure you want this Troubleshooter? I've just had the worst two hours of my life with him! His good points? He's thick-skinned and nothing seems to upset him. Kevin?" There is a pause. "Are you sure he's the kind of man you need? Well, if you say so."

The young lady looks at Troubleshooter. She's much friendlier now. "My boss seems to think you're just what we need," she says taking him by the arm. "I've obviously been seeing you in the wrong light." Troubleshooter smiles. "Evidently, my dear young lady," he replies. "But I am a professional and a natural *high-flyer*. Troubleshooter is going to make a name for himself in the City!"

luncheon	Mittagessen
high-flyer	Überflieger

I. Answer the questions.

1. Why is Troubleshooter in London?
2. Why does he go on a tour of the City with a young lady?
3. What happens at the end of the story?

II. Mark the correct ending to the sentence.

1. If a meeting is 'delayed' (line 4) it is …
   a) held at another time.
   b) cancelled.
   c) stopped in the middle.
2. The phrase 'This one's on me' (line 15) means …
   a) here's another glass of wine for you.
   b) I'll pay for this.
   c) let me make lunch for you next time.
3. If you are 'thick-skinned' (lines 22-23) you …
   a) don't feel the cold very easily.
   b) you stay calm in difficult situations.
   c) you are overweight.
4. If you see somebody 'in the wrong light' (line 27) you …
   a) don't understand them.
   b) don't like them.
   c) have the wrong impression of them.
5. A 'high-flyer' (line 28) is somebody who …
   a) wants to have a successful career.
   b) wants to be a pilot.
   c) is aggressive and rude.

III. Look at the map of the City (page 7) and identify these famous landmarks.

1. The Bank of England
2. The Stock Exchange
3. Lloyd's of London
4. St Paul's Cathedral
5. Tower Bridge

IV. Say these words out loud.

1. architecture
2. ignorant
3. ridiculous
4. pause
5. evidently

V. What's a City Slicker (line 8)? (Look up the word in a good dictionary!)

VI. Match the underlined idiom (1-4) to its meaning (a-d).

1. Why do they always drop names? It's so embarrassing, isn't it?
2. She made a name for herself as a designer.
3. The name of the game in business is sheer hard work.
4. We can't put a name to the actor on TV last night. Did you see him?

a. a vital aspect
b. to mention famous people's names in order to impress others
c. to remember what somebody is called
d. to get a good reputation

13E

Career goals

Module C tapescripts

1C

The Polhill Garden Centre is in the southeast of England, about thirty miles from London. It's a successful family business.

"This is a family business. My father started the business. I've carried it on. I'm now the Managing Director. It started about thirty years ago. We were growing *chrysanths* and *bedding* plants in those days for sale in the London markets. We very quickly realized that retailing was the way to go and we formed a garden centre in about the 1980s and since then we've continued to *prosper*.

Most of our customers come from the city. They are retired. They enjoy a day out in the country and they love *pottering* around places like this. We pull from a very large area, mostly greater London. Lots of our customers enjoy a day out into the country. Lots of them spend nearly the whole day here wandering through different departments. We can park up to 2,000 cars and we probably have about 20,000 customers per week coming through the shop. One of the most successful departments that we have is our restaurant. We call it Polly's *Pantry*. It acts as a customer *draw* to our Centre and many people spend a lot of hours chatting, having cups of coffee and deciding what they're going to buy in the Centre."

Some of the departments in the Garden Centre do not belong to the Novell family. They are called concessions.

"We sell a lot of products here. Some of them are sold in-house, that's by the Garden Centre company, other products are sold by concessions. Concessions are shops within our large shop who pay a rent to us for the floor space. The butcher is a concession and he pays us rent for the space that he occupies. He is a good attraction for the Centre because people can come up and buy their local produce here from him and it all helps as a draw towards the Centre and makes us a larger and a better-expanding company."

A big business like this employs many people and not just the staff who deal with the customers.

"A business of this size takes a lot of administration. We have ten people employed in the office and they are responsible for the day-to-day running of the place; *payroll*, paying the wages. They're also responsible for ordering the products by computers, via a modem, to our suppliers. We need to quickly be able to replace the products that we sell and this is the quickest way of doing it.

We employ a lot of *knowledgeable* staff who understand how plants grow and are able to tell the customers how to look after them. We always have to remember that plants are our number one product and that without these the rest of the Centre won't work."

chrysanth	Chrysantheme	draw	Anziehungspunkt, Attraktion
bed	pflanzen, setzen		
prosper	erfolgreich sein	payroll	*hier*: Gehälter
potter	herumschlendern	knowledgeable	kenntnisreich
pantry	Speisekammer		

2C

The Prince's Youth Business Trust exists to help young people who want to start up on their own. Hugh Pierce is one of their business advisors.

"My career in banking started in 1960 when I worked on the branch banking side for fifteen years. In 1975 I switched to the international side of banking where I spent twenty years and since August 1982 my career has *revolved* around all aspects of the bank's business in Latin America.

The Prince's Youth Business Trust has a success rate for the businesses it helps of 66% and the help it gives is principally through loans, the average is two and a half thousand pounds, plus a business advisor. A business advisor is an absolute essential and a condition of anybody who gets support from The Prince's Youth Business Trust."

One young person who is getting help from The Prince's Youth Business Trust is Ben. He is a photographer and Hugh is his business advisor.

"Ben's business can be described as fashion and portrait photography. Now I take a wider view because what he's actually doing is building images of people and of places. But the best person to describe Ben's business is Ben himself. Now I know nothing about photography and *curiously* I think that is an advantage because it stops me interfering in what is his business. It frees me up to talk objectively about his business from my perspective, which is commercial and financial. So I contribute commercial *expertise* and experience and financial guidance and a *listening board*, a sounding board, if you like, that he can *bounce* his ideas from. If I knew a lot about photography I might be tempted to say, 'Well, why don't you try this shot?' or 'If you develop it that way ...', which is wrong. It's his business, his ideas. I'm just advising him in the commercial realities."

Hugh insists that young people starting out in business must prepare a business plan.

"I think for many business advisors a business plan is absolutely *key*. It tells the client where he is, where he wants to get to and how he's going to get there. If you like, it forces him, or her, to think about that business. It can sound a theoretical exercise. I can assure you it's not. It's hard work. There's nothing magical. It's just hard work and hard, focused thought.

The general recommendation is that a business advisor meets the client once every two to three months, perhaps more often in the early years. Now, Ben and I meet every month and our meetings tend to follow the same pattern."

Another feature of the business world is the business cycle, the ups and downs every business goes through.

"A business cycle is really a way of saying that business has its ups and downs. When it's up, it's very, very good but don't get over-optimistic. When it's down don't get over-depressed because in both situations the young person has to take their decisions and they shouldn't be over-influenced by the ups and they shouldn't be over-influenced by the downs and a business advisor listening to them and talking with them can help them to, in their own mind, *smooth out* the effect of those ups and downs.

The Prince's Youth Business Trust has a record of success in start-up businesses *unequalled*. Two-thirds of businesses that The Prince's Youth Trust helps last for more than three years. Now,

I know from my experience in commercial banking, that is an extremely high proportion. One of the most successful examples is a company called Dockspeed. Now, Dockspeed are in the transport business and currently have a fleet of 26 lorries and an annual turnover of £6 million."

The Prince's Youth Business Trust has many successes to its credit.

revolve	(sich) drehen	key	das Wichtigste
curiously	seltsamerweise	smooth out	glätten
expertise	Sachverstand, -kenntnis	unequalled	unübertroffen, ohnegleichen
listening board	*etwa*: Zuhörer		
bounce	aufprallen lassen		

3C

Ted Roffey has worked at Headley Brothers for forty-two years and he has seen great changes in the printing industry. His first job at the age of fifteen was feeding paper to the printing presses, doing exactly the same job as this machine but it was very different forty-two years ago.

"The paper was on your right hand side, you took the sheet off, into the *platen*, the platen would go up, and print and come back again, as it came back you took the sheet out with the left hand and replaced it with another sheet from the right hand and so on."

Quite soon Ted moved from the machine room to learn the traditional skills of the *compositor*.

"After eighteen months or so an apprenticeship *came up* in the composing department and I moved away from the *messy* - what we thought was the messy - side of the industry into the composing department."

The traditional methods of the printing trade were *passed on* to the young apprentices by the older men as they had been for generations. This was the age of hot metal. John Pitt explains.

"It was called hot metal because that was what it was. The machinery created *type* out of hot *lead*, so the work in that environment was very *smelly*, very hot, very noisy, and involved a certain amount of danger. Those such as Ted who started in the hot metal era have seen their work *switch* from composition using hot metal to *film* planning work and from there into computer page *make-up*."

Nowadays Ted composes pages with a computer and its powerful word processor.

"When I came into the trade and first started learning the system, it was important that you were good at English, you understood English and you could spell. Nowadays, the system I've got now, we've got what we call a *spell-checker* whereby the job that I set, I run it through a spell-checker system and it'll pick out 95% of the words which I've typed in incorrectly. Now I do the whole process that perhaps three or four men did: I set the type, I make it into pages, I import pictures into it, I import colour pictures into it. Now going back a few years that would have meant a compositor, a type setter, somebody to *cast the type*, somebody to make the pages up and so on and so on."

Machines that can do the work of four men can create unemployment. So has redundancy been a problem at Headley Brothers?

"Nobody was ever made redundant when new technology came in. Everybody was always catered for and natural *wastage* took place; when people retired they were not replaced. Nobody was put out of work and anybody who wanted to be retrained could be retrained wherever they wanted to."

Headley Brothers has become more efficient and more productive, but have all these changes been good for the work force?

"A change for me has meant coming to work dressed in reasonably clean clothes to work in a clean environment on work which I feel now is certainly far more rewarding than what it was many years ago, and it's far more interesting."

platen	(Druck)platte, Walze	switch	ändern, umstellen
compositor	(Schrift)setzer(in)	film	(Druck)film
come up	frei werden	make-up	Aufmachung, Layout, Umbruch
messy	dreckig, schmutzig		
pass on	übertragen	spell-checker	Rechtschreibprüfer(in), Korrektor(in)
type	Schriftsatz, Buchstaben		
lead	Blei	cast	gießen
smelly	übelriechend, stinkend	wastage	Personalabbau

4C

Pat Daniels is a working, married woman with two grown-up daughters. She lives in Chatham, one of the towns on the River Medway. Pat was born and grew up in Kent. Money was important to her from an early age.

"Well, I can remember as a little girl getting pocket money, but it was about six pence a week. It gradually went up to a shilling and then to half a crown, which is two and six, all in old money, and occasionally I had an aunt come to see me who used to give me pocket money as well whenever she left. And I used to save that up. But I only ever spent it on sweets and a few toys. It wasn't very much and I never saved any of it. The other thing I used to do, was - my parents still joke about it now - I used to try to get as much as I could for my money. So I'd never go into a sweet shop and buy something for three pence, it was always something, you know, four for a penny, so I'd come out with lots. And I think I'm still a bit like that today.

When I was a little bit older, when I was getting a little bit more pocket money, I didn't spend it all on sweets. I did open a post office savings account and that gives you a small *deposit* which is tax free. So Christmas presents and birthday presents used to go in here as well. And that built up to some money that I used to be able to spend on holidays and for Christmas presents for people.

When my own children started to get pocket money, we encouraged them to open post office savings accounts because as children they don't have to pay tax on a post office savings account, and they put money into that, and again, that used to pay for any *treats* that they wanted to save up for or to buy Christmas or birthday presents. As they got older and they earned a little bit more money through pocket money or *chores* that they did, they both opened a post office investment account and that gave a little bit more interest.

When my children became teenagers they opened bank accounts, and with a bank account you get a bank statement, and you get a *cash card* and this enables you to get money out of the machine. At the age of sixteen they got a cheque book, but they weren't able to get a *cheque guarantee card* until the age of eighteen. So once the teenagers had opened - my children had opened - a bank account we were then able to pay their pocket money direct into the bank account, and any clothes allowance that we wanted to let them have went straight into their bank account and then they were able to go shopping themselves, draw money from the machine, and use their cheque book when they became eighteen.

When I first got a job I used to spend all my money. Every penny I earned I spent. I used to spend it on clothes, going to the cinema, just generally enjoying myself, entertaining myself. I never gave a thought to saving any money at all. In my day I didn't open a bank account. Any money I had left over at the end of the week I used to go out and spend. And as far as *pensions* are concerned, I never even gave that a thought. It was just a word not in my vocabulary. I didn't even think about the future. But of course today children have to *budget* and have to think about the future because it's so uncertain. Many people save with a *building society* and you get a book like this. The interest is paid net of tax, that means they take the tax off the interest before they pay it to you. Since the 1980s in Britain the government have encouraged people to save by introducing tax free savings schemes. There are special names for these schemes. One is called TESSA and it's Tax Exempt Special Savings Account, and there are special conditions attached to these accounts. One of the conditions is that you have to leave your money in there for five years, at least. Then there's a PEP, P-E-P, that stands for Personal *Equity* Plan. Equity means stocks and shares and this allows you to invest in stocks and shares without paying tax on the interest.

One of the things my husband and I had to consider once we had two daughters was the possibility of paying out for weddings and in fact my oldest daughter got married last year. But fortunately we opened a savings account which enabled us to pay for the wedding."

deposit	Guthaben, Einlage	pension	Rente, Pension
treat	besondere Freude	budget	wirtschaften, einplanen
chores *pl*	Hausarbeit	building society	Bausparkasse
cash card	Geldautomatenkarte	equities *pl*	Stammaktien, Dividendenpapiere
cheque (guarantee) card	Scheckkarte		

5C

The Advertising Association which represents the interests of the advertising business in the United Kingdom is headed by Andrew Brown. Andrew is the Director General.

"Advertising has a primary function which is about the provision of information. But the important thing in commercial advertising is to acknowledge its role in a competitive economy. In the UK it's about £12 billion, about 25% of which goes on television, and a slightly greater percentage goes into the press. The press remains the largest medium in the UK. A brand is an idea really that exists in a consumer's head. It is more than just a name. All products have names but brands are products that have values over and above simple, physical attributes. They generate trust, people believe in them, people recognize them and they stand for something over and above just the physical attributes. *Trainers* at one level have a very simple physical function, which is associated with athleticism. The difference between the brands is strongly felt, particularly amongst the youth, by their association, by the belief about which performers actually choose which brands. The UK is regarded worldwide as the centre of excellence for advertising. It is a talent business in all aspects and therefore you do need high *calibre* thinkers, people who are interested in *tackling* any type of problem in a genuinely innovative kind of way. And therefore curiosity and creativity are not characteristics *solely constrained* to people in creative departments inside agencies."

Andrew entered the advertising business at an early age with one of the top UK agencies.

"I was only eighteen so I joined as a postboy but I joined J. Walter Thompson which was the biggest agency in the UK at the time and I stayed there for twenty-eight years and I worked my way up through the business becoming an account executive. I then did three and a half years in what was called - still is called - account planning, which is really a strategic department looking at research and briefing. And then I moved into more senior account management and was a director of the company for ten years with responsibility for managing a number of different accounts.

Humour is used in British advertising to a greater extent than it is in other markets in the US and in some parts from central Europe. I think British audiences like it. One of the advantages that humour has is that it makes TV spots, for example, little *vignettes* of entertainment in their own right. There are fashions about slogans. I mean all slogans really mean is a summarizing of the proposition that the brand or service is making in a succinct and hopefully memorable way so that the association between the brand and its purpose and its promise is memorable and retained in the minds of audiences. There are some slogans which are really part of culture in the UK because they have been persevered with and invested in by their brand owners for years and years and years and they are part of common language. 'Have a Break, Have a KitKat', the famous 'Go To Work on an Egg', 'Guiness is Good for You'. Now some of those don't exist anymore but they're still part of culture and they're part of long term advertising investment and they clearly define what those brands stand for, or did stand for at the time when all that investment was being made."

trainer	Turnschuh	solely	allein, nur
calibre	Format	constrain	beschränken
tackle	angehen	vignette	prägnante Kurzdarstellung

6C

As General Manager of Ettington Park, Kevin Poulter is responsible for the management structure of the hotel staff.

"We have a very flat organizational structure. There are seven departmental managers who report through to me and they include the Head Chef, the Food and Beverage Manager, the Rooms Manager, Finance Manager, *Maintenance* Manager and our Personnel and Training Manager. We have a leisure club which includes the usual indoor swimming pool, gym area, *jacuzzi*, sauna and so forth."

The Ettington Park Hotel caters for corporate clients who wish to use the conference facilities and in recent years there has been an increase in corporate activity days. Kevin was interested in the hotel and catering business from an early age.

"I finished my education in full and I knew that the hospitality and tourism industry was something that I wanted to specialize in and then went on to college and studied an OND (Ordinary National Diploma) in Hotel and Catering Management and then went on to join the professional institute, which is the Hotel and Catering Management Association. There is also the opportunity of going on to do degree courses, either a BA or BSc. I chose, in actual fact, to go down the former route and then go straight into a graduate scheme within a hotel company.

When I joined the hotel some two and a half years ago I identified some clear objectives. One of them was to establish a sound sales marketing plan and working towards that on a monthly basis. Secondly was to develop and improve the team of people that work here. We are in an industry that we are related to the customer on a one to one basis and, without doubt, the service that one receives is the measure for success by way of the consumer. The third priority and objective that I've set for myself is to improve the quality of product and I'm glad to say I think over the *refurbishment* programme we have completed that project and without doubt the major one and how I am measured is by way of the financial performance and profitability of the unit.

Stratford is very forward thinking in its marketing of Stratford as a destination. It's a brand that's known internationally anyway because of the Shakespearean connection and within the last eighteen months the areas and the district councils have got together and established a limited company which is dedicated to promote Stratford as a destination. And they like to work very closely with both the hoteliers as well as the local attractions here. This hotel is show business, we sell theatre, but you're only as good as your last performance, and so therefore we tried with part of our training and induction process to empower and to give all the staff here and the troops the opportunity of expressing themselves."

maintenance	Instandhaltung, Pflege	refurbishment	Verschönerung; Renovierung
jacuzzi	Whirlpool		

7C

This is the Marks & Spencer store on Kensington High Street in London. Chris Brown is working here for three months. He is gaining experience as a management trainee.

"To get a first interview at Marks & Spencer I had to fill out an application form and this is your only chance really to sell yourself and get that interview. On the application form you have to demonstrate skills such as leadership, *assertiveness*, teamwork, and you have to draw on your life experience to actually impress the recruiters at Marks & Spencer. And that's quite *gruelling* because you have to impress them in one hour, which in such a short period is hard work."

Hilary Woodland: "After the first interview, if they are recommended and they do well from the first interview, they're invited to attend an *assessment* centre, which is a twenty-four hour process whereby they go through three exercises which are management problems which they have to solve. And what we're looking for there is for them to show us the management behaviour they told us they have at the interview. If they are successful from that, then they get a job offer in writing. Your training as a graduate takes a year, it can take nine months if you're very, very good but the average is one year. And you will go in two stores to do that training. And your management training covers everything from how to motivate your staff, to how to lay a section out, to how to discipline your staff, to how to work effectively in teams; it's the whole range of management skills."

As *Deputy* Manager of the store, Gail Hovey will monitor Chris Brown's progress during his training period.

"Chris, during his three months, will learn the basics of running a sales floor. So Chris has responsibility for Ladies *Formal Wear*. So, although he's only here for three months, he will be expected to perform at a supervisor's level by the time he leaves."

Gail is not a university graduate like Chris. She chose a different route to become a manager. Like this young man, Gail began her career doing work experience with Marks & Spencer while she was still at school.

"I applied at the age of seventeen for work experience and was successful in that application. I then did temporary seasonal work over the Christmas period and then at the end of my school-leaving time I applied for Marks & Spencer's management career and was successful.

In this store I'm responsible for 410 staff. As a senior management team we would decide how many staff we needed to run the store. We would advertise those vacancies either in the local paper or in a shop window and based on letters that are written to the store we would then have a recruitment day. During that recruitment day the applicants would fill in an application form and they would then be interviewed by the supervision team or the junior management team. Following their success they would then be employed.

Marks & Spencer has a high reputation with our customers. And that reputation is gained through *word of mouth* from one customer telling another customer of the service that they have received from Marks & Spencer. I think that reputation is well deserved because of the emphasis that we place right from the minute that the staff enter the store on customer care."

assertiveness	Bestimmtheit	deputy	stellvertretend
gruelling	aufreibend, äußerst strapaziös	formal wear	Gesellschaftskleidung
assessment	Einschätzung, Beurteilung	word of mouth	Mundpropaganda

8C

With excellent transport communications by road, rail and air the National Exhibition Centre in Birmingham is a popular location for many international events. This week the British Equestrian Trade Association, BETA, is holding its annual trade fair. Linda Metcalfe is the organizer.

"The NEC is, in our opinion, having moved our exhibition here three years ago, the best *venue* for an exhibition in the UK. It has a comprehensive range of business facilities. There is a business centre, and they have faxes, telephones, secretarial assistance available and can basically *accommodate* any business requirement. The visitors here are the retailers, manufacturers and importers related to the equestrian and country clothing trades. The exhibitors come here, obviously, to speak to customers and potential customers. It gives them an opportunity to have a shop window, a chance to display the goods that they sell. They also probably spend a while *eyeing up* the competition and checking out how other companies in their sector are doing."

Charlie Chaplin: "We like to keep an eye on what's happening, not just in this country, but worldwide. So we like to see what everyone else is up to, what new ideas they've got. We try and find out *incognito*, by sending people around, as much as possible, so they can come back with new ideas, maybe new technologies on *fabrics* or developing things. We don't copy, but we would take it one step further and improve on it."

Linda Metcalfe: "We maintain our communications with our exhibitors through an extensive database, initially inviting them to have a look at what the trade fair consists of, and then as soon as we have our exhibitors established for that year we then mail them regularly to keep them up to date with the various forms they need to complete for the services, for example, the *badges* they will need when they're on the site, we try and prepare in advance if at all possible. We publish a catalogue for the trade fair so therefore we need to ask them how they would like their entry to appear in that catalogue. So there are many mailings that go out to the exhibitors. The exhibitor base covers twenty countries outside the UK, the visitors come from forty-four countries around the world so we're very broadly international I'd say."

German manufacturer: "Well, I think it's quite important for us to be here because we are the *bit* manufacturer in Germany so we have to be represented here and compared to the other trade fairs I would say it's a very important trade fair because it's very international and the business facilities are very good here and we really appreciate them."

American woman: "This is my second year at BETA and compared to the trade shows that are available to us in North America this is by far superior. We're just delighted with the quality and the *craftsmanship* and the friendliness of the English. We're thrilled!"

venue	Veranstaltungsort	badge	Abzeichen, (Namens)schild
accommodate	entsprechen, (be)dienen		
eye up	begutachten, mustern	bit	Kandare (*Gebissstange des Pferdes*)
incognito	unerkannt		
fabric	Stoff	craftsmanship	Handwerkskunst

9C

Tibb & Britain is a large mixed goods distribution centre that is dedicated to servicing just one supermarket chain: J. Sainsbury. Brian Nixon is the General Manager and Carol Bushen is the Administration *Clerical* Supervisor.

Brian: "We are a regional distribution centre that covers the Southeast, delivering to 65 Sainsbury stores. The centre is dedicated solely to Sainsbury's. The *fleet* size - we have 75 *trailers* and 46 units to deliver those goods."

The goods are stored in a large warehouse that has a cool storage area for *chilled* goods as well as an *ambient* area, which stores goods at normal or ambient temperature.

Carol: "The two sections we have within the warehouse are chill and ambient, chill being a temperature-controlled section and the ambient which is the normal, everyday temperature."

Brian: "Increasing demand has been put on distribution in the form of *line growth* by the housewife or the customer in the stores demanding more choice. This is increasing line growth in the region of about 20%. For example, eighteen months ago we only had 2,000 chilled lines coming through this operation. We now have 3,500."

A sophisticated computer system helps to control the ordering and flow of goods through the system. The computer software is known as DISCO.

Carol: "DISCO is the software that Sainsbury's use in all their depots. It stands for the distribution within the *stock* control and distribution of goods. There is no paperwork involved at all, it is all done on the computer."

Brian: "What happens is that the goods are received onto the system, the system then produces a *bar coder label*. The label is attached to each pallet as it comes into the warehouse. The operators use the *scan guns* which are *affixed* to their *fork-lift trucks* to scan the bar codes. That sends messages back to the computer, which in turn, returns the message onto the screen that the driver has affixed to his truck and gives him information as to where to put that pallet within the warehouse."

clerical	Büro-, Schreib-	stock	Vorrat, Bestand
fleet	*hier*: Fuhrpark	bar code(r label)	Strichkodierung
trailer	Anhänger	scan gun	Bar-Code-Lesegerät
chill	frisch, kühl	affix	anbringen
ambient	Umgebungs-, Raum-	fork-lift truck	Gabelstapler
line growth	Produktlinien-Wachstum		

10C

The Twining family have been importing tea into Britain for nearly three hundred years. The business was started by Thomas Twining and today it is managed by Sam Twining.

"Thomas Twining is a fascinating story. As a young man he'd worked as an apprentice for an East India merchant, really an importer, who was buying his tea from the East India Company who had the monopoly to trade with China. And young Thomas must have learned his product knowledge and how to taste tea working for the East India merchant."

Tea was heavily taxed in the eighteenth century and only very rich people could afford to drink it. But Thomas Twining saw a business opportunity.

"At the age of 31, he goes off and buys a coffee house. He could have bought any one of two and a half thousand. He chooses one very carefully, close to where the aristocracy were building their new homes after the Fire of London. And so he got to a position where he had a coffee house, introduces tea, which he knows only the aristocracy can afford to buy because it's so heavily taxed, and has it in a position very close to where they're living. That was a very clever *move*."

With the help of modern technology, the Twinings family business is still selling tea, but not just in Britain.

"When we have bought it and it comes in from China, India, Sri Lanka, wherever, we *blend* it and we pack it and it is all controlled from here by our seven tea tasters, then we will re-export it around the world. And in fact 90 countries buy tea from us. It's terribly important to have a good teapot, but even more important is to have that very fine, thin, *bone china* cup because drinking a good tea is like drinking a fine wine, and the thinner the cup is on your lip the better the taste of the tea will be. So Royal Worcester and Twinings work well together."

The Royal Worcester porcelain factory also has a long history. It is called 'Royal' because it received a royal warrant. Rachel John, the Marketing Manager, explains.

"In 1788 King George III and his wife, Queen Charlotte, came to the city of Worcester. They visited the porcelain factory and they actually decided that they would like a service made for themselves. They were so delighted when they received the service that they granted the company the royal *warrant* the following year."

To be a successful exporter, the company must carefully research its different markets around the world with their different cultures.

"There are many cases where we have developed specific products for specific markets. For example, if I were to show you this dish here, now this isn't something that perhaps you would see a great deal of in the UK. It's called a *shell dish* and this was specifically produced for Japan, for the wedding market, because brides in Japan, they give their guests a present for attending the wedding. Well, this little cup is actually for the Arabic market. Obviously the coffee they drink there is very, very strong and they only want to drink a little at a time, so we actually produce these very small Arabic coffee cups, and as you notice, there are no handles!"

move	Schritt, Zug	warrant	Berechtigung
blend	(ver)mischen	shell dish	Muschelgeschirr
bone china	feines Porzellan		

11C

Dockspeed is an international road *haulage* company which specializes in the transportation of *refrigerated* products. Andy Ingleston started the business eleven years ago with one lorry and the help of the Prince's Youth Business Trust. Today, Dockspeed has 27 lorries, 62 drivers and an annual turnover of over £7 million.

"We made a conscious decision to position this company in an area of the marketplace which was not of interest to the larger companies within this sector. We now offer overnight *groupage* services to every capital city in Europe. We collect product from all different collection points throughout the UK and we group it together on site here - an industry phrase is 'groupage' for bringing several *consignments* together to make into one full vehicle."

Dockspeed carries goods that must be delivered quickly and on time - *perishable* products that have a short shelf life.

"We have, for example, three vehicles leave every evening for Brussels, four for Paris and they carry anything from small samples to full loads. That means that we could be sending a vehicle on a quiet night with a shoebox full of pieces. Now that is not the sort of business that would *lend itself to* the railways. They are interested in large amounts of traffic that will fill one hundred rail waggons."

The control room has to keep the lorry fleet busy every day of the year by arranging the goods to move around Europe's highways in the most efficient way possible.

"The control room is manned from five o'clock in the morning until midnight via a shift system. There's a constant communication flow updating customers where their product is, what time deliveries were made, accepting orders, processing orders - because as an order is received it has to be logged into our computer system - producing documentation, obviously route planning is particularly important, you've got to be in a situation where you don't have vehicles passing each other wasting diesel, empty vehicles cost money. We've got to be planning when that vehicle's empty, to get him a reload to come back, be it to the UK or come back to the depot."

In the interest of safety, the drivers are strictly regulated. They can only drive for nine hours a day. The *tachograph* makes sure that there is no overtime.

"This is a tachograph *chart*. This is the tachograph. Each one of these traces shows the speed at which the driver is travelling, at the top there we can see the driver's average speed for his journey for that particular day. The tachographs have to be carefully examined and with 27 vehicles and 62 drivers there's *an awful lot* of charts coming in every week which have to be examined."

In this highly regulated and complex business, Dockspeed has been a great success story. Why?

"There's no substitute in any business for hard work. We like to think that we can triumph in the face of *adversity*. Flexibility is important, good staff are important, pay people well you get good staff, and make it organized so that everybody feels part of the team."

haulage	Transport, Spedition	lend oneself to	sich für etw. eignen
refrigerate	(tief)kühlen	tachograph	Fahrtenschreiber
groupage	Sammelladung	chart	Diagramm
consignment	Versendung, Verschickung	an awful lot	eine ganze Menge
perishable	verderblich	adversity	Not

12C

Fifteen miles down the road from the Guardian Insurance office in Ipswich is one of Britain's busiest ports.

"Felixstowe Docks is the largest container port in the United Kingdom. From here ships sail to the Americas, to the Far East and all over Europe. And naturally there's a need for insurance of every kind here at Felixstowe. Many of the processes here are manual, there's heavy lifting *gear*, and the employees at the docks need to be protected against those risks. That's why the employer will be providing employer's liability insurance, which basically protects them in the event of the employee's suffering illness, injury, or whatever, if it's caused as a result of a fault of the employer. Public liability is not a huge factor here because this is a container port here at Felixstowe, there are no passenger ferries that travel from Felixstowe. Having said that, there are members of the public in various capacities that do use the port here, people like Customs and *Excise*, or the police, all need from time to time to come into Felixstowe Port, and so they do need to be covered by public liability insurance and that is what the Port of Felixstowe Authority will provide.

Many of the cargoes that are being carried around Felixstowe contain very high value - cigarettes, electrical goods - individual containers can be worth many, many thousands of pounds and so theft is a particular aspect and so insurance can be provided for the owners of that cargo and the Port of Felixstowe Authority to cover them against the risk of theft. Vehicle insurance is very wide here at Felixstowe. The sort of vehicles you have on the complex are not the normal sort of private cars. There's lots of plant and machinery to take cargo around the complex and so there would be particular types of commercial vehicle insurance required here at Felixstowe."

Moving from the docks to the ships that use them, there are basically two types of marine insurance. The insurance of the ship, or the *hull* as it is called, and the insurance of the cargo that the ship carries.

"Hull insurance or ship insurance is required by the ship owner because ships, in the main, particularly those ones travelling here at Felixstowe, are worth many millions of pounds and a loss at sea would be catastrophic for a ship owner. Cargo insurance is about the protection of the items being carried by ships in the containers here at Felixstowe and the cargoes can vary enormously and can have very high values and so each consignment needs to have the appropriate level of insurance attached to it."

And if there is a shipping accident here at Felixstowe, how would the insurance claims be settled?

"Well, claims can be fairly complicated on the marine side. Ships are very large, they can *capsize*, there can be fairly large oil *spillages*, machinery can *topple over*. The process is a fairly complicated one in terms of sorting out the claim and would involve people like loss *adjusters*, marine *surveyors*, *accountants* even, to actually establish the amount of claim to be paid in any circumstance."

gear	Vorrichtung
Excise	*Verwaltungsabteilung für indirekte Steuern*
hull	Schiffskörper
capsize	kentern
spillage	verschüttete Menge, Verlust, Spillage
topple over	umkippen
adjuster	(Schadens)sachverständige(r)
surveyor	Gutachter(in)
accountant	Buchhalter(in), Wirtschaftsprüfer(in)

13C

The principal trade association for the UK banking industry is the British Bankers' Association. Roger Miles is the BBA's Head of Communications.

"The Square Mile is one of the world's major international financial centres now for a number of reasons. I think we have a history of being a maritime and therefore a trading nation. But we also have an extraordinary concentration of activity, volume of activity and markets in London. As a very rough *index* we have around five hundred foreign banks in London which, to my knowledge, is the greatest number of foreign banks in any city in the world. In the form of the stock exchange in London, we actually have the world's strongest international equities market. Although New York and Tokyo have a larger equities market by volume, that is for share trading, their markets are very much more driven by local needs for companies within their own countries or regions. The distinctive strength of London is that we are an international share market where shares of the world's companies change hands and indeed other forms of capital to support trading activity worldwide.

Apart from the markets themselves there are a number of broader reasons why companies like to do business in the City. Perhaps the most obvious one, the City is called the Square Mile, it's rather less than two kilometres square, with a concentration of expertise in financial services and professional support, in the law, accountancy, various other supporting activities. There's a strong infrastructure. Particularly since the deregulation in the 1980s we've seen a rapid growth in service technology, for example, the new, *ring-main* of *fibre-optic* communications means that these enormous volumes of trading through the markets can travel at the speed of light around the City from *dealing* desk to dealing desk uninterrupted. It is very striking, the *sheer* volume of activity going on in the City, taking for example, the money markets, latest best figures that we have seen indicate that around 1.6 trillion dollars - that's 1.6 with eleven zeroes after it - of money are flowing through the world's money markets and the City of London has around a third share of that.

I myself had a rather mixed approach to banking. I originally took an English degree. I then spent a while training as an accountant and worked in corporate public relations for just over ten years before coming into working with the British Bankers' Association in my current job."

index	Messzahl	dealing	Handel, Transaktionen
ring-main	Hauptleitung	sheer	rein
fibre-optic	faseroptisch		

Key to exercises

Retail and wholesale 1

1A

Text

I. 1. true - **2.** true - **3.** false - **4.** true - **5.** true
II. 1. general public - **2.** small retailers - **3.** large quantities
III. 1. department - **2.** staff - **3.** customer - **4.** order - **5.** manufacturer
IV. 1. employ - **2.** purchase - **3.** import - **4.** supply - **5.** enable
V. 1. employs - **2.** staff - **3.** purchases - **4.** imports - **5.** customers - **6.** orders - **7.** supply
VI. 1. Geschäftsführer(in) - **2.** Endverbraucher - **3.** Gartengeräte - **4.** Geschäftsschluss - **5.** Auftragseingang
VII. 1. /stɑːf/ - **2.** /tuːl/ - **3.** /ˈdepəʊ/ - **4.** /ˈməʊdəm/ - **5.** /rɪˈsiːt/
VIII. 1. *Example*: Yes, I think having a garden centre is a good business in Britain. British people like gardening and like to spend time (and money) at garden centres. **2.** *Example*: I think I would choose David Novell's job because he has the most varied work.

Exercises

I. 1. I work in personnel (*or*: human resources). **2.** I work in a children's hospital. **3.** I work in research and development. **4.** I work in a health insurance company.
II. 1. I work in a jewellery shop. I'm responsible for looking after the customers. **2.** I'm a secretary. I'm responsible for dealing with the correspondence (including reports and statistics) and coordinating appointments. **3.** I'm an engineer. I'm responsible for customer service and organizing seminars.
III. 1. A 'horse race' is a race for horses. A 'race horse' is a type of horse. **2.** 'Milk chocolate' is a type of chocolate. 'Chocolate milk' is milk with chocolate in it.
IV. 1. alarm clock - **2.** contact lenses - **3.** credit card - **4.** youth hostel - **5.** babysitter - **6.** bathroom
V. 1. def - **2.** def - **3.** def - **4.** def - **5.** non-def (Mr Schneider, who originally came from Germany, has worked here for twenty years.) - **6.** def
VI. 1. Is that the woman you work with? **2.** The goldfish we bought died after three days. **3.-5.** *no object relative pronoun* **6.** The accident we saw yesterday was shown on TV.
VII. 1. receipt - **2.** order - **3.** product (*or*: production) - **4.** delivery - **5.** employment (*or*: employee, employer) - **6.** purchase - **7.** development - **8.** use
VIII. company - department - staff - chance - travel - conference
IX. *Example*: I work in an insurance company. I am a receptionist / telephonist there. I am responsible for answering the phone and connecting callers to the people they want to talk to. If visitors come to the company, I welcome them and show them where to go. I like my job because I meet a lot of people. I am never bored. However, I would like a job nearer to home. At the moment I travel over an hour to get to my place of work. That means two hours' travelling every day. It's very tiring.

1B

Text

I. 1. b) - **2.** c) - **3.** b)
II. 1. refund - **2.** receipt
III. 1. current - **2.** deposit
IV. 1. She wants to make sure that Clare bought the plant at the garden centre. **2.** She needs a registration document, a certificate of insurance and an MOT certificate. **3.** She asks the bank clerk to check how much money she has got on her current account.

V. 1. *Example*: No, I don't think so. I think many people in Germany would not go back to a shop and return something they don't want or are not happy with. Once they have bought something, they usually keep it. It's what they are used to. **2.** No, they don't. British post offices can be part of a supermarket or other shop. In Germany there are not many post offices like this (at the moment).

Exercises

I. 1. d. - **2.** a. - **3.** b. - **4.** c.
II. 1. May I open the window, please? **2.** Could I interrupt you for a second? **3.** May I borrow your pen? **4.** Excuse me? Could I disturb you?

III. ▸ Hello! Please come in. Let me take your coat. Would you like a drink?

▸ Thanks. That'd be great.

▸ Would you like a glass of wine?

▸ Mmm, that sounds nice.

▸ Would you like to try some New Zealand wine I've just bought?

▸ New Zealand wine? Yes, that'd be lovely.

▸ Would you like to come into the kitchen and take a look at the bottle before I open it?

▸ OK.

IV. 'Do you like tea?' is a general question. 'Would you like tea?' is a specific question; you ask it when you are offering someone tea at the moment of speaking.
V. 1. What don't you like doing? **2.** What would you like? **3.** What wouldn't you like to do? **4.** What do you like doing?
VI. ▸ I think he's coming at half past five. ▸ Yes, that's a good idea. ▸ What time'd be best? ▸ OK. I'll ring the restaurant now.
VII. 1. Are - **2.** Are - **3.** Do - **4.** Have
VIII. ▸ Could I have ten first-class stamps, please? ▸ Yes, of course. ▸ No, thanks. ▸ That's £2.80, please. ▸ Thanks. And twenty pence change. ▸ Thanks.

1C

I. c)
II. 1. b) - **2.** b) - **3.** c) - **4.** a)
III. 1. c. - **2.** d. - **3.** a. - **4.** b.
IV. 1. products - **2.** Produce - **3.** produce - **4.** produced

1D

I. 1. He wants to give them some advice on how to write a business plan. **2.** He didn't ask for payment immediately after finishing his report for the young couple. (However, the signmaker wrote 'Payment on completion of work' on his invoice.) **3.** Not very good. He is £280 in the red.
II. 1. b. - **2.** a. - **3.** c.
III. 1. c. - **2.** a. - **3.** b.

A variety of firms 2

2A

Text

I. 1. has got - **2.** three - **3.** not - **4.** doesn't work
II. 1. sole, responsibility - **2.** solicitor, partnership - **3.** director, fountains - **4.** public, shares
III. 1. proprietor - **2.** to be made redundant - **3.** assets - **4.** practice - **5.** liability - **6.** turnover - **7.** stock exchange - **8.** profit
IV. 1. The Centre can help him with financial and legal advice. **2.** Winch & Winch is a partnership but The Fountain Workshop is a limited liability company. **3.** It must file accounts when it has a turnover of more than £350,000. **4.** A PLC can raise money more easily and more efficiently than a private company.
V. 1. He means he doesn't want to have to deal with any problems. **2.** He is referring to financial trouble. **3.** A managing director has an obligation to manage the day-to-day affairs of the company properly and correctly. **4.** A company like Brands Hatch Leisure needs to expand its business by offering new events and to do this it needs to raise capital.

Exercises

I. 1. c. - **2.** d. - **3.** b. - **4.** a.
II. 1. The fact is that a sole trader takes all the responsibility for the financial side of the business. **2.** The problem is that in a partnership you are not able to limit your personal liability. **3.** The advantage is that in a limited liability company you are not liable with all your assets. **4.** The thing is that a PLC is affected by the price of its shares.
III. *Example*: The main thing about bicycles is that they are cheap. The disadvantage is that you cannot transport heavy loads on them. The problem with cars is that they are expensive to buy and expensive to run (*unterhalten*). They also pollute the environment. The advantage of a car is that you can use it in summer and winter and drive wherever you want. The advantage of buses is that they are cheap to use. The disadvantage is that they only go at certain times of the day.
IV. 1. financial - **2.** commercial - **3.** legal - **4.** various - **5.** efficient - **6.** famous
V. 1. /ˈkʌmpənɪ/ - **2.** /ˈbɪznɪs/ - **3.** /ˈkɒliːgs/ - **4.** /ədˈvɑːntɪdʒ/ - **5.** /laɪəˈbɪlɪtɪ/ - **6.** /ˈpremɪsɪz/ - **7.** /ˈtɜːnəʊvə/ - **8.** /ɪgˈzekjətɪv/
VI. 1. better, than - **2.** more comforting, than - **3.** as, as - **4.** greater than - **5.** easier, than
VII. capital - profits and losses - duties - disagreements

2B

Text

I. 1. paint a house - **2.** a week - **3.** her cousin's getting married and she has been asked to be a bridesmaid - **4.** to fill in a holiday form - **5.** work overtime - **6.** they are going to be very busy at the end of the month
II. 1. They will find the colour scheme for the house. **2.** She must fill in a holiday form because she wants to take a day off (work). **3.** She probably finishes work at five o'clock.
III. 1. /ˈkʌləˌskiːm/ - **2.** /beɪʒ/ - **3.** /... ðəˈθɜːtɪˌfɜːst/ - **4.** /ˈwəʊnˌtaɪ/ - **5.** /ɪmplɔɪˈiː/
IV. 1. He really would like to say no. **2.** It means 'Friday next week'. **3.** A bridesmaid looks after the bride at a wedding.

Exercises

I. 1. c. - **2.** d. - **3.** a. - **4.** b.
II. Yes, she does. ('Would you mind?' = *Würde es Ihnen etwas ausmachen?*)
III. No, it isn't.

IV. 1. Would it be all right if I used your phone? **2.** Would you mind if I went home at one o'clock on Friday afternoon? **3.** Would it be OK if I had two weeks' holiday in January? **4.** Would it be all right if I worked at home tomorrow? **5.** Would you mind if I started work later in the morning? **6.** Would it be OK if I didn't move office?
V. 1. I'd like you to work a little longer today. **2.** I want us to work this Sunday. **3.** I'd like you to knock before you come in. **4.** I'd like everyone to come to the Christmas party.
VI. 1. Where do you come from? **2.** Whose motorbike is this? **3.** How long did the journey take? **4.** What's this called in English? **5.** How far is it from Glasgow to Edinburgh? **6.** How often do you see each other? **7.** How long have you worked in this company? **8.** How do you get here? **9.** Why are you smiling? **10.** When did (*or*: does) your train arrive?
VII. was made redundant - began operating - as - grew - found - to do - a partner (*or*: someone) - business (*or*: company) - continued to grow - was - have carried on growing - turnover

2C

I. 1. b)
II. 1. c) - **2.** a) - **3.** b) - **4.** c)
III. 1. c. - **2.** a. - **3.** b.
IV. 1. /ˈævərɪdʒ/ - **2.** /fəˈtɒgrəfə/ - **3.** /ekspəˈtiːz/ - **4.** /rekəmenˈdeɪʃən/ - **5.** /dɪˈsɪʒən/
V. 1. advise - **2.** success - **3.** lend - **4.** support - **5.** photograph - **6.** contribution - **7.** recommend - **8.** decide - **9.** meeting - **10.** preparation

2D

I. 1. Troubleshooter visits a photographer to give him some advice. **2.** He is already receiving advice from another organization: the Prince's Trust. **3.** The young model punches Troubleshooter on the chin and he falls to the ground. His picture appears in 'The Daily Splash'.
II. 1. c) - **2.** a)
III. 1. a)
IV. 1. There are a lot of cheap houses. **2.** The person didn't understand the joke immediately. **3.** I'm going to the toilet.

Technology at work 3

3A

Text

I. 1. Converting photographs into digital files - **3.** Printing - **4.** Binding - **5.** Dispatch
II. The pages are folded and then the sections are fed into hoppers and dropped onto a conveyor belt. The sections are then gathered together and glued into the cover.
III. He uses passive forms when he wants to describe the process in an unemotional way. He uses active forms when he knows the name of the people who are performing the actions and wants to give his description a more personal touch.
IV. 1. Modern technology plays a very large role. For example, scanners are used to convert photographs into digital files and files are transferred by ISDN or modem. The office is equipped with 35 PCs. They have a computer database with details of all their customers. Computers are used to produce invoices. All their PCs are linked in a network. There is also a mainframe network for subscriptions. They use e-mail and fax, too. **2.** All Invicta's presses are manufactured in Germany. **3.** There are three shifts during the day and weekend shifts as well. Staff are sometimes asked if they will work overtime. Also Ingrid Eissfeldt says that the company has an increasing volume of work in Europe.

V. 1. mail - **2.** staff - **3.** shift
VI. 1. There are no secretaries because everyone has their own PC. **2.** They use them to produce customer invoices and write letters, for example. **3.** They can send it by e-mail, fax, courier or mail.
VII. 1. database - **2.** invoice - **3.** subscription
VIII. 1. ISDN is faster than using a modem. **2.** *Example*: I think working shifts is a good idea. Some people like to work during the evening or at night. It means that they can be at home during the day, for example. Also you can earn more money if you work shifts. Personally I would prefer to work during the day. However, if I had to work shifts, I would do so.

Exercises

I. 1. are used - **2.** are prepared - **3.** are transmitted - **4.** can be printed - **5.** is sent - **6.** are gathered, (are) glued - **7.** are packed, sorted and put - **8.** are produced - **9.** has to be used - **10.** may be asked
II. 1. I was told something very interesting yesterday. **2.** Our order for forty dictionaries was lost. **3.** The money was never seen again. **4.** $10,000 was stolen from a bank. **5.** All items of clothing are checked before they leave the factory. **6.** The workforce has had to be reduced by 20%. **7.** You will be met at the airport. **8.** Your work permit cannot be renewed.
III. Resources mustn't be wasted; no wasted materials, no wasted time and no wasted space. And it means outmoded processes have to be thrown out. It's an ongoing process and everyone in the company has to be involved. Responsibility has to be moved to the point where employees and customers meet. The important decisions have to be made by the employees - not the management - because they are closest to the customers. More decision-making powers have to be given to the employees. They should be supported by the company administration. This can only be done through creative teamwork and not in a climate of conflict and tension.
IV. 1. Random Access Memory - **2.** Compact Disk, Read-Only Memory - **3.** Integrated Services Digital Network - **4.** Gigabyte - **5.** Megahertz - **6.** three dimensional
V. 1. He went outside to get some fresh air. **2.** We drove along the country roads to avoid the traffic. **3.** They got up early to get to the airport on time. **4.** She emigrated to Florida to get away from the cold weather.
VI. 1. I'm leaving now so as not to be late. **2.** They're bringing us the parcel personally in order not to have to pay the delivery charges. **3.** She is living alone so as not to have to depend on her parents any longer. **4.** We'll be quiet in order not to wake up the baby.
VII. 1. personal - **2.** personnel - **3.** wallet - **4.** briefcase - **5.** employer - **6.** employee - **7.** diary - **8.** calendar - **9.** economical - **10.** economic

3B

Text

I. 1. They want to buy furniture and office equipment. **2.** Yes, she is. She shows them the furniture and what you can do with it and explains what the computer can do.
II. 1. thing we need - **2.** nice - **3.** show how much money is coming in and going out - **4.** tested
III. 1. desk - **2.** swivel chair - **3.** bookcase - **4.** cupboard - **5.** filing cabinet
IV. 1. hole punch(er) - **2.** scissors (*not in the text*) - **3.** drawing pins - **4.** paper clips - **5.** stapler
V. 1. headed notepaper - **2.** envelopes - **3.** compliment slips
VI. 1. b. - **2.** a. - **3.** d. - **4.** c.

Exercises

I. 1. If you'd like to follow me. **2.** If you'd like to wait here for a second. **3.** Perhaps you'd like to fill in this form. **4.** Perhaps you'd like to show me what you've brought with you today. **5.** If you'd like to come with me.
II. Visitor: I'd like to see Donald Ryan, please.
Receptionist: Could I have your name, please?
Visitor: Yes, it's Jeremy Rushton.
Receptionist: Would you like to take a seat for a moment.
Visitor: Thank you.

Receptionist: Could I get you a cup of coffee?
Visitor: Do you think I could have a cup of tea?
Receptionist: Of course ... here you are.

III. 1. Would you like one? **2.** Shall I get one for you, too? **3.** The ones from Ireland didn't. **4.** ... but the French ones are sweeter. **5.** Your one is much better. **6.** No, use the ones over there. **7.** Can I have one with cream in it? **8.** The white one! There are three white ones! **9.** I wouldn't have one in my house! **10.** We want to buy her one, too!

IV. 1. don't you? - **2.** do you? - **3.** don't you? - **4.** haven't you? - **5.** have you? - **6.** does it? - **7.** isn't it? - **8.** are they?

V. 1. are - **2.** are - **3.** is - **4.** Has - **5.** are, were - **6.** Is - **7.** have - **8.** Don't, they are

VI. 1. some - **2.** some - **3.** is, it - **4.** isn't, it hasn't

VII. 1. The information we received about Headley Brothers was very interesting. **2.** Thank you for the advice you gave us. **3.** She has made great progress in English since Christmas. **4.** Would you like some more toast or a piece of cake?

VIII. 1. Are - **2.** does - **3.** is - **4.** Has

IX. 1. Die Daten sind auf der Festplatte. **2.** Die Vereinigten Staaten sind eines der reichsten Länder der Welt. **3.** Keine Nachrichten sind gute Nachrichten. **4.** Sind die Medien nur an Skandalen und Katastrophen interessiert?

3C

I. b)

II. 1. a) - **2.** c) - **3.** a) - **4.** b)

III. 1. became available - **2.** entered - **3.** was introduced

IV. 1. /əˈprentɪs/ - **2.** /əˈprentɪʃɪp/ - **3.** /rɪˈdʌndənsi/ - **4.** /tekˈnɒlədʒi/

V. 1. efficiency - **2.** traditional - **3.** danger - **4.** environmental - **5.** importance - **6.** redundancy

3D

I. 1. He goes to PC World to buy the latest, state-of-the-art office equipment. **2.** He decides not to buy the new computer equipment he has chosen after all. He goes back to the museum and picks up his old typewriter and is happy that he has saved so much money.

II. 1. b) - **2.** c) - **3.** b) - **4.** b) (VAT is 17.5% in Britain at present.)

III. 1. retten - **2.** sparen - **3.** aufheben - **4.** sparen, ersparen - **5.** speichern

Banking 4

4A

Text

I. 1. c) - **2.** b) - **3.** a) - **4.** a) - **5.** a)

II. 1. She means a business plan, a stake and security. **2.** She means if the business did badly or failed and lost a lot of money.

III. 1. to think about the good and bad points of a plan - **2.** to invest your own money in a business - **3.** to show that you will be able to pay your bills

IV. 1. the cheque - **2.** the customers - **3.** the business - **4.** security

Exercises

I. 1. c. - **2.** d. - **3.** e. - **4.** a. - **5.** b.
II. 1. j. - **2.** h. - **3.** i. - **4.** f. - **5.** g.
III. 1. If we had begun our journey ... - **2.** ... they're increasing train fares? - **3.** They've established a committee ... - **4.** It's not easy to tolerate that sort of behaviour ... - **5.** They've postponed making a statement ...
IV. 1. lent - **2.** borrowed - **3.** lending - **4.** lend
V. 1. /tʃek/ - **2.** /prɒpə'zɪʃn/ - **3.** /kə'mɪtmənt/ - **4.** /'seɪfgɑːd/
VI. 1. safeguard - **2.** cheque - **3.** commitment - **4.** proposition
VII. 1. a standing <u>or</u>der - **2.** a <u>busi</u>ness plan - **3.** a <u>cur</u>rent account - **4.** a <u>cash</u> dispenser
VIII. 1. make - **2.** done - **3.** make - **4.** making - **5.** doing - **6.** made - **7.** do - **8.** making
IX. a. - d. - b. - e. - f. - c.

4B

Text

I. 1. c) - **2.** b) - **3.** a) - **4.** c) - **5.** b)
II. 1. Zins - **2.** Einzugsermächtigung - **3.** Kontoführungsgebühren - **4.** das Konto überziehen
III. 1. c) - **2.** a) - **3.** b)
IV. 1. Wait a moment. **2.** We don't need anything else.
V. 1. A 'direct debit' is when you give the bank permission to withdraw money from your account to pay a bill. A 'standing order' is when you tell the bank to pay a bill at regular intervals, for example the monthly rent. **2.** Yes, he is polite and informative (without being pushy). **3.** They need to fill in some forms in order to open their joint account. They will probably have to give information about themselves such as their dates of birth, their addresses, their jobs etc.

Exercises

I. 1. Yes, I have. - **2.** Yes, it is. - **3.** Yes, I would. - **4.** No, I don't. - **5.** No, I won't. - **6.** No, I'm not.
II. 1. opened - **2.** had bought - **3.** Would we pay - **4.** will you be able to see - **5.** had been - **6.** have not reached
III. 1. have - **2.** did - **3.** does - **4.** was
IV. 1. She'll ring you unless you ring her. **2.** He'll take the job unless it's badly paid. **3.** We can go out later unless you're too tired. **4.** Come and see us at the weekend unless you're busy.
V. 1. 'll do - **2.** 'm going to buy - **3.** are you going to paint - **4.** 'll show - **5.** 'll see - **6.** 'm going to be sick
VI. 1. unhelpful - **2.** inefficient - **3.** unfriendly - **4.** uncomfortable - **5.** unreliable - **6.** unemployed - **7.** unnecessary - **8.** unsuitable - **9.** illogical - **10.** impossible

4C

I. a), b), d)
II. 1. a) - **2.** c) - **3.** b) - **4.** b)
III. 1. Savings Account - **2.** Plan
IV. 1. The children did small jobs around the house like cutting the grass, washing the car etc. **2.** The children were given money to buy clothes. **3.** Interest is paid after taxes have been taken off.
V. *Example*: Personally, I don't think it is necessary for me to plan my finances in the way Pat Daniel does. I'm in a different situation. I'm not married and I don't have any children so I don't have the responsibility that she does. I don't earn much money and that means I can't save much, either. Generally speaking, however, I do think it is important to budget. It's not good to be in debt or to have to borrow money from the bank to buy something you want.

4D

I. 1. He wants to lend her some money. **2.** Irene is Troubleshooter's mother. She doesn't like the idea at all.
II. 1. a) - **2.** c) - **3.** b) - **4.** c) - **5.** c)

III. 1. Banks lend you money when times are good. However, they want you to pay it back when times are bad. - **2.** a better (*or*: lower) rate of interest - **3.** the text that is small and difficult to read - but which often contains extremely important information
IV. 1. a shop where goods can be bought in large quantities and at low prices - **2.** a small metal box with a lock which you keep cash in - **3.** the part of a shop where you pay - **4.** a machine you can get money from - **5.** the money which comes into and goes out of a business
V. 1. b. - **2.** c. - **3.** a.

Advertising 5

5A

Text

I. 1. false - **2.** false - **3.** false
II. 1. It's a small part of the market. **2.** It's bad because the consumer will buy the product once but never again. **3.** You can get five colour page insertions in the national newspapers or a week-long poster advertising campaign. **4.** Posters in key locations cost more because more people will see them. **5.** Slogans can actually make their way into the language that people use. **6.** The editing is also crucial because the communication has to be crisp and succinct.
III. 1. consumer - **2.** once - **3.** broadsheet - **4.** currently - **5.** eventually - **6.** crucial
IV. 1. You can't do good advertising if you do not understand the nature of the brand. **2.** People may buy the product but only on one occasion. **3.** 'You and your Baby' would be a better place for the advertisement. **4.** Obviously key locations will make a difference to how much a particular poster will cost. **5.** Going back a long time we have 'Guinness - Pure Genius'. **6.** Once the film has been shot, we then begin a fairly lengthy process of editing.
V. 1. It's in the former docklands in east London. **2.** Brands exist really in the consumer's head. Brands are products that have values over the simple, physical product itself. **3.** *Example*: Products such as skateboards or training shoes. **4.** *Example*: A popular German slogan in British advertising was Audi's ‚Vorsprung durch Technik'.

Exercises

I. 1. of living - **2.** on paying - **3.** on landing - **4.** of getting - **5.** of watching - **6.** of hurting - **7.** of doing - **8.** by listening
II. 1. She lives in an enormous eight-room flat. **2.** It was an exhausting 24-hour flight to Australia. **3.** We went for a thirty-kilometre walk along the Welsh coast. **4.** She gave him a ten-pound note. **5.** There's a new eighteen-hole golf course near our house. **6.** It was a long twenty-page article.
III. 1. Koch, boss - **2.** darf nicht, must not - **3.** vernünftig, sensitive - **4.** Bedeutung, opinion - **5.** letzten Endes/schließlich, possibly - **6.** tatsächlich, current
IV. 1. /sək'sɪŋkt/ - **2.** /'dʒi:niəs/ - **3.** /kæm'peɪn/ - **4.** /'kru:ʃl/ - **5.** /ɪn'vɪsɪdʒ/
V. 1. credit card - **2.** crossed cheque - **3.** data processing - **4.** building site - **5.** curriculum vitae - **6.** working conditions - **7.** industrial revolution - **8.** order form - **9.** forwarding agency - **10.** raw materials - **11.** accounts department - **12.** trade fair - **13.** curriculum vitae - **14.** forwarding agency - **15.** crossed cheque - **16.** accounts department - **17.** trade fair
VI. *Broadsheets*: The Daily Telegraph, The Independent, The Times. *Tabloids*: Daily Mail, The Express, The Mirror. *Example*: The broadsheets are quality newspapers with well-researched articles in which fact is separated from comment. The tabloids are sensational papers with large headlines, a lot of photographs and short texts.

5B

Text

I. 2. Nicola's question - **3.** Nicola's presentation - **4.** Everyone gives their views
II. 1. They are pleased with the campaign. **2.** David sounds unhappy. He thinks they have a branding problem. Sally also has reservations about the anti-roll execution.
III. 1. b) - **2.** a) - **3.** c) - **4.** b) - **5.** b)
IV. 1. the research debrief - **2.** branding - **3.** the anti-roll execution - **4.** the advertising campaign
V. 1. start - **2.** ask - **3.** big rise - **4.** in general - **5.** as long as - **6.** go
VI. 1. *Example*: I think I am greatly influenced by advertising. Advertising is everywhere. You can't get away from it. Advertising has become part of our culture and our way of thinking. **2.** *Example*: In my experience meetings tend to be much longer than necessary. A lot of time is wasted because a lot of people want to talk about things which are not important for the group as a whole.

Exercises

I. 1. 66¢ - **2.** £8.42 - **3.** $63.36 - **4.** £1.89 - **5.** $151 - **6.** £5,675
II. 1. 10¢ - **2.** note - **3.** greenback - **4.** euro
III. 1. 'four hundred and fifty-six pounds' - **2.** 'nine hundred and eighty-nine dollars and thirty-four cents' - **3.** 'sixty-five thousand, four hundred and eighty-two pounds' - **4.** 'six thousand, one hundred and twenty-five dollars' - **5.** 'twenty-four thousand, six hundred and fifty-eight pounds' - **6.** 'six hundred and seventy-nine thousand, seven hundred and ninety-seven dollars'
IV. *Up*: soar, rocket - *Down*: plunge, tumble, slump
V. 1. rose - **2.** raise - **3.** rises - **4.** raise - **5.** rise - **6.** raising
VI. 1. The actual number of unemployed people is 3,645,987. Last month it was lower but we don't know by how much. **2.** There were 3,645,987 more unemployed people this month than last month.
VII. 1. worrying - **2.** encouraging - **3.** exciting - **4.** disappointing - **5.** threatening - **6.** annoying
VIII. All of them.

5C

I. f)
II. 1. a) - **2.** c) - **3.** b) - **4.** c) - **5.** c) - **6.** c)
III. 1. ... in a new and different way. - **2.** I started at the bottom of the hierarchy and moved up. - **3.** ... advertising campaigns for different companies. - **4.** ... the message the brand or service is making ... - **5.** ... have been around a long time.
IV. 1. /ˈætrɪbjuːt/ - **2.** /kjʊəriˈɒsəti/ - **3.** /kriːeɪˈtɪvəti/ - **4.** /vɪnˈjet/ - **5.** /æθˈletɪsɪzəm/
V. 1. believable - **2.** excellent - **3.** curious - **4.** creative - **5.** responsible - **6.** memorable - **7.** cultural - **8.** strategic

5D

I. 1. He shows him his design for an advertising poster. **2.** Yes. His posters received a lot of attention and Morrison was able to sell all his toy bazookas. **3.** At the beginning of the story Mr Morrison had not sold one bazooka and at the end of the story he was sold out.
II. 1. a) - **2.** b) - **3.** b)
III. 1. c. - **2.** d. - **3.** a. - **4.** b.

Tourism and travel 6

6A

Text

I. 1. lines 9-11 - **2.** line 22 - **3.** line 35
II. 1. Shakespeare, Warwick Castle and the Cotswolds. **2.** Many people come for a special occasion such as a birthday or wedding anniversary. **3.** It buys from nominated suppliers.
III. 1. c) - **2.** b) - **3.** b) - **4.** c) - **5.** a)
IV. 1. /ˌlukʃəri həʊˈtel/ - **2.** /ˈwɒrɪk/ - **3.** /ˈbʌdʒɪt/ - **4.** /əˈwɔːd/ - **5.** /vedʒəˈteəriən/
V. 1. ... does not eat meat. - **2.** ... is the head of a kitchen. - **3.** ... is the list of food you can order at a restaurant. - **4.** ... is a drink.
VI. 1. Many tourists are attracted to Stratford-upon-Avon. - **2.** ... many different kinds of ... - **3.** ... tell their friends that we are good. - **4.** I do what the other hotels in the group do.

Exercises

I. 1. as - **2.** although - **3.** because - **4.** While
II. 1. The hotel was successful but it was obvious that it could have been even more successful. **2.** We advertised the hotel in the local and national press although it was not enough to increase room occupancy very significantly. **3.** We have a very flat hierarchy so we involved the staff in the discussions. **4.** Some of the staff's ideas were accepted whereas others were rejected. **5.** After we recognized the advantages of tailoring requirements to companies' needs, we began to offer conference facilities. **6.** The number of business guests increased rapidly as soon as we started to offer corporate packages.
III. 1. urgently - **2.** great - **3.** immediately - **4.** extremely - **5.** hard, excellent - **6.** magnificent, marvellous - **7.** happy, rarely - **8.** satisfactorily, well
IV. 1. exports - **2.** magnet - **3.** industry - **4.** supplier - **5.** comfortably - **6.** anniversary - **7.** requirement - **8.** advertisement
V. 1. please turn over - **2.** annual general meeting - **3.** free on board - **4.** enclosure - **5.** stamped addressed envelope - **6.** value added tax - **7.** as soon as possible - **8.** for example
VI. 1. He's training to be a waiter. **2.** He means the guests. **3.** A 'liqueur' is a sweet after-dinner drink like brandy. 'Liquor' is used to describe alcoholic drinks in general.
VII. 1. A 'suite' has more than one room and is usually more elegant than a 'bedroom'. **2.** They are very large rooms with special four-poster beds (*Himmelbett*) in them. **3.** They say /ˈsɔːnə/ and /ˈkrəʊkeɪ/. **4.** A beautiful part of England between Oxford and Gloucester famous for its picturesque villages and stone cottages. **5.** National Exhibition Centre (*Messegelände östlich von Birmingham*).

6B

Text

I. Jones - Tenerife - two - Jason Beach Hotel - double - sea - half - bath - shower - £1,151.90
II. 1. She doesn't want her husband to make all the decisions by himself. **2.** It costs more because you can have the privacy of your own balcony looking out to sea. **3.** She probably means health insurance.
III. 1. ... means you have to provide your own meals. - **2.** ... is two weeks. - **3.** ... is their last (*or*: family) name. - **4.** ... all meals are included. - **5.** ... is an extra charge for a sea view.
IV. 1. To 'make up one's mind' means to decide something and to 'have in mind' means to think of something. **2.** You are 'lucky' when you have a lot of luck. You need luck when you go to a casino, for example. When someone smiles, they are usually 'happy'. The opposite of happy is sad. **3.** The 'bath' is part of the 'bathroom'. You put water into it to have a bath.
V. 1. Gatwick, Stanstead and Heathrow. **2.** *Example*: It's not my idea of a holiday. For me there are too many people in too little space. When I go on holiday I like to get away from people. I also don't like lying around on the beach all day.

Exercises

I. 1. We had a look at some brochures. **2.** They didn't have a swim in the sea. **3.** She had a chat with her friends. **4.** Did you have a ride along the beach on a donkey? **5.** We had a walk into the village nearly every evening. **6.** They sat on the balcony and had a drink of the local wine.
II. 1. He took a shower before dinner. **2.** She took a photograph of the sun going down. **3.** It was Christmas Eve last year when they took the decision to emigrate. **4.** They've spent all day taking care of the children. **5.** She stood on the top of the hill and took a deep breath. **6.** She took a step towards him and slapped him in the face.
III. 1. Who did you bump into? **2.** What (*or*: Who) did you sit next to? **3.** Who were you talking to? **4.** Who (*or*: Where) did you get a phone call from? **5.** What (*or*: Who) did you come across? **6.** What did you get bitten by?
IV. 1. Jason Beach Hotel, White Sands Hotel - **2.** Gatwick, Stanstead - **3.** seven, fourteen - **4.** full, half
V. 1. 'the sixth of January' - **2.** 'the fourteenth of March' - **3.** 'the twenty-first of May' - **4.** 'the first of July' - **5.** 'the thirtieth of September' - **6.** 'the eighth of November'
VI. 1. bored - **2.** knight - **3.** knot - **4.** see - **5.** write - **6.** cheque
VII. e. - j. - b. - g. - h. - a. - f. - c. - i. - d.
VIII. *From top to bottom and from left to right*: television in room, television room, telex, fax, cooperation with travel agencies, near airport, hotel car park, hotel garage(s), quiet rooms, children welcome, wheelchair access, lift, conference facilities, restaurant, caters for special dietary needs, number of beds, bar, garden or park, radio in room, telephone in room, cooking facilities in room, outdoor swimming pool, indoor swimming pool, sauna, solarium, tennis, indoor tennis court, bowling, golf club, sailing, riding, ski lift, historical building

6C

I. a), b), d), e)
II. 1. b) - **2.** a) - **3.** c)
III. 1. c) - **2.** a) - **3.** b)
IV. BA means 'Bachelor of Arts', BSc means 'Bachelor of Science'. These are the first degrees at British and US universities. If you start university right after school, you will be about 22 years old when you get a Bachelor's degree.

6D

I. 1. He has to suggest some improvements. **2.** Kevin has a lot of good ideas which he passes on to him. **3.** He is disappointed because Troubleshooter is given all the credit for his ideas.
II. 1. a) - **2.** c) - **3.** c) - **4.** a) - **5.** b) - **6.** a)
III. Both words have only two syllables, not three.
IV. 1. die Richterbank - **2.** Hinterbänklerin - **3.** Reservebank
V. *Example*: On the one hand I think that zoos are very interesting. It's fun to see all the exotic animals there. At the same time, however, zoos always depress me a little. The animals always look so sad, especially those animals which are used to having a lot of space like lions, monkeys or polar bears. Let me put it this way: I wouldn't mind if zoos did not exist!

Human resources 7

7A

Text

1. ... helping people to find a job. - **2.** ... for all jobs you need to know how to operate a computer. - **3.** ... how to present herself at an interview.
II. 1. She arranges an interview for Kirstin with a prospective employer, talks to him about Kirstin's application and sends him her CV. She also gives Kirstin some advice about what to do at the interview and promises to call her back. **2.** She does not find a job for Kirstin. She only advises her. In other words, it is Kirstin who must go to the interview and show the employer that she's the right person for the job.
III. 1. the consultants - **2.** information about the applicant - **3.** the test - **4.** a prospective employer
IV. 1. c) - **2.** b) - **3.** a) - **4.** a) - **5.** c)
V. 1. personal assistant - **2.** information technology - **3.** curriculum vitae
VI. 1. *Example*: To me it means speaking slowly, clearly and politely on the phone. **2.** *Example*: I think she means basic office skills like operating a computer and answering the phone as well as the applicant's ability to read, write and do maths. **3.** *Example*: I think she is very helpful and understanding. **4.** *Example*: I think it is important to ask questions about the job and not to say anything negative about a previous employer.

Exercises

I. 1. Under no circumstances are you allowed to park here. **2.** At no time was the managing director informed of the union's decision. **3.** Not until a month later did he find out who his boss was. **4.** Not until she had been with the company for six months did she know why she had been given the job.
II. 1. Hardly had he arrived at the office when the sun came out. **2.** Seldom have I been to such a wonderful concert. **3.** Little did they appreciate the problems we were facing. **4.** Not only did we lose our money. We also lost our credit cards.
III. 1. friendly - **2.** fine - **3.** charming - **4.** attractive
IV. 1. It's nice and quiet here, isn't it? **2.** We'll get back nice and early tomorrow morning. **3.** Your car's nice and clean. **4.** Your office is nice and tidy!
V. 1. 'Temporary staff' are people who are employed for a short period of time (eg six months or a year). 'Permanent staff' have unlimited contracts. **2.** A 'secretary' works in an office and deals with correspondence. A 'receptionist' sits at a reception and answers the telephone. She or he also looks after visitors. **3.** An 'employer' gives work to people. An 'employee' takes work.
VI. d. - b. - c. - a.
VII. 1. c. - **2.** a. - **3.** e. - **4.** f. - **5.** b. - **6.** d.
VIII. advertisement - rang (*or*: called, phoned) - asked (*or*: invited) - interview - CV - offered - accepted
IX. for - hours - customers - people - computer - last - important - exams (*or*: examinations)

7B

Text

I. 1. lines 4-8 - **2.** lines 21-22 - **3.** lines 36-37
II. 1. She was a receptionist. She worked for four years. **2.** She wanted to travel. **3.** He asks her about her previous job and why she thinks she's suitable for the new job.
III. 1. c) - **2.** b) - **3.** a) - **4.** c) - **5.** b) - **6.** a) - **7.** b)
IV. 1. Ich arbeitete in der Telefonzentrale. **2.** Ich werde die Stelle ausschreiben müssen. **3.** Ich bin an Terminarbeit gewöhnt. **4.** Ich kann auch ziemlich bestimmt auftreten, wenn es notwendig ist.
V. 1. *Example*: I think she did well. She sold herself well but she wasn't arrogant. I'm sure she got the job. **2.** *Example*: I think working abroad must be a rewarding experience. I would love to do it. You can meet new people, learn a foreign language and get to know another country and its way of life.

Exercises

I. 1. He dislikes working shifts. **2.** I admit losing (*or*: to having lost) the money. **3.** Did you forget to bring the magazine? **4.** They are looking forward to going to the party. **5.** Thank you for helping. **6.** I object to having coffee in a smoky café. **7.** I didn't forget to order the books last week. **8.** She suggested having the meeting later.
II. 1. She told me to read all the local papers. **2.** She told me to apply for as many jobs as possible. **3.** She advised me to be polite on the phone. **4.** She advised me to arrive for the interview on time. **5.** She advised me to smile at the interviewer. **6.** She told me not to worry if I wasn't successful the first time.
III. 1. If you 'keep records of the mail' you make sure everybody in the company gets their post and that all outgoing post is taken to the post office. If you 'keep copies of the mail' you make photocopies of the correspondence. **2.** A 'testimonial' is a general report about somebody's character and abilities. A 'reference' is a written report which supports a person's application for a specific job. **3.** An 'interviewer' asks questions. An 'interviewee' answers them. **4.** If you 'stay late' you don't go home from a party or other event until it is very late. If you 'stay up late' you don't go to bed until it is very late.
IV. where did you hear - doing - were told - attracts - have been interested - was - telling - had - sells - working - was - had had - are you doing - am working - applying

7C

I. 1. Chris Brown is c. - Gail Hovey is b. - Hilary Woodland is a. - **2.** Chris Brown talks about a. - Gail Hovey talks about b. - Hilary Woodland talks about c.
II. 1. b) - **2.** a) - **3.** b) - **4.** c) - **5.** c) - **6.** b)
III. 1. c) - **2.** b) - **3.** a)
IV. *Example*: No, I wouldn't like to work in the retail business. I think it must be very hard being on your feet all day. It must also be difficult to deal with customers in a friendly way all the time. I would prefer to work in an office or outside.

7D

I. 1. He is interviewing some people for a job. **2.** No, he doesn't. All the applicants for the job were unsuitable.
II. 1. c) - **2.** b) - **3.** a) - **4.** b) - **5.** a)
III. 1. b. - **2.** c. - **3.** a.
IV. You use this expression to tell somebody that they should not be so inquisitive (*neugierig*).

Communications 8

8A

Text

I. 1. b) - **2.** a) - **3.** c)
II. 1. Team briefing means informing the workforce about what is happening in a company. Chris likes the idea because he thinks it's a two-way system. It informs the workforce about certain decisions but it also gives the workforce a chance to say what it thinks about those decisions. **2.** She uses the Internet, e-mail and post. **3.** She doesn't do traditional things like shorthand.
III. 1. a) - **2.** c) - **3.** a)
IV. 1. communication strategy - **2.** agents - **3.** forms
V. 1. looked critically at - **2.** main part - **3.** at one time in the past had - **4.** if
VI. 1. *Example*: No, I don't agree. It's easy for senior managers to inform the shop floor about deci-

sions they have made but it is much more difficult for the workers to tell the management what they think. **2.** *Example*: I think the Internet can be very useful. I use it very often myself. It's helping me to learn English and it also has practical advantages. For example, I recently booked a holiday via the Internet. It was a very easy and efficient way of doing it.

Exercises

I. were - appeared - were not - wanted to send - had to interrupt - could be transmitted - brought out - could send - was - turned out - were - came out - had - bought - wanted to make - improved - boomed - did not the same happen
II. 1. I have lived in Dublin for three years. **2.** I have had a new car for six months. **3.** I have lived in my own flat for three weeks. **4.** My brother has been in Canada since 1995. **5.** John has been a software engineer for five years. **6.** He has not been in the office for two weeks.
III. 1. did you live - **2.** Did you buy - **3.** has bought - **4.** have not been - **5.** haven't seen - **6.** has had, hasn't heard, 's been successful
IV. 1. just - **2.** recently - **3.** yet - **4.** before - **5.** already - **6.** last week
V. 1. used to work - **2.** is used to speaking - **3.** used to write - **4.** were used to looking after
VI. 1. for - **2.** in - **3.** with - **4.** in - **5.** about - **6.** from - **7.** about - **8.** to
VII. 1. e. - **2.** i. - **3.** f. - **4.** h. - **5.** c. - **6.** b. - **7.** d. - **8.** a. - **9.** g. - **10.** User is wearing a Walkman!

8B

Text

I. 1. b) - **2.** a) - **3.** b) - **4.** a)
II. 1. c) - **2.** a) - **3.** b) - **4.** b) - **5.** b)
III. 1. *Example*: Yes, they are. Trade fairs are an opportunity to see what other companies are doing, establish contacts and meet customers. **2.** *Example*: Yes, I think good personal relations with customers are vital for business. If you get on well with your customers then it makes it easier to do business. People like to feel comfortable with others.

Exercises

I. 1. waiting - **2.** leave - **3.** meeting - **4.** getting - **5.** being
II. 1. b. - **2.** a. - **3.** d. - **4.** c.
III. 1. won't you? - **2.** would you? - **3.** will you? - **4.** will you? - **5.** would you? - **6.** will you?
IV. 1. if - **2.** mind - **3.** could - **4.** as - **5.** of - **6.** to - **7.** by - **8.** of - **9.** in - **10.** by
V. speaking - was wondering - has just gone out - Do you know - will definitely be - met - sent - seems to be - rang - 'll try - calling
VI. 1. zipcode - **2.** check - **3.** vacation - **4.** apartment - **5.** fall
VII. 1. pavement - **2.** pupils - **3.** motorways - **4.** taxi - **5.** boot

8C

I. 1. a), c) - **2.** b)
II. 1. b) - **2.** b) - **3.** c) - **4.** a) - **5.** b)
III. 1. place - **2.** somewhere to show their products - **3.** look closely at - **4.** details of where the firm's stand is and what it does - **5.** what a horse has in its mouth
IV. 1. Equestrian - **2.** Exhibition

8D

I. 1. He is angry because he is disturbed by a man using a mobile phone. **2.** He 'turns into' a secretary because it's the only way that he will be able to establish business contacts with the man. If the man recognized Troubleshooter, he wouldn't give him the job.
II. 1. a) - **2.** b) - **3.** b) - **4.** c) - **5.** a)
III. 1. The expression 'I've been to lunch' means I am back from lunch. The expression 'I've gone to lunch' means that I am not back from lunch or I'm still at lunch. **2.** The expression 'leave a note' means

to put a message somewhere so that somebody can read it. The expression 'make a note' means to write something on a piece of paper so that you don't forget it. **3.** The expression 'take somebody to lunch' means to invite somebody to have lunch with you. The expression 'take lunch to somebody' means to carry or transport lunch to somebody who can't get up or move very easily.
IV. 1. mind your own business - **2.** bed & breakfast - **3.** research and development - **4.** Member of Parliament (*or*: Military Police) - **5.** miles per hour - **6.** Gross National Product

Distribution 9

9A

Text

I. 1. They are logistics, vehicles, warehouses and good communications. **2.** Coolchain is a distribution company. It stores fruit and vegetables and distributes them to regional distribution centres. **3.** There are the importers and the UK grower. **4.** Some of the importers use Coolchain's warehousing and packing facilities, others don't because they have their own.
II. 1. He grows soft fruit. **2.** They use Coolchain for marketing and distribution. **3.** They are very important because they pick the fruit every day and receive instructions from a central office. **4.** It's important because soft fruit is very delicate and has a short shelf life.
III. 1. logistics - **2.** vehicles - **3.** chain - **4.** retailer
IV. 1. cooperative - **2.** soft fruit - **3.** modem - **4.** punnet
V. 1. /lə'dʒɪstɪks/ - **2.** /'prɒdju:s/ - **3.** /'vi:əkl/ - **4.** /fru:t/ - **5.** /'rɑ:zbəri/
VI. 1. distribute - **2.** facilitate - **3.** delivery - **4.** communicate - **5.** process - **6.** import - **7.** operate - **8.** order
VII. 1. A 'warehouse' is a large building where goods are stored. A 'packhouse' is a place where goods are packed. **2.** A 'retailer' is a person who sells products to the general public. An 'importer' is a person who brings in goods from a foreign country. **3.** A 'fax link' means communicating by fax. A 'modem link' means communicating by e-mail. **4.** 'Picking' fruit is taking it off the tree or bush where it grows. 'Packing' fruit is putting it into a box or punnet.

Exercises

I. 1. e. - **2.** c. - **3.** d. - **4.** b. - **5.** a. (*other answers possible*)
II. *Examples*: **1.** going to rain this afternoon - **2.** train to Birmingham leaves in forty minutes - **3.** qualifications and experience
III. 1. Nach unseren Unterlagen ist er bereits drei Mal im Gefängnis gewesen. **2.** Die Arbeit wurde nach ihren Anweisungen durchgeführt. **3.** Können Sie die Schuhe nach Größen sortieren?
IV. 1. spring, summer, autumn, winter - **2.** January, February, March, April, May, June, July, August, September, October, November, December - **3.** Monday, Tuesday, Wednesday, Thursday, Friday, Saturday, Sunday
V. 1. Ostern - **2.** Pfingsten - **3.** Allerheiligen - **4.** Heilig Abend - **5.** Zweiter Weihnachtstag - **6.** Neujahr - **7.** Karfreitag - **8.** Fastenzeit
VI. *Examples*: **1.** presents, turkey, Queen's speech - **2.** chocolate, boat race, daffodils (*Osterglocken*) - **3.** alcohol, Auld Lang Syne (*Lied: Nehmt Abschied, Brüder*), New Year's resolutions (*Vorsätze*) - **4.** more turkey, visiting friends, feeling tired
VII. 1. tin - **2.** box - **3.** jar - **4.** glass - **5.** tray - **6.** punnet - **7.** pallet
VIII. consignment - bays - load - pallets - environment - coolchain
IX. 1. acknowledging - **2.** confirmation - **3.** negotiations - **4.** expanding - **5.** forwarder - **6.** agreement - **7.** competitors - **8.** informative

9B

Text

I. 1. b) - **2.** b) - **3.** a) - **4.** a)
II. 1. Now we've got a boy and a girl. **2.** Here's a photograph of him. **3.** Which member of the family does he look like (*or*: resemble)? **4.** She's leaving hospital tomorrow.
III. 1. Wem findest du, ähnelt er? **2.** Lieben Gruß an sie.
IV. 1. b) - **2.** c) - **3.** b)
V. 1. It must be between ten and eleven in the morning. **2.** They probably don't have many trays in the shop and many customers would like to use them.
VI. *First category*: definitely, holiday, strawberries, certainly, family, wonderful - *Second category*: tomorrow, delighted - (*no words in the third category*)
VII. 1. sail - **2.** meat - **3.** hear - **4.** sea - **5.** sun - **6.** wood
VIII. 1. *Example*: They know where the produce was grown and can be sure that it's fresh. They also know the farmer and can be sure of good service. **2.** *Example*: Yes, I could imagine working on a farm. I would like the idea of being outside or looking after animals.

Exercises

I. 1. She often pops in ... - **2.** He's just popped over ... - **3.** They've popped down ... - **4.** I am just popping out ...
II. 1. Er schaute kurz ins Zimmer hinein. **2.** Sie steckte den Brief in den Briefkasten. **3.** Ich schiebe schnell diesen Kuchen ins Rohr.
III. 1. sale - **2.** on sale - **3.** sales - **4.** Sales - **5.** for sale
IV. 1. when somebody who works in a shop talks to a customer about a product - **2.** when people put all the things they don't want into their car boot and drive to a large car park or field to try and sell it to the general public - **3.** a person who travels to shops, companies or other organizations and tries to sell his or her firm's product
V. 1. Fine, thanks. **2.** Thank you very much. **3.** Thank you. **4.** Thanks. (I think I've got hay fever.) **5.** You're welcome. **6.** How do you do. (*or*: Pleased to meet you.) **7.** Yes, of course. What is it? **8.** Oh, that's a pity. **9.** Yes, I will. **10.** Thank you. That's very kind of you. (*other answers possible*)
VI. 1. c. - **2.** a. - **3.** b.
VII. have you had - For - attracting - produce - slightly lower - to find - will tell - difficult - applying - business - don't want to do - be
VIII. 1. wasteful - **2.** impatient - **3.** greedy - **4.** selfish - **5.** mean - **6.** lazy - **7.** materialistic - **8.** rude (*other answers possible*)

9C

I. a), c), e), f)
II. 1. b) - **2.** b) - **3.** b) - **4.** b) - **5.** c) - **6.** a)
III. 1. c. - **2.** d. - **3.** b. - **4.** e. - **5.** a.
IV. 1. Sortiment - **2.** auf Lager - **3.** ausverkauft

9D

I. 1. He has set up a courier service. **2.** Not really. It's only just been established. However, Troubleshooter thinks it can develop. **3.** Yes, he does. He delivers parcels, answers the phone and, most of all, deals with angry customers.
II. 1. c) - **2.** a) - **3.** b)
III. 1. a small business can turn into a big one - **2.** to stay by the phone and answer it when it rings - **3.** to have a short sleep - **4.** to manage a difficult situation well - **5.** unhappy people who are paying Troubleshooter for his services
IV. 1. c. - **2.** a. - **3.** b. - **4.** d.
V. 1. d. - **2.** g. - **3.** f. - **4.** b. - **5.** a. - **6.** c. - **7.** e.

Export and import 10

10A

Text

I. 1. manufactures porcelain - **2.** Italy, Germany and France - **3.** agents and distributors - **4.** agent receives money from Royal Worcester for the amount of porcelain he or she sells. A distributor buys the porcelain from Royal Worcester and then sells it to the customer directly - **5.** market research - **6.** to ask customers what they think of future designs for porcelain
II. 1. commission - **2.** market research - **3.** taste - **4.** tableware
III. 1. for (*or*: in) - **2.** on - **3.** from - **4.** in - **5.** on
IV. 2. is put onto - **3.** is sent to the - **4.** a lead time - **5.** are manufactured - **6.** are packed - **8.** is raised
V. 1. lead time - **2.** carton - **3.** invoice - **4.** letter of credit
VI. 1. Countries have different tastes regarding porcelain so what sells well in one country will not necessarily sell well in another. **2.** Porcelain is very fragile so it has to be packed well before it leaves the factory. **3.** Customers who pay on time can be given open credit facilities. Customers who are not so reliable have to use a letter of credit.

Exercises

I. b), d), e) can follow - a), c) can't follow
II. a), b), d), e) can follow - c) can't follow
III. 1. by - **2.** in - **3.** by - **4.** on
IV. 1. into - **2.** off - **3.** up - **4.** back
V. 1. buy - **2.** invite
VI. 2. Chinese, the Chinese - **3.** French, the French - **4.** German, the Germans - **5.** Greek, the Greeks - **6.** Indian, the Indians - **7.** Italian, the Italians - **8.** Japanese, the Japanese - **9.** Spanish, the Spaniards - **10.** Turkish, the Turks
VII. *Example*: I once had a holiday on the Greek island of Lesbos. It was three years ago. I went with my girlfriend. Lesbos is quite a big island so we travelled around a lot by bus and stayed in different villages. It was very hot so we spent a lot of time on the beach. We swam, played chess and read. The local people were very friendly and we got to know some of them. I would like to go back there again one day.
VIII. 1. b. - **2.** f. - **3.** a. - **4.** c. - **5.** e. - **6.** d. (The opening and close of the letter are missing as well as the sender's and recipient's address.)

10B

Text

I. 1. b) - **2.** a) - **3.** c) - **4.** b)
II. 1. c) - **2.** a) - **3.** a) - **4.** a)
III. 1. It's a receipt, an identification document and an entitlement document. **2.** If the ship sinks and the tea is lost Twinings can claim money from their insurance company. **3.** It shows where the tea has come from and where it is going.
IV. 1. bought, (the week) before - **2.** all the preparations have been completed - **3.** After (*or*: As soon as) - **4.** gives, load
V. 1. a contract - **2.** seeing that everything is in order - **3.** the different documents - **4.** a certificate of insurance - **5.** a certificate of origin

Exercises

I. 1. Can I make you some tea? **2.** We showed the customs officer our passports. **3.** They offered the elderly couple their seats. **4.** He bought his girlfriend a necklace.
II. 1. Send them to her. **2.** Lend it to them. **3.** Give it to her. **4.** Teach it to them.

III. 1. The guests were met ... - **2.** The agent was thanked ... - **3.** The distributor was asked ... - **4.** Both candidates were offered ...
IV. 1. Describe your present job to us. **2.** Can you suggest to me who I should invite to dinner? **3.** She explained the difference between 'buy' and 'purchase' to her colleagues. (*or*: She explained to her colleagues the difference between 'buy' and 'purchase'.)
V. 1. catch - **2.** buy - **3.** understand - **4.** arrive at - **5.** annoy - **6.** receive - **7.** become - **8.** prepare
VI. 1. consignment - **2.** distributors - **3.** consultants - **4.** consumption - **5.** applicants - **6.** cancellations - **7.** division - **8.** resignation
VII. 1. e. - **2.** g. - **3.** d. - **4.** c. - **5.** a. - **6.** h. - **7.** f. - **8.** b.
VIII. The highest price would be CIF Felixstowe because this would include all the costs from Israel to the British port.

10C

I. 1. a), b), c) - **2.** a), c)
II. 1. a) - **2.** b) - **3.** a) - **4.** b) - **5.** b)
III. 1. a) - **2.** b) - **3.** c) - **4.** b)
IV. 1. /mə'nɒpəli/ - **2.** /ærɪ'stɒkresi/ - **3.** /ˌbəʊn'tʃainə/ - **4.** /'pɔːsəlɪn/ - **5.** /'wɒrənt/ - **6.** /braɪd/

10D

I. 1. He wants to export English wine to France. **2.** No, it's not. He doesn't sell any wine in France. **3.** He gets into trouble at customs.
II. 1. ... get paid according to the amount of goods you sell - **2.** ... the currency of the European Union - **3.** ... you want to have more than you really need - **4.** ... to the government on certain goods you bring into - or take out of - a country - **5.** ... to carry your papers and files
III. 1. fangen - **2.** erwischen - **3.** erreichen - **4.** - (*Aufmerksamkeit*) erregen - **5.** erblicken - **6.** hängenbleiben mit - **7.** verstehen - **8.** (*Feuer*) fangen

The transportation of goods 11

11A

Text

I. 1. false. It uses different means of transport. - **2.** true - **3.** false. It is part of public-sector and private-sector industry. - **4.** true
II. 1. b) - **2.** c) - **3.** a)
III. 1. freight - **2.** public-sector industry - **3.** freight forwarders - **4.** the West Country - **5.** the Channel Tunnel - **6.** road congestion
IV. 1. industries and services which are owned by private individuals - **2.** England, Wales and Scotland - **3.** what comes out of a car engine, such as carbon monoxide - **4.** a person who buys something in a shop
V. 1. Our trains can transport goods all around Britain. **2.** Our trains can transport as much as fifty lorries can transport. **3.** Customers have economic reasons for the choice they make.
VI. 1. /freɪt/ - **2.** /ɒn'ruːt/ - **3.** /kən'dʒestʃən/ - **4.** /ɪg'zɔːst iˌmɪʃn/ - **5.** /iːkəˌnɒmɪk kraɪ'tɪəriə/
VII. 1. *Example*: No, I don't. Transporting freight by train is still much more costly and much less efficient than transporting freight by lorry. Many business people don't worry about the environment. They just want to be successful and make money. **2.** *Example*: No, I don't. A lot more could be done such as building more efficient cars and restricting the speed limit on motorways.

Exercises

I. 1. had gone - **2.** had already begun - **3.** had never been - **4.** hadn't had
II. 1. will have reached - **2.** will have doubled - **3.** will have been - **4.** will have increased
III. 1. by - **2.** until - **3.** by - **4.** until
IV. 1. You can't say 'am' *and* 'in the morning'. **2.** You don't say '21.00 hours'; you say 'nine o'clock in the evening'.
V. 1. 'twenty to five' - **2.** 'twenty-three minutes past eleven' - **3.** 'quarter to two' - **4.** 'half past eight' - **5.** 'quarter past eleven'
VI. for - since - goods - white - machines - furniture - explosive - dangerous
VII. *Example*: I think the British government will try to encourage companies to use rail freight facilities by increasing road tax or by raising the price of petrol or by introducing a new 'green' tax on certain means of transport.
What's a meeting? ('to take minutes' = *ein Protokoll schreiben*)

11B

Text

I. 1. move into it - **2.** to move by themselves or use a removals company - **3.** use the services of a removals company - **4.** hire a van for the day and do the move himself
II. 1. Frank gets lost and Joe blames Katie. **2.** Some of their belongings are broken.
III. 1. b) - **2.** a) - **3.** b)
IV. 1. quotation - **2.** dinner service - **3.** fraction - **4.** van - **5.** exhausted
V. 1. to move your belongings from one house to another - **2.** pay to use it for a short period of time - **3.** you want to know where you are or where you want to go - **4.** you've had a very eventful day
VI. 1. cheaper - **2.** unpack - **3.** busy - **4.** right - **5.** spend

Exercises

I. 1. I was wondering if I could use your fax machine? **2.** I was wondering if I could borrow your mobile for a moment? **3.** I wondered if I could borrow your dictionaries? **4.** I wondered if I could have your car for an evening?
II. 1. sorry - **2.** afraid - **3.** wondering - **4.** mind
III. 1. 'll tell - **2.** leave - **3.** 'll see, arrives - **4.** 'll hear, talk
IV. 1. You shouldn't have told me! + b. - **2.** You must have heard me! + e. - **3.** You might have warned me! + d. - **4.** You could have phoned me! + a. - **5.** You may have hurt me! + c.
V. Underground - airport - Terminal - check-in desk - ticket - suitcase - bag - luggage - hand luggage - boarding pass - Gate - security check - passport control - departure lounge - duty-free shop - screen - flight - took off - baggage reclaim - conveyor belt - customs - friends

11C

I. a), c), e), f)
II. 1. b) - **2.** a) - **3.** b) - **4.** a) - **5.** b) - **6.** a) - **7.** b)
III. 1. b) - **2.** a) - **3.** c) - **4.** c)
IV. 1. We made sure there was no other similar companies doing the work we wanted to do. **2.** We enjoy trying to master a difficult situation.

11D

I. 1. She's asked him to transport a box of marshmallows to Luxembourg. **2.** It's attractive because he can have as many free samples as he want. **3.** He has to charter an aeroplane.
II. 1. b) - **2.** c) - **3.** b) - **4.** a)
III. 1. c. - **2.** b. - **3.** a. - **4.** d.

Insurance 12

12A

Text

I. 1. true - **2.** true - **3.** false - **4.** true
II. 1. 'Buildings insurance' provides cover against the risk of a building being damaged by fire or flood, for example. 'Contents insurance' provides cover against the risk of the contents of a building or house being damaged or stolen. **2.** A 'storm' is a strong wind with rain or snow. A 'flood' is a sudden increase in the level of water. **3.** If you're 'under-insured' you haven't got enough cover and the insurance company won't pay you enough money to repair or replace what has been damaged or lost. If you're 'over-insured' you have too much cover. **4.** 'Damage' is done to property. 'Injury' is personal. It involves people.
III. He talks about employers' liability insurance, public liability insurance, products liability insurance. He also speaks about buildings and stock insurance and business interruption insurance.
IV. 1. employers' liability insurance - **2.** public liability insurance - **3.** products liability insurance - **4.** business interruption insurance
V. 1. liability - **2.** negligence - **3.** compensation - **4.** party
VI. 1. parties - **2.** negligent - **3.** liable - **4.** compensation
VII. 1. *Example*: I think houses are more expensive in Germany than in other parts of the world and this is why many people are not home owners in Germany. One of the reasons why houses are more expensive is that land (*Grund*) is expensive in Germany. The other reason is that houses are built very solidly and thoroughly. **2.** *Example*: I find insurance very complicated. I think there's always a danger that you are 'over-insured'. At the moment I've got health insurance, contents insurance for my flat, accident insurance and insurance for my car. I hope that's enough.

Exercises

I. 1. of - **2.** to - **3.** to - **4.** from - **5.** to - **6.** on - **7.** against - **8.** on
II. 1. c. - **2.** a. - **3.** d. - **4.** e. - **5.** b.
III. 1. apologized for - **2.** is applying for - **3.** believe in - **4.** laughed at
IV. 1. listening to - **2.** speak to - **3.** belongs to - **4.** happened to - **5.** insisted on - **6.** concentrate on - **7.** rely on - **8.** live on
V. 1. Wir suchten meine Schlüssel. **2.** Wir schauten das Foto an. **3.** Wir passten auf das Baby auf.
VI. 4. (suffer)
VII. 4. (manufacturer)
VIII. 2. (uninterrupted)
IX. contributions - misfortunes - premium - claim - compensation - contract - document

12B

Text

I. 1. false - **2.** true - **3.** true - **4.** false - **5.** true - **6.** false - **7.** not say
II. 1. *Example*: Yes, I think they will. Phil Hickley is helpful and friendly and the couple seem to like what his company can offer. **2.** *Example*: They know a bit. They know about no-claims discounts but they are not sure about the different types of cover or what can affect the premium.
III. 1. a) - **2.** b) - **3.** b) - **4.** b) - **5.** a)
IV. 1. 'Third-party, fire and theft insurance' provides cover if you have an accident and damage somebody else's car. It doesn't cover your own car, however. 'Fully-comprehensive insurance' covers your car *and* the other person's car. **2.** The 'make' of a car is the name of the manufacturer, eg VW. The 'model' of a car is the type of car, eg Golf. **3.** A 'cover note' is a short, temporary document telling you that your car is insured. An 'insurance policy' is a legal document giving all the details of the cover for

your car. **4.** A 'claim' is when you ask your insurance company to pay out for loss or damage. A 'premium' is the money you pay to the insurance company for cover.

Exercises

I. 1. bill - **2.** account - **3.** diary - **4.** agenda - **5.** lonely - **6.** alone - **7.** insurance - **8.** assurance - **9.** lend - **10.** borrow - **11.** woman - **12.** wife
II. *Examples*: **1.** A week is a long time in politics. / Our company has a policy of giving responsible positions to new employees. **2.** It's difficult to control a car when you're driving over ice. / Can you check this letter? Are there any spelling mistakes in it? **3.** My friend designed this chair. This is his first drawing. / They constructed their house out of wood. **4.** My son likes going to school but he doesn't like doing his homework. / Is doing the housework a satisfying job? **5.** What's the price of a small car in Germany? / Who won first prize in the swimming competition?
III. 1. reduction - **2.** assistance - **3.** delivery - **4.** enclosure - **5.** choice - **6.** restriction - **7.** advice - **8.** agreement
IV. c. - f. - a. - d. - e. - b.

V. ▸ Good afternoon. Can I help you?
▸ Yes. I've got an appointment with Mrs Summerfield at half past four.
▸ Could you give me your name, please?
▸ It's John Sweeney from Infotech.
▸ She won't be long, Mr Sweeney.
▸ OK. Thanks very much.

VI. see - appointment - Sorry - afraid - somebody - waiting - kind - Would

12C

I. d)
II. 1. b) - **2.** a) - **3.** c) - **4.** b) - **5.** b) - **6.** a) - **7.** b)
III. 1. b) - **2.** b) - **3.** a) - **4.** c)
IV. 1. a boat which transports people, cars and buses - **2.** goods powered by electricity such as hair dryers, CD players, washing machines etc - **3.** is to make sure nobody brings illegal goods (eg drugs) into the country. It is also your job to make sure people pay duty - **4.** turns over and sinks - **5.** when an oil tanker hits an iceberg and the oil spills out into the sea

12D

I. 1. Some pallets were knocked over and eventually a greenhouse was destroyed. (In the middle five other 'accidents' take place!) **2.** He started the chain of events by knocking over the pallets. **3.** Yes and no. He is insured so his insurance company can handle any claims. However, he is not sure if he has paid his premiums.
II. 1. c) - **2.** b) - **3.** b) - **4.** a)
III. 1. c. - **2.** a. - **3.** b. - **4.** d.

The City and international trade 13

13A

Text

I. 1. b) - **2.** b) - **3.** b) - **4.** a)
II. 1. balance of payments - **2.** currency - **3.** billion
III. 1. c) - **2.** b) - **3.** a) - **4.** a) - **5.** a)
IV. 1. The 'balance of payments' is the difference between what a country pays for its imports and what it receives for its exports (including invisibles such as banking and insurance). The 'balance of trade' is the difference in money value between the visible imports and visible exports of a country. **2.** A 'million' is a 1 and six noughts (1,000,000) and a 'billion' is a 1 and nine noughts (1,000,000,000). **3.** 'Insurance' is used together with 'health', 'car' or 'travel' etc. 'Assurance' is only used with the word 'life'. The two words mean the same, however. **4.** The 'City of London' is the part of London where the Bank of England, the Stock Exchange and Lloyd's are situated. The 'centre of London' is the middle of London where all the shops, cinemas and theatres are to be found (eg Leicester Square).
V. 1. money - **2.** shares - **3.** company - **4.** companies - **5.** investors
VI. 1. /ɪnˈvɪzəbl/ - **2.** /ˈbɪljən/ - **3.** /kəˈtæstrəfi/ - **4.** /ˈmɜːtʃənt/ - **5.** /ˈspekuleɪtə/

Exercises

I. 2 (a person or object insured / a building made of wood)
II. 1. The world's largest cigar, weighing 110 kg, was insured for nearly £18 million. The cigar, rolled to celebrate the launch of a new brand, took 315 hours to make. **2.** In 1901 the first car insured at Lloyd's was covered by a marine policy. Cars were such a novelty at the time that the underwriters wrote a policy on the basis that the car was a ship navigating on dry land. **3.** A killer whale captured off the Canadian Pacific coast and towed to an aquarium in Seattle was insured for $8,000 against various emergencies, including rescue attempts by other whales.
IV. 1. annual general meeting - **2.** approximately - **3.** as soon as possible - **4.** Bachelor of Arts - **5.** Bachelor of Science - **6.** carbon copy (*or*: cubic centimetres) - **7.** curriculum vitae - **8.** European Union - **9.** Greenwich /ˈgrenɪtʃ/ Mean Time - **10.** Master of Business Administration - **11.** miscellaneous (*Verschiedenes*) - **12.** North Atlantic Treaty Organization - **13.** nota bene (= take special note of) - **14.** or nearest offer (*Verhandlungsbasis*) - **15.** Organization of Petroleum Exporting Countries - **16.** personal assistant (*or*: Press Association, public address system) - **17.** personal identification number - **18.** please turn over - **19.** répondez, s'il vous plaît - **20.** stamped addressed envelope - **21.** value added tax - **22.** very important person - **23.** with effect from - **24.** World Health Organization - **25.** words per minute (*other answers possible*)
Scores: If you know more than 21 ➔ excellent; if you know more than 17 ➔ good; if you know more than 13 ➔ not bad; if you know fewer than 8 ➔ could be better!
V. *Positive*: affable, alert, ambitious, artistically-minded, bashful, bold, brave, caring, cautious, committed, conscientious, considerate, cooperative, courageous, courteous, creative, critically-minded, determined, diplomatic, easy-going, enterprising, fair, firm, full of drive, generous - *Negative*: aggressive, bloody-minded, callous, cruel, evasive (*other answers possible*)
VI. 1. holiday - **2.** good - **3.** the same result for both teams - **4.** exhibition - **5.** machinery - **6.** tool for cutting
VII. 1. *Most* people prefer more freetime to more money. **2.** We discussed the facts and figures. **3.** The answer depends *on* a lot of factors. **4.** Our prices are not *as* high as our competitors'. **5.** We need more *information* before reaching a decision. **6.** *What* do you call this part of the machine in English? **7.** The technician he spoke to *said* he didn't know the answer. **8.** Thank you very much for your order. I'*ll* send the goods today. **9.** Retailers *often have* problems manufacturers don't understand. **10.** Sales have fallen by 15%. **11.** *We used to manufacture* photocopiers. **12.** Here is the menu. What *would* you like? **13.** Yes, I agree with you, Simon. What's your *opinion*, Susan? **14.** He suggested *advertising* the post in the local paper. **15.** Fifty *people* work in the office here. **16.** Can you *tell* me something about your

distribution policy? **17.** Would you explain *to* me how the machining centre works, please? **18.** We'll see *each other* again tomorrow, John. Bye. **19.** Please read our conditions on the *reverse side* carefully. **20.** We don't want *you to* have difficulties with your payment. **21.** If the goods are faulty *take* them back to the shop where you bought them. **22.** Please let us have your order *by* next Friday. **23.** Mr Epson is used to *repairing* these printers. **24.** I'm not *interested* in your excuses. Tell me what happened. **25.** She doesn't smoke and I don't *either*.

13B

Text

I. 1. not say - **2.** true - **3.** not say - **4.** not say - **5.** not say
II. 1. exports his product to the US. - **2.** his product will be turned away at US customs. - **3.** will have to think about using the services of a factoring company. - **4.** it is the most secure method of payment.
III. 1. b) - **2.** b) - **3.** a) - **4.** c) - **5.** a) - **6.** c) - **7.** a)
IV. 1. to find out the financial strength and the amount of trust you can put in a company - **2.** an arrangement between a supplier and a factoring company by which the supplier sells the rights to the factoring company to collect the accounts - **3.** a document sent by the seller to the buyer showing which goods have been sold - **4.** the rise and fall of the value of one currency against another - **5.** an order from one person to another for a certain sum of money to be paid at a certain date to a specified person

Exercises

I. 1. unless - **2.** provided - **3.** as long as - **4.** Supposing
II. 1. However - **2.** whichever - **3.** Whoever - **4.** wherever
III. 1. Was sind die Zugangsvoraussetzungen für den diplomatischen Dienst? **2.** Allen Bedingungen der Gewerkschaft muss zugestimmt werden. **3.** Ich würde unter keinen Umständen in Kalifornien leben wollen. Und du? **4.** Sehr gute Englischkenntnisse sind Voraussetzung für ein MBA-Studium.
IV. 1. b. - **2.** d. - **3.** e. - **4.** f. - **5.** g. - **6.** h. - **7.** c. - **8.** a.
V. 1. d. - **2.** e. ('plaice' = *Scholle*) - **3.** a. ('to hold something against somebody' = *jmdm. etwas übelnehmen*) - **4.** b. - **5.** c. (You have *missed* the history lectures!) - **6.** g. - **7.** f.

13C

I. d)
II. 1. b) - **2.** a) - **3.** b) - **4.** a)
III. 1. c) - **2.** a) - **3.** b) - **4.** b) - **5.** a)
IV. 1. /ˈekwəti:s/ - **2.** /streŋθ/ - **3.** /ekspɜ:rˈti:z/ - **4.** /ˈɪnfrəstrʌktʃə/ - **5.** /ˈvɒlju:m/
VI. *Example*: Yes, it would attract me. I could imagine, for example, working in the foreign exchange department at one of the City's banks. I'm interested in financial matters and I would like to work in an international atmosphere. It would also be a challenge to work abroad for a number of years and get to know England, the English and the English way of life a bit better. Who knows? Maybe one day I'll get the chance!

13D

I. 1. He's been invited to attend a meeting there. **2.** The lady has come to pick Troubleshooter up. As the meeting has been delayed for two hours Troubleshooter suggests going on a tour of the City together. **3.** After one or two arguments the young lady is convinced that Troubleshooter is the right person to help her company with their problems.
II. 1. a) - **2.** b) - **3.** b) - **4.** c) - **5.** a)
IV. 1. /ˈɑ:kɪtektʃə/ - **2.** /ˈɪgnərənt/ - **3.** /rɪˈdɪkjələs/ - **4.** /pɔ:z/ - **5.** /ˈevɪdəntli:/
V. A City Slicker is a person who is quick and clever (in contrast to somebody who comes from the country).
VI. 1. b. - **2.** d. - **3.** a. - **4.** c.

Wordlist

The numbers refer to the modules in which the word or expression occur for the first time. The words and expressions in Module C are listed after the corresponding tapescripts (see page 227).

A

abacus 2D	Abakus (*Rechenbrett*)
accommodate 8C	entsprechen, (be)dienen
account director 5A	*etwa*: Projektleiter(in)
account for 6A	ausmachen
accountant 12C	Buchhalter(in), Wirtschaftsprüfer(in)
acorn 9D	Eichel
activity day 6A	Aktiv-, Erlebnistag
adjuster 12C	(Schadens)sachverständige(r)
adversity 11C	Not
affix 9C	anbringen
afield 10A	entfernt
ambient 9C	Umgebungs-, Raum-
an awful lot 11C	eine ganze Menge
assertiveness 7C	Bestimmtheit
assessment 7C	Einschätzung, Beurteilung
assignment 11D	Aufgabe, Auftrag

B

backbone 8A	Rückgrat
badge 8C	Abzeichen, (Namens)schild
balance of payments 13A	Zahlungsbilanz
bar code(r label) 9C	Strichkodierung
basic cost 6B	Grundpreis, -kosten
bazooka 5D	Panzerfaust
bearing 5A	Auswirkung
bed 1C	pflanzen, setzen
bill of exchange 10B	Wechsel
bill of lading 10B	Seefrachtbrief
bindery 3A	Buchbinderei
bit 8C	Kandare (*Gebissstange des Pferdes*)
bits and pieces 3B	Krimskrams
blend 10C	(ver)mischen
board of directors 2A	Vorstand
bone china 10C	feines Porzellan
bookcase 3B	Bücherregal, -schrank
booklet 12B	Broschüre
bounce 2C	aufprallen lassen
bounce 4A	(*Scheck*) platzen
brand 5A	Marke
branding 5B	*eine ‚Marke' aus einem Produkt machen*
briefcase 2D	(Akten)tasche, -mappe
briefing 8A	Informationsgespräch
brisk 6D	flott, forsch

budget 4C — wirtschaften, einplanen
building society 4C — Bausparkasse
business director 5A — *etwa*: Bereichsleiter(in)
business plan 1D — Geschäftsplan

C

calibre 5C — Format
cane 1A — Rohr
capsize 12C — kentern
cargo 10B — (Schiffs)fracht, -ladung
cascade down 8A — stufenförmig nach unten führen
cash card 4C — Geldautomatenkarte
cash flow 3B — Cashflow (*Überschuss nach Abzug aller Kosten*)
cast 3C — gießen
chair 5B — den Vorsitz führen bei
chart 11C — Diagramm
chase 4D — jagen
chef 6A — Küchenchef(in), Koch, Köchin
cheque (guarantee) card 4C — Scheckkarte
chief executive 2A — Geschäftsführer(in)
chill 9C — frisch, kühl
chores *pl* 4C — Hausarbeit
chrysanth 1C — Chrysantheme
clear 11D — (*Zoll*) passieren
clerical 9C — Büro-, Schreib-
clipart picture 3B — Clipart (*Computerbildchen*)
code 9D — *hier*: adressieren
come up 3C — frei werden
commercial director 3A — *etwa*: Bereichsleiter(in)
commission 10A — Provision
commitment 4A — Engagement
Companies House 2A — *Handelsregister in GB*
compliment slip 3B — Empfehlungskärtchen
comply 13B — einwilligen, erfüllen
compositor 3C — (Schrift)setzer(in)
congestion 11A — Stau
consignment 10B — Ladung
consignment 11C — Versendung, Verschickung
constrain 5C — beschränken
consultant 7A — Berater(in)
contents insurance 12A — Hausratversicherung
convey 8D — übermitteln, -bringen
conveyor belt 3A — Förder-, Fließband
coolchain 9A — Kühl(ungs)kette
cope 9D — zurechtkommen
corporate 6A — *hier*: Geschäftsleute
corporate 12A — Firmen-, Unternehmens-
corporate team-building programme 6A — *Programm zur Steigerung der Teamfähigkeit, zur Integration von Mitarbeitern*
count out 2D — (*Sport*) auszählen
cover 12A — (Versicherungs)schutz; Deckung

cover note 12B vorläufiger Versicherungsschein
craftsmanship 8C Handwerkskunst
crisp 5A frisch, knackig
crop 9A Ernte
curiously 2C seltsamerweise
current account 1B Girokonto
CV 7A Lebenslauf

D

database 3A Datenbank
day-to-day 1B Alltags-, täglich
dealing 13C Handel, Transaktionen
debrief 5B Nachbesprechung
deposit 4C Guthaben, Einlage
deposit account 1B Sparkonto
depot 1A (Lager)haus
deputy 7C stellvertretend
dispatch 3A Versand
distribution 1A Verteilung, Vertrieb
dome 6D Kuppel
draft 10B Wechsel
drainpipe 12D Abflussrohr
draw 1C Anziehungspunkt, Attraktion
draw up 6A festsetzen, aufstellen
draw up 7A abrufen
drawing pin 3B Reißzwecke
dreadful 11B schrecklich
duchy 11D Herzogtum

E

economies of scale 6A *Vorteile durch hohe Stückzahl*
embarrassment 4A Verlegenheit
en route 11A unterwegs
entitlement 10B Berechtigung
envisage 5A sich vorstellen
equestrian 8B Reit-, Reiter-
equities *pl* 4C Stammaktien, Dividendenpapiere
excess 12B Selbstbeteiligung
Excise 12C *Verwaltungsabteilung für indirekte Steuern*
execution 5B Ausführung
exhaust 11A Auspuff
expertise 2C Sachverstand, -kenntnis
extend 8D *hier*: aussprechen
extension lead 3D Verlängerungskabel
eye up 8C begutachten, mustern

F

fabric 8C Stoff
factoring 13B Finanzierung offener Buchforderungen
feed into 3A zuführen

fertilizer 1A — Dünger
fibre-optic 13C — faseroptisch
file 3A — Datei
file accounts 2A — (Geschäfts)bücher einreichen
filing cabinet 3B — Aktenschrank, -regal
film 3C — (Druck)film
firm up 8B — unter Dach und Fach bringen
fix up 12B — (*Versicherung*) abschließen
fleet 9C — *hier*: Fuhrpark
fluctuation 13B — Schwankung
fork-lift truck 9C — Gabelstapler
formal wear 7C — Gesellschaftskleidung
forwarder 11A — Spediteur(in)
fraction 11B — Bruchteil
free-range (eggs) 9B — (Eier) von freilaufenden Hühnern
freight 11A — Fracht(gut)
full board 6B — Vollpension
full costing 6B — Gesamtkalkulation
fully-comprehensive insurance 12B — Vollkaskoversicherung
future 13A — Future, Termingeschäft

G

gallon 10D — Gallone (*ca. 4,5 Liter*)
gear 12C — Vorrichtung
get on top 7B — *hier*: negativ beeinflussen
go ahead 6A — stattfinden
go ahead 6B — es machen
go along 7A — *hier*: sich bewerben
go through 1B — (*Betrag*) eingehen
grand piano 12A — Flügel
groupage 11C — Sammelladung
grower 1A — Züchter(in)
gruelling 7C — aufreibend, äußerst strapaziös

H

half board 6B — Halbpension
hanging file 3B — Hängeregister
hassle 2A — Ärger
haulage 11C — Transport, Spedition
have sb on 5D — jmdn. auf den Arm nehmen
headed notepaper 3B — Briefpapier mit Briefkopf
headkeeper 6D — Oberwärter(in)
hence 9A — also
high-flyer 13D — Überflieger
hole punch 3B — Locher
Home Counties 1A — *an London grenzende Grafschaften*
hopper 3A — Einfülltrichter
hull 12C — Schiffskörper

I

implement 6D	durchführen
incognito 8C	unerkannt
incorporation 2A	Gründung
index 13C	Messzahl
ink 3A	Druckfarbe, Tinte
insertion 5A	Anzeige
instalment 4D	Rate
intermodal transport 11A	Transport auf verschiedenen Verkehrsmitteln
invoice 3A	(Waren)rechnung, Lieferschein
issue with 12B	ausstellen
IT 7A	Informationstechnik

J

jacuzzi 6C	Whirlpool
joint account 4B	gemeinsames Konto

K

keep 3B	*hier*: führen
keep records 7B	aufzeichnen, dokumentieren
key 2C	das Wichtigste
kick off 5B	beginnen
knowledgeable 1C	kenntnisreich

L

lawnmower 1A	Rasenmäher
lead 3C	Blei
lead time 10A	Liefer-, Produktionszeit
lend oneself to 11C	sich für etw. eignen
letter of credit 10A	Kreditbrief, Akkreditiv
liability 2A	Haftung
line growth 9C	Produktlinien-Wachstum
listening board 2C	*etwa*: Zuhörer
loan 4A	Darlehen
luncheon 13D	Mittagessen

M

mainframe 3A	Groß-
maintenance 6C	Instandhaltung, Pflege
make 12B	Marke, Fabrikat
make one's mark on 6D	seinen Stempel aufdrücken, sich profilieren
make up 3C	Aufmachung, Layout, Umbruch
man 9D	besetzen
manufacturing director 8A	Produktionsleiter(in)
market 7B	Absatzmärkte erschließen, vertreiben
meet deadlines 7B	Termine einhalten
memo 3B	Notiz, Mitteilung
merchant 6A	Händler(in)

messy 3C	dreckig, schmutzig
mists *pl* **of time** 5A	Dunkel der Vergangenheit
moan 6D	schimpfen
monitor 3B	überwachen, kontrollieren
mortgage 4B	Hypothek
MOT (*abbr for* **Ministry of Transport**) 1B	*TÜV*
move 10C	Schritt, Zug
multiple 9A	Ladenkette

N

nap 9D	Nickerchen
nappy 5A	Windel
newssheet 13A	Informationsblatt
niche 5A	Nische
no room to swing a cat 7D	sich (vor Enge) nicht rühren können
no-claims discount 12B	Schadenfreiheitsrabatt
notice 7B	Kündigung

O

office junior 7A	Bürogehilfe, -gehilfin
on top of 6B	von zusätzlich
onward 9D	weiter
open account 10A	Barkonto
operater 11A	Unternehmer(in)
option 13A	Optionsschein
origin 10B	Herkunft
overdraft 13B	Überziehung
overheads 1D	allgemeine Kosten

P

PA 7A	persönliche(r) Assistent(in)
package 7A	präsentieren
packhouse 9A	Abpackhalle
packing list 11D	Packliste
paint feature 3B	Maloption
pantry 1C	Speisekammer
paper clip 2D	Büroklammer
paperwork 2B	Unterlagen
partnership 2A	Personengesellschaft
pass on 3C	übertragen
pay up 12A	(be)zahlen
payroll 1C	*hier*: Gehälter
pension 4C	Rente, Pension
perishable 11C	verderblich
personal assets *pl* 2A	persönlicher Besitz
petty cash 7B	Portokasse
piece of cake 6D	Kinderspiel, Klacks

pile up 9D	sich stapeln
platen 3C	(Druck)platte, Walze
plug into 3D	anschließen an
policy 12B	Versicherungsschein, Police
polythene 3A	Polyäthylen, Plastik
pop in 9B	hineintun
porcupine 6D	Stachelschwein
portfolio 10A	(Akten)mappe
potter 1C	herumschlendern
power 3D	Strom
preferential rate 4D	Vorzugsrate
premises *pl* 2A	Firmengelände
premium 12A	Prämie
present with 1D	präsentieren, überreichen
prime time 5A	Haupteinschaltzeit
print out 1B	Auszug, -druck
proposition 4A	Vorhaben
prosper 1C	erfolgreich sein
provided 5B	angenommen, gesetzt den Fall
public liability insurance 12D	Haftpflichtversicherung
punch 2D	schlagen
punnet 9A	Körbchen

Q

quotation 11B	(Preis)angebot, Kostenvoranschlag
quote 2A	(*Aktien*) notieren
quote 2D	zitieren

R

raise the point 5B	auf etw. zu sprechen kommen
ramp 6D	Rampe
raspberry 9A	Himbeere
rates *pl* 2D	Kommunalsteuern
record 12B	Dokument, Unterlage
recruitment agency 7A	Personalagentur
refrigerate 11C	(tief)kühlen
refurbishment 6C	Verschönerung; Renovierung
registration document 1B	Kraftfahrzeugbrief
removals company 11B	Umzugsfirma
reservation 5B	Vorbehalt
retail and wholesale 1A	Einzel- und Großhandel
revenue 10D	Einnahmen, Einkünfte
revolve 2C	(sich) drehen
ring-main 13C	Hauptleitung
roadside 5A	Straßenrand
room occupancy 6A	Zimmerbelegung
run out 9D	(*Zeit*) davonlaufen

S

safeguard 4A	Absicherung
sales manager 10A	Verkaufsleiter(in)
sales representative 3A	Vertreter(in)
scan gun 9C	Bar-Code-Lesegerät
scribble 8D	kritzeln
self-catering 6B	Selbstversorgung
service industry 6A	Dienstleistungsbranche
set to 4D	loslegen mit
share 2A	Aktie
sheer 13C	rein
shell dish 10C	Muschelgeschirr
shift 11A	verlagern
shorthand 8A	Kurzschrift, Stenografie
smelly 3C	übelriechend, stinkend
smooth out 2C	glätten
sneeze 7D	niesen
sole trader 2A	Einzelunternehmer(in)
solely 5C	allein, nur
solicitor 2A	Rechtsanwalt, -anwältin
spell-checker 3C	Rechtschreibprüfer(in), Korrektor(in)
spillage 12C	verschüttete Menge, Verlust, Spillage
spreadsheet 3B	Tabellenkalkulation(sprogramm)
stake 4A	Einsatz, Anteil
standing order 4A	Dauerauftrag
stapler 3B	Hefter, Tacker
stationery 3B	Büromaterial
stay in credit 4B	im Kreditrahmen bleiben
stipulate 13B	verlangen, vorschreiben
stock 9C	Vorrat, Bestand
stock exchange 2A	Börse
storey 2B	Stock(werk), Etage
subscription 3A	Abonnement
subsidiary 9D	Tochter-
succinct 5A	knapp
sundries *pl* 1A	Verschiedenes
supplement 6B	Zuschlag
surveyor 12C	Gutachter(in)
switch 3C	ändern, umstellen
switchboard 7A	Vermittlung, Zentrale
swivel chair 3B	Drehstuhl, -sessel

T

tableware 10A	Tafelgeschirr, -besteck
tachograph 11C	Fahrtenschreiber
tackle 5C	angehen
tailor for 6A	zuschneiden, abstimmen auf
take the biscuit 6D	alles übertreffen, das Höchste sein
take through 5B	*hier*: berichten von, vorstellen
take up 7B	weitermachen, -arbeiten

targeting 5A (*Zielgruppen*) Abzielen, Ansteuern
testimonial 7B Referenz
the small print 4D das Kleingedruckte
third-party, fire and theft 12B Teilkasko(versicherung)
till 3D Kasse
topple over 12C umkippen
total cost 6B Gesamtpreis, -kosten
trailer 9C Anhänger
trainer 5C Turnschuh
transparency 3A Dia(positiv)
treat 4C besondere Freude
trolley 3D Einkaufswagen
troubleshooter 1D Krisenmanager(in)
turning 11B Abzweigung
turnover 2A Umsatz
type 3C Schriftsatz, Buchstaben

U

unequalled 2C unübertroffen, ohnegleichen
up-and-coming 2D kommend, aufstrebend
update 3D auf den neuesten Stand bringen

V

vacancy 7B offene Stelle
VAT 3D MwSt. (*Mehrwertsteuer*)
venue 8C Veranstaltungsort
vignette 5C prägnante Kurzdarstellung

W

warehouse 9A Lager(haus)
warrant 10C Berechtigung
wastage 4C Personalabbau
web site 8A Website (*Onlineangebot*)
word of mouth 7C Mundpropaganda
word processing 3B Textverarbeitung
work force 8A Arbeiter-, Belegschaft
write-off 12B Totalschaden

Y

yummy 11D jamjam, lecker